CARIBBEAN BY CF

Have a great cruise!

DOCUMENTATION
Passenger Name _____
Ship Name _____
Captain's Signature _____
Date of Voyage _____
Cabin Number _____

THE COMPLETE GUIDE TO THE CARIBBEAN CRUISE EXPERIENCE

CARIBBEAN
By Cruise Ship

BY ANNE VIPOND

YOUR PORTHOLE
COMPANION

™

OCEAN
CRUISE
GUIDES
Vancouver, Canada △ San Clemente, USA

Published by:
Ocean Cruise Guides Ltd.
614 – 888 Beach Avenue
Vancouver, B.C.
V6Z 2P9
Phone: (604) 685-0593 Fax: (604) 685-2479

Editors: Mel-Lynda Andersen, William Kelly.
Contributing Editor: Michael DeFreitas
Contributing Photography:
Michael DeFreitas, Fred Jensen, Gordon Persson
Cover Artwork by Alan H. Nakano.
Cover Design by Hoy Jacobsen & Co.
Cartography: Doug Quiring
Design and Production: Ocean Cruise Guides Ltd., Vancouver.
Printed and bound in Canada by Printcrafters Inc.
Publisher: William Kelly

Canadian Cataloguing in Publication Data

Vipond Anne, 1957 –
Caribbean by cruise ship

Includes index.
ISBN 0-9697991-3-6

1. Cruise ships--Caribbean Area--Guidebooks. 2. Caribbean Area--Guidebooks. I. Title
F2165.V56 1996   917.2904'52   C96-910467-7

Photo Credits: All photography by Anne Vipond unless otherwise noted. Gordon Persson, VII, 25 (bottom); Fred Jensen, 16, 80 (top); Bob Krist, 26 (top), 63; Michael DeFreitas 31 (middle), 45, 76, 83, 89, 91 (bottom); Alan Nakano, 32 (illustration) 66, 94 (illustration); Royal Caribbean Cruise Line 38; Rio Grande Press, Inc., 65 (top & bottom); St. Croix Landmark Society, 53, 58, 60, 67-69; Mary Evans Picture Library, 54, 62, 64; George Brizan, 59; William Richards, VP Records, 84; Florida Division of Tourism, 91 (top); George Rhodes, 96.

P roducing a travel guide that is both informative and entertaining is always a challenge, and such projects require the assistance of many people and organizations. We appreciate the help and direction received on Caribbean history from Dr. Margaret Krigger at the University of Virgin Islands. We also received valuable help from Carol Wakefield of the St. Croix Landmarks Society. Others who generously shared their expertise were Dr. Alina Szmant, University of Miami, who specializes in marine life; Fred Wickstrom, a professor of music at the University of Miami; and Frank Lepore of the National Hurricane Center in Miami. We also appreciate the co-operation of George Brizan, leader of the National Democratic Congress of Grenada, and Robert McCoy of Rio Grande Press Inc.,Glorieta, New Mexico.

We would like to acknowledge the cruise lines that provided photography and information. In particular, Larry Dessler at Holland America Line, Rich Steck at Royal Caribbean Cruise Line, Helen Burford at Celebrity Cruises, Ernest Beyl at Seabourn Cruise Line, and Erik Elvejord at Windstar Cruises. We also thank the public relations departments of Carnival Cruise Lines, Norwegian Cruise Line and Princess Cruises.

In addition, we thank the many tourism departments which were, without exception, generous with their time and resources. This includes the tourism staffs of Antigua, Barbados, British Virgin Islands, Puerto Rico, St. Kitts and U.S. Virgin Islands where Juel Anderson and her associates were especially helpful.

A special thank you to John and Nan Vipond, Joyce Kelly, Fred and Marnie Jensen, Gordon Persson and Raymond Norris-Jones.

Contents

Basseterre, St. Kitts

T he island-dotted Caribbean Sea is perfectly suited to a cruise vacation. Nowhere else in the world can travellers visit such a diversity of destinations, in a tropical setting, and do so on any type of cruise vessel – from the dazzling new megaships to the small sailing ships which anchor off secluded beaches for picnic lunches.

Sailing vessels have long plied these tranquil waters, riding the constant trade winds which temper the region's heat and humidity. Then, in the 1960s, the concept of cruising was pioneered in the Caribbean when jet planes became the new mode of transatlantic travel and shipping companies sought new roles for their ocean liners. Today the Caribbean is the most popular cruising area in the world. The beauty of its beaches is legendary and, with almost no tidal range, its turquoise waters remain clear and warm year round – ideal conditions for swimming, snorkeling and other water sports.

Yet there's more to the Caribbean than white sand and swaying palm trees. The West Indies were once the most important colonial region in the world. Each island has its own history and local flavor, an exotic mix of African, European, Indian and Asian cultures called Creole. The African influence is most evident – in the people them-

selves, their love of rhythmic music and the bold use of color in everything from folk art and batik clothing to the colonial architecture, be it a
canary yellow fort, a flamingo pink church or a lime green government
building. West Indian houses boast bright wooden shutters and gingerbread fretwork, and even local fishermen paint their skiffs a combination of rainbow reds, yellows and blues, inspired no doubt by the aquamarine sea which shimmers across the colorful corals and tropical fish.

There is no mystery to the appeal the Caribbean holds for travellers
yearning to escape the grey grip of winter. The senses are reawakened
in the Caribbean, where the air is soft and warm, carrying the fragrance
of flowers and sweet spices. Cruise ships often pull into port as dawn is
breaking, treating their passengers to the magic of a seaborne arrival as
the golden pink sun rises above a rippled sea and the verdant shores of
a volcanic island draw ever nearer. The departure is equally special, the
ship easing away from shore and heading out to sea as the setting sun
casts its Caribbean colors across the sky. For a vacation of relaxation
and romance, nothing surpasses a cruise to these islands of endless
summer.

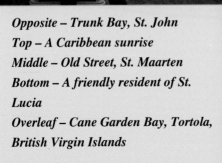

Opposite – Trunk Bay, St. John
Top – A Caribbean sunrise
Middle – Old Street, St. Maarten
Bottom – A friendly resident of St.
Lucia
Overleaf – Cane Garden Bay, Tortola,
British Virgin Islands

PART I

GENERAL INFORMATION

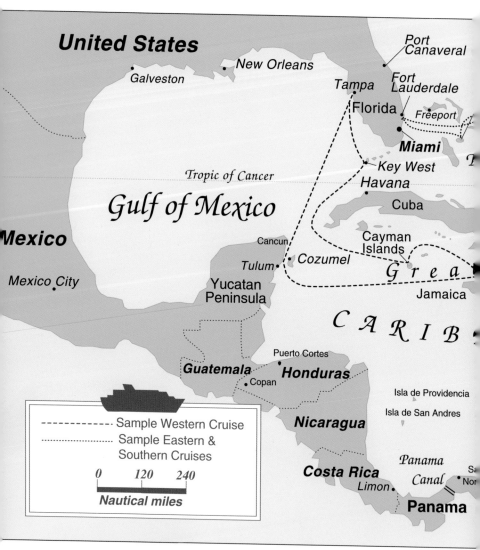

WHICH CRUISE?

The Caribbean Sea, a vast body of water containing dozens of islands, is visited by an assortment of cruise vessels on a range of itineraries. Such selection makes choosing a cruise seem somewhat daunting. However, the cruise lines have made it easier by dividing the Caribbean into service areas and offering cruises to each one. They use a variety of base ports, the major ones being Florida's Miami and Fort Lauderdale, and Puerto Rico's San Juan. Other base

CARIBBEAN CRUISES

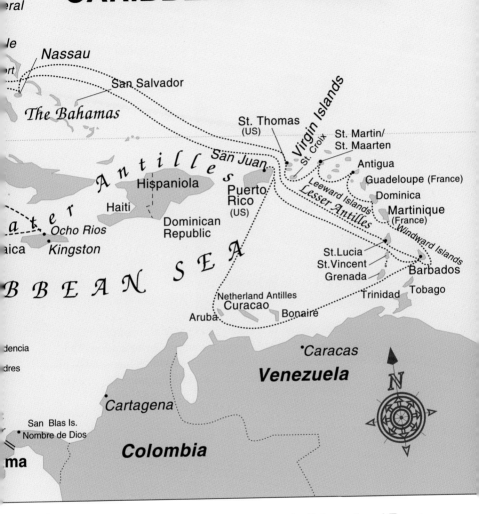

ports include Port Canaveral (for cruises to the Bahamas), and Tampa and New Orleans for cruises to the Western Caribbean.

The Western Caribbean includes such destinations as Jamaica, Grand Cayman and the Mexican island of Cozumel. An Eastern Caribbean cruise usually takes in the Virgin Islands, St. Maarten and other islands including the Bahamas. Southern Caribbean cruises stop at a few Eastern ports but also proceed southward along the Lesser Antilles, often right to the Venezuelan coast, some ports of call being Martinique, Barbados and Curacao.

A Caribbean cruise is a chance to relax, have fun and be pampered by the friendly and attentive staff for which cruise ships are renowned.

The West Indies extend in a wide, 2,500-mile arc from Florida to Venezuela, separating the Atlantic Ocean from the Caribbean Sea. They are comprised of the Greater Antilles, which are the larger islands of Cuba, Haiti/Dominican Republic, Jamaica and Puerto Rico, and the Lesser Antilles, which are the smaller islands to the east and south. The Lesser Antilles are further divided into the Leeward and Windward groups, terms from the days of sail in reference to the prevailing trade winds which blow from the east and reach the Windward Islands first.

The many cruise ships plying the Caribbean can spread out and offer a variety of routes and combinations of ports. The cruise lines are well aware it's the Caribbean's diversity that makes it such an appealing vacation destination and so arrange their itineraries to give passengers the best of everything. One island might be Dutch flavored, another a showpiece of Spanish architecture, a third rich in French culture, and a fourth steeped in British history. One port might be included specifically for duty-free shopping and yet another for its natural beauty of volcanic mountains and tropical rainforests. Generally speaking, a 7-day cruise will stop at three to five ports of call, and a 10-day cruise will call at six to eight ports.

Highlights of a Western cruise include superb diving and snorkeling at the coral islands of Grand Cayman and Cozumel, as well as the opportunity to visit Mayan ruins on the Yucatan peninsula. Eastern cruises usually include stops at the half-Dutch/half-French island of St. Maarten/St. Martin and at the famous duty-free port of Danish-founded Charlotte Amalie on St. Thomas in the U.S. Virgin Islands. A Southern Cruise ventures into less-travelled waters and quieter ports where tourism is not as highly developed and the authentic West Indian lifestyle is still predominant.

The large ships pull into the popular ports while the smaller luxury ships and sailing vessels tend to visit the quieter, less developed islands. Some of the cruise lines include private beach stops in their itineraries, anchoring off tiny undeveloped islands or remote beaches where passengers can spend a day on shore enjoying the water sports and snack bar facilities provided by the cruise company.

When to Go?

The weather varies little throughout the year in the Caribbean due to the moderating effect of the surrounding water and steady breezes. The average temperature is about 80 degrees (26 Celsius) and this fluctuates less than 10 degrees between the warmest and coldest months. The hottest, wettest months are in summer and they mark the start of the hurricane season which starts in July and continues through to November. The topography of each island determines its local climate,

St. John's, Antigua, is one of numerous ports where cruise liners dock in the heart of town, near heritage buildings and upscale shopping areas.

A modern cruise liner and a luxury sailing ship share dock space at Frederiksted, St. Croix.

with the low-lying islands receiving about half the rainfall of the mountainous ones, their leeward sides being dryer than the windward sides.

The most popular months for Caribbean cruising are mid-October to mid-April, with the peak season starting at Christmastime and lasting to the end of March. The major cruise lines offer special Christmas and New Year's itineraries with the ships decked out in festive greenery and the holiday season celebrated with carolers, traditional fare and even a visit from Santa for the children on board. New Year's Eve cruises are also very popular and some ships feature special bands (with a big-band or jazz focus) to bring in the new year.

The selection of ships cruising the Caribbean is exhaustive. Megaships, modern liners, small luxury ships and sailing vessels all offer Caribbean itineraries. Megaships and modern liners provide similar cruise experiences with on-board facilities that include swimming pools, fitness centers, show lounges, casinos and beauty spas. The main difference between the two types of ship is their size, with modern liners carrying between 500 and 1,500 passengers compared to the newer megaships which accommodate up to 2,500 passengers. The 'floating resort' concept applies to both types of ship but is achieved on a larger scale on the megaships. A few classic liners also ply Caribbean waters.

In contrast to the large ships are the small luxury ships carrying 100 to 300 passengers. Being aboard one of these upscale vessels is similar to being on board a billionaire's private yacht. The service is attentive and personalized, and although the on-board facilities are not as extensive as on the large liners, all appointments are of the highest quality and some of the features are unique, such as a stern that folds out into a swimming platform from which passengers can partake in various water sports while the ship is at anchor.

The romance of sail is captured in the sailing vessels which range from small windjammers to large clipper-style ships carrying a few hundred passengers. While all have an engine on board to help propel the vessel under calm conditions, the sails are used much of the time in the trade winds of the Caribbean. Passengers can usually participate in sail handling through informal classes on board. Life on these vessels is unstructured, the cabins are compact and the meals less elaborate than on large ships, although some sailing vessels – such as the Windstar fleet – offer luxury accommodations and service.

SHORE EXCURSIONS

Shoreside activities in the Caribbean include sightseeing, shopping, adventure tours such as submarine rides, recreational pursuits such as snorkeling and sailing, and simply lazing on a beach. Most cruise lines offer organized shore excursions for the convenience of their passen-

Private beach stops include this one at Catalina Island, Dominican Republic, where cruise passengers are tendered ashore for a relaxing day of sunbathing, swimming and other watersports.

The Caribbean's coral reefs and tropical fish, enjoyed by divers and snorkelers, can also be viewed by glass-bottom boat, semi-submersibles and on board an Atlantis submarine (shown here) which dives to depths of 90 feet and offers underwater exploration in air-conditioned comfort.

gers and these are usually described in a booklet enclosed with the cruise tickets. On-board presentations are also given by the ship's shore excursion manager. There is a charge for these excursions but they are usually fairly priced and the tour operators used are reliable and monitored by the cruise company to ensure they maintain the level of service promised to passengers, with the added advantage that the ship will wait for any of its overdue excursions.

However, pre-booked shore excursions are not the only option when exploring ports of call. Choices include renting a car, hiring a taxi, using the pubic transport system or simply setting off on foot to see the town and outlying area. With a bit of preparatory reading and a reliable map in hand, a person can see and do a great deal in the time available and often return with a better perspective of the port or island. Just make sure you're back to the dock in plenty of time.

In the Caribbean, many 'shore' activities actually take place in the water – swimming off soft sand beaches, snorkeling among coral gardens, scuba diving to shipwrecks inhabited by tropical fish, and skimming across the water on a windsurfer, catamaran or 12-meter racing yacht. For those who prefer to stay dry, submarine rides and glass bottom boats afford effortless views of the underwater world.

Airborne excursions include helicopter and seaplane flights for panoramic views of island-dotted waters. There are also boat trips to secluded beaches, river rafting through mangrove forests, and hikes through tropical rainforests where waterfalls, crater lakes and freshwater pools create a paradisal setting for the exotic birds, plants and animals living there. Most of the islands are small and easily toured within a few hours, with look-outs providing vistas of beach-lined bays, offshore cays and distant islands.

In addition to the Caribbean's natural beauty, its colonial history can be explored on island drives to such points of interest as Nelson's Dockyard on Antigua and Brimstone Hill Fortress on St. Kitts. Some of the islands' former sugar plantation estates are open to the public, their grand mansions now museums and the grounds now parkland contain-

Racing aboard an America's Cup 12-meter yacht at St. Maarten is one of the Caribbean's most popular shore excursions, even for passengers who have no sailing experience.

Many of the Caribbean islands have championship golf courses open to the public, including this popular one at Mullet Bay Resort, St. Maarten.

ing picnic tables and botanical gardens. The ports themselves often have numerous historical sites with colonial forts, churches and government buildings lining narrow cobblestone streets where restored warehouses now contain shops and restaurants. A number of ports have local botanical gardens for easy viewing of the many indigenous and exotic plants that grow in the region.

Beaches are usually within walking distance or a short taxi ride away and most are open to tourists although it's not unusual for there to be a small admission charge. The beaches on volcanic islands can vary in color while those on flat coral islands have white sand. Those on the Caribbean side of an island are sheltered; those on the Atlantic side will have a surf. Beachfront hotels often rent lounge chairs, beach umbrellas and the use of lockers and change facilities to the public as well as watersports equipment. Many Caribbean resorts also let non-guests use their tennis courts for a fee, and public golf courses can be found on most islands. Dive and snorkel shops are often located in port or among the beach resorts. On the mountainous islands containing lots of rivers, run-off during spells of heavy rain will send sediment into the water and reduce visibility for divers.

Ship-organized shore excursions cover a wide range of activities – from island tours to boating and dive expeditions – and are attractive for their convenience. You are transported to and from the ship, any needed equipment is provided, and you know ahead of time how long the tour will last and how much it will cost.

Island drives often include panoramic lookouts such as this one at the Estate St. Peter Greathouse on St. Thomas. The view is looking north to Megans Bay and Hans Lollik Island.

Renting a car is an option on most islands, however there are a few drawbacks. Driving is often on the left, the roads can be narrow and winding, and a temporary driver's licence is usually required in addition to the rental fee, bringing the total cost above that of hiring a taxi for a few hours, especially if you're travelling in a small group and can split the cab fare. However, it's fun to strike out on your own, and the roads are often quiet once you get away from the port area. Good islands to explore with a rented car include Barbados (with manicured lanes, a scenic east coast and numerous countryside attractions), St. Kitts (with a new highway to the Southeast Peninsula) and the U.S. Virgin Islands. To save time and ensure the availability of a rental car, it's best to reserve ahead of time through your travel agent. Major car rental companies operate on most islands.

If you decide to take a taxi tour, chat with a few drivers and choose one who is friendly and shows promise as a tour guide. Most drivers are a wealth of information and represent an opportunity to learn more about the local people while seeing the island's natural and historical sights. Always agree beforehand on the price of the tour and exactly which stops are included. If you enjoyed the tour, a tip is appropriate. Fares to popular destinations are usually set by the local taxi association and posted near the cruise ship pier. At some ports, such as Jamaica's Ocho Rios and Basseterre on St. Kitts, a taxi director is stationed at the cruise pier to quote fares and direct passengers to qualified drivers. Other ports may provide pierside information booths.

A tranquil sunrise is enjoyed by a boater at Port Everglades, one of Florida's base ports for cruises to the Caribbean.

Ernest Hemingway's former home, with many of his personal effects still in place, is a popular attraction at Key West, Florida.

A statue of Christopher Columbus graces the front of Government House in Nassau, capital of the Bahamas. Pastel pink buildings and white gloved bobbies are part of this bustling port's British colonial charm.

A cruise ship anchors off George Town on Grand Cayman, where coral-filled waters and miles of white sand beach have transformed this British outpost into a vacation paradise.

Cozumel's port of San Miguel, once a sleepy fishing village, is famous for its nearby coral reefs and Mayan ruins.

The tiered falls at Dunn's River are near the port of Ocho Rios, a resort area on Jamaica's lush and mountainous north coast.

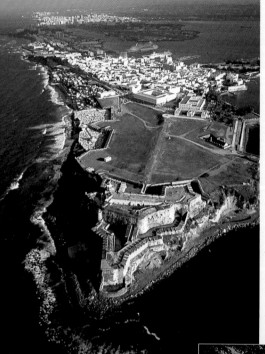

The massive fortress of El Morro guards the entrance to San Juan, Puerto Rico. One of the best-preserved ports of colonial Spain, it is also an important base port for Caribbean cruises.

Charlotte Amalie on St. Thomas, one of the world's busiest ports of call, is famous for its duty free shopping.

A 20-minute ferry ride from St. Thomas, Cruz Bay is a pretty port on St. John, an island blessed with beautiful beaches and protected parkland.

Christiansted on St. Croix was the colonial capital of the Danish West Indies before they became the U.S. Virgin Islands.

Sint Maarten's Dutch port of Philipsburg has great shopping and dozens of sandy beaches nearby.

Road Town is the main port of the British Virgin Islands, where infamous rum-drinking pirates once roamed and sailing yachts now fill the anchorages.

Marigot on Saint Martin, part of the French West Indies, is a pleasing port of sidewalk cafes and elegant shops.

St. Kitts, Britain's mother colony in the West Indies, was once protected by Brimstone Hill Fortress with its sweeping views out to sea.

Antigua's sheltered bays and beautiful beaches have long attracted yachtsmen, royalty and rock stars.

At Pointe-a-Pitre, the main port of Guadeloupe, a West Indian market flourishes amid the town's French colonial buildings and boutiques.

A morning arrival at Fort-de-France, Martinique, reveals the town's yacht-filled harbor and soaring spire of Saint-Louis Cathedral.

Dominica, a rugged island of unspoiled rainforests and cascading waterfalls, was a stronghold for Carib natives and is where some of their descendants now live.

St. Lucia's idyllic bays and beaches include Marigot Bay, its beautiful setting used in the filming of Dr. Doolittle.

The inner harbor at St. George's on Grenada is one of the most picturesque in the Caribbean.

The British heritage of Barbados is preserved in its plantation great houses, such as St. Nicholas Abbey which was built around 1650.

Caracas, capital of Venezuela, is a vibrant city of shady plazas, historic monuments and modern skyscrapers. Located 40 miles from the coast on a lush mountain plateau, the city enjoys a pleasant climate.

Aruba's pastel-painted port of Oranjestad is filled with duty-free shops and situated close to beaches of powdery white sand.

Dutch gabled buildings line the canal-like entrance to Willemstad on the island of Curacao.

The wonderful thing about preparing for a cruise is the lack of effort required. You must pack of course, and you may want to read up on the ports of call you'll be visiting. But as soon as you step on board the ship, the work is done. Your luggage will be brought to your cabin by a smiling steward. Your meals will be served in a sumptuous dining room. Your cabin will be kept spotless by a steward who moves in mysterious ways – never disturbing you but there when needed. Your time will be your own to do as you please, yet the days will fly by. So, to ensure you make the best use of your time aboard, here are some tips on what to take – and what to expect.

Documentation

A valid passport is the best proof of citizenship a traveller can carry. American and Canadian citizens are not required, however, to carry a passport when visiting countries of the Caribbean, including Mexico. You will need a birth certificate or a certified copy of one, accompanied by an official photo identification such as a driver's license. For American travellers, a U.S. naturalization certificate, accompanied by an official photo identification, is also acceptable. All non-U.S. and non-Canadian citizens must carry a valid passport or, in the case of a U.S. resident alien, an Alien Registration Receipt Card.

Before your departure, leave a detailed itinerary with a family member, friend and/or neighbor. Be sure to include the name of your ship, its phone number and the applicable ocean code, as well as your cabin number – all of which will be included in your cruise documentation. With this information, a person can place a satellite call to your ship in an emergency. Another precaution is to photocopy on a single sheet of paper the identification page of your passport, your drivers license and any credit cards you will be carrying in your wallet. Keep one copy of this sheet with you, separate from your passport and wallet, and leave another one at home.

Most travel agents recommend a travel insurance policy at the time of booking. A comprehensive policy will cover travel cancellation, delayed departure, medical expenses, personal accident and liability, lost baggage and money, and legal expenses.

Health Precautions

You may already have supplementary health insurance through a credit card, automobile club policy or employment health plan, but you should check these carefully. Whatever policy you choose for your trip, carry details of it with you and documents showing that you are covered by a plan.

No vaccinations are necessary for a Caribbean cruise but to avoid traveller's diarrhea, it's best to drink bottled water when ashore and never eat a piece of unfamiliar fruit you see hanging from a tree. The poisonous manchineel tree, which grows near beaches, bears fruit resembling small green apples. Contact with these or the tree's leaves, sap or bark will cause a chemical burning. Signs usually identify these trees but the best approach is to stay on designated paths to avoid hazardous vegetation.

All large ships have a fully-equipped medical center with a doctor and nurses. Passengers needing medical attention are billed at private rates which are added to their shipboard account. This invoice can be submitted to your insurance company upon your return home.

Modern cruise ships use stabilizers to reduce any rolling motion when underway, so seasickness is not a widespread or prolonged problem with most passengers. However, there are a number of remedies for people susceptible to this affliction. One is to wear special wrist bands, the balls of which rest on an acupressure point. Another option is to chew Meclizine tablets (often available at the ship's front office) or take Dramamine pills. It's best to take these pills ahead of time, before you feel too nauseous, and they may make you feel drowsy. A third solution is to wear a Scolpolamine patch behind one ear, but these are known to produce side effects such as dizziness and blurred vision. Check first with your doctor before deciding on any medication.

Fresh air is one of the best antidotes to motion sickness, so stepping out on deck is often all that's needed to counter any queasiness. Other simple remedies include sipping on ginger ale and nibbling on dry crackers and an apple. Lying down also helps. Should you become concerned about your condition, simply visit the medical center on board for professional attention.

What to Pack

Pack casual attire for daytime wear – both on board the ship and in port. Cool, loose cottons and silks are best. Wear a wide-brimmed hat, preferably of straw, and comfortable shoes or sandals. Also, take along a light windbreaker for rain forest hikes and nighttime strolls on deck. A light sweater will come in handy when the air conditioning in dining rooms, stores and museums is much cooler than the temperature outside. Colorful tops and shorts can be purchased at good prices at ports along the way.

Sunscreen is also important, one with a protection factor of 15 or higher, to shield your skin from the sun's burning rays. Apply generously before going outside and reapply frequently if you are spending time at the beach, even when the sky is overcast.

Your evening wear should include something suitable for the two or three formal nights held on board most ships. Women wear gowns or cocktail dresses and men favor suits. For informal evenings, the women wear dresses, skirts or slacks, and the men wear jackets with either a shirt and tie or an open-necked sports shirt.

Most ships have coin-operated launderettes with an iron and ironing board. Passengers can pay to have their laundry done for them, as well as steam pressing and dry cleaning.

Basic toiletries, such as soap, shampoo and hand lotion, are often provided, and a hair dryer may or may not be installed in the bathroom, something you can determine at the time of booking. The on-board shops usually carry toiletries as well. Beach towels are supplied, upon request, for use on shore.

Keep prescribed medication in original, labeled containers and carry a doctor's prescription for any controlled drug. If you wear prescription eyeglasses or contact lenses, consider packing a spare pair. And keep all valuables (travellers cheques, camera, expensive jewelry) in your carry-on luggage, as well as all prescription medicines and documentation (passport, tickets, insurance policy). Last but not least, be sure to leave room in one of your suitcases for souvenirs.

Life Aboard

Cabins vary in size but all are, at the very least, clean and comfortable. Telephones and televisions are standard features on almost all ships, and storage space includes a closet for hanging dresses and suits, and drawers to hold your other clothes and miscellaneous items. Valuables can be left in your stateroom safe or placed in a safety deposit box at the Front Office. Security, however, is rarely a problem on board a ship and passengers can feel at ease in any of the ship's public areas day or night. Should you have any inquiries or need assistance, simply visit the Front Desk, also called the Purser's Office.

Breakfast and lunch on board a cruise ship are usually open seating, with meals served between set times. For dinner you will be asked, when booking your cruise, to indicate your preference for first or second sitting. Some people prefer first sitting as it leaves an entire evening afterwards to enjoy the stage shows and other venues. On the other hand, the second sitting allows plenty of time, after a full day in port, to freshen up and relax before dinner. Room service is also available for all meals and in-between snacks.

Extra Expenses

There are few additional expenses once you board a cruise ship. All meals (including room service) are paid for, as are any stage shows, lectures, movies, lounge acts, exercise classes and other activities held in the ship's public areas. Personal services and shore excursions, however, are not covered in the basic price of a cruise. Neither are any alcoholic drinks you might order in a lounge or with a meal. Most ships are cashless societies in which passengers sign for incidental expenses which are itemized on a final statement and settled by credit card, personal cheque or cash.

Although tipping is a cruising tradition, no passenger is obligated to give out tips at the end of a cruise. However, most passengers do tip because cruise ship service is usually worth rewarding. Cruise lines normally provide guidelines on how much to tip various staff, but a general rule is to tip the cabin steward about $3.00 per passenger per day, your waiter the same amount, and your busboy half that amount. Tips are usually given the last night of the cruise.

Miscellaneous

Each island has its own legal tender, but American currency is accepted everywhere in the Caribbean, as are major credit cards and travellers cheques. Cab fares are usually paid in cash. It's a good idea to carry some small U.S. bills for minor purchases rather than receive large amounts of local currency in change. Travellers cheques should be cashed on board the ship unless you are planning a large purchase.

Passengers can phone home from the ship, either through the ship's radio office or by placing a direct satellite telephone call. This is expensive, however, and unless the call is urgent, you may want to wait and place it from a land-based phone. The pre-paid telephone calling card is an easy way for passengers to place long distance calls while in port. Sold on board some ships, these cards allow the user to make international and domestic calls from any touchtone phone. Pre-paid Caribbean calling cards are sold at some ports of call, and public phones are usually located at or near the cruise pier. AT&T calling centers are also found at major ports of call.

The Caribbean spreads across three time zones. Islands east of Dominican Republic are on Atlantic time while those extending westward to the Cayman Islands are in the Eastern time zone. Cozumel, lying off the Yucatan peninsula, falls within the Central time zone.

Vacation Photos

Photographs are often the cheapest and most cherished souvenirs we have of our vacation, and even casual photographers will enjoy capturing the vibrant colors of the Caribbean on film. If you are taking a brand new camera on your trip, shoot and develop a roll of film at home beforehand to make sure the camera works properly and that you understand all its features. Second, pack more film than you anticipate using rather than waste holiday time looking for shops that sell fresh film at reasonable prices. For automatic cameras, 200-ASA print film is probably your best choice for all-around lighting conditions. Make sure you've got fresh batteries in the camera and remember to have fun with your picture taking. Be spontaneous and creative rather than analytical when framing a shot. The subject matter should fill the frame so move in closer if there's a lot of superfluous space in your viewfinder.

Shopping

The Caribbean is famous for its 'free ports' where the selection and savings on luxury goods are among the world's best. With few local manufacturing industries to protect, most Caribbean countries charge no duty on imports, nor is there sales tax, resulting in savings of up to 50%. These savings are passed on to visitors who, in turn, are allowed a duty-free allowance on goods they take home.

Each country's allowance is determined by its customs laws. In addition to liquor and tobacco allowances, U.S. residents can return home with $600 worth of duty-free goods bought anywhere in the Caribbean, plus another $600 worth of purchases from the U.S. Virgin Islands. This duty-free allowance applies to each family member, and families travelling together can pool their exemptions. Canadian residents are allowed a duty-free exemption of $300 (Cdn). Travellers from other countries should confirm their allowable exemptions. Before you embark on your cruise, you may want to visit your local customs office and register valuables you plan to take with you (i.e. cameras, jewelry) so that you have no problem reimporting them duty- and tax-free. Separate from goods bought at duty-free prices are those that are duty exempt. Any item purchased in its country of manufacture is duty exempt such as locally made handicrafts. Loose gems – emeralds, diamonds, rubies and sapphires – are also duty exempt.

Your ship's port lecturer will offer valuable advice on what to look for and where to shop at each port of call. Although recommended merchants often pay a promotional fee to the cruise line, they must guarantee the integrity of goods they are selling to the line's passengers. If you are considering an expensive purchase, it's prudent to shop at stores known or recommended by the cruise line because a few disreputable dealers have been known to engage in shady practises such as offering complimentary cleaning of a person's diamond ring, only to replace the stone with a fake.

Despite such potential pitfalls, shopping in the Caribbean is an exciting and rewarding experience. The world's leading jewelers are located at the main shopping ports, as are virtually all major watch manufacturers. Shops on board the large ships also carry leading brands of liquor, perfume, watches, jewelry, crystal and china at duty-free prices.

When buying a piece of jewelry, its quality grades, carat weight, gold content and purchase price should all be noted on the receipt, an important document for insuring the item when you return home. Gold content is measured in karats, with one karat equalling 1/24 part gold. Pure gold is 24 karats while an alloy containing, for example, 75% gold is 18 karats. Precious stones are weighed in carats, one carat equalling 200 milligrams.

Diamonds are graded for clarity and color. Only trained gemologists can accurately determine a diamond's grade, but there are a few features you can look for. If, for instance, you are buying a cluster ring or tennis bracelet, look to see if all the stones are fairly well matched without any one being a different color than the rest. To test for brilliance, stand back from the bright lights of the showcase and see if the gems maintain their sparkle. Good buys in the Caribbean include large single diamonds and tennis bracelets.

The world's finest emeralds are mined in Colombia and many of these stones are brought directly to the Caribbean where jewelers sell them at impressively low prices. Emeralds, like diamonds, are sold by weight but the cut of the stone is less important than its color. The darker the emerald, the higher its value, yet a person should buy the color they personally prefer. All emeralds are flawed and be suspicious of someone offering you a dark green stone with no visible flaws at a low price, for it might be a fake. Also, a green oil is sometimes rubbed on an emerald to hide its flaws and deepen its color – until the oil wears off – so it's important to buy an emerald from a reputable dealer.

While the selection of brand-name luxury goods, including leather, linen, perfumes, cameras and electronics is truly tantalizing, not to be overlooked are the locally made goods. Look for Caribbean clothing made of high-quality, sea island cotton. Batik and tie dye processes are often used to color the clothing with bright floral patterns. Colorful Caribbean artwork, widely influenced by Haitian primitive art, ranges from folk art to fine art. Wood crafts, basket weaving, pottery and doll making are practised throughout the islands and these unique souvenirs can be bought at local markets and craft shops. Each island's colorful postage stamps, often depicting tropical flowers or birds, also make nice Caribbean keepsakes.

Straw hats, widely sold at Caribbean craft markets, provide cool and effective protection from the tropical sun.

C ruising the Caribbean provides many opportunities to ponder the complex workings of a modern cruise ship. Where once a voyage took months from South America to Florida, now it takes only a matter of days. Even a modern yacht, equipped with highly efficient sails, an auxiliary engine and satellite navigation equipment, can transit the Caribbean with a fraction of the effort required during Columbus's time.

The complexities of ships prompted mariners to develop their own nomenclature. A colorful vocabulary, it has been adapted with lyrical precision to describe each task. As quoted in Smythe's Sailor's Word-Book, "How could the whereabouts of an aching tooth be better pointed out to an operative dentist than Jack's, 'Tis the aftermost grinder aloft, on the starboard quarter.'"

During the 15th century, when commerce with distant lands became increasingly profitable, trading countries began investing in improvements in ship design. This resulted in stronger, faster ships with better sailing characteristics. Chart making was also improved, as were navigational instruments, all of which resulted in greater confidence in ocean travel and exploration. It is this legacy of discovery, combined with tales of daring and adventure, that has given shipboard travel an aura of romance and mystique.

Sea travel attained elegance in the 20th century when grand transatlantic ocean liners were introduced. Opulent and breathtaking inside, graceful and inspiring to view from shore, these ships usually had an extended bow, rounded stern and raked funnels. Although design aspects have changed, today's cruise ships retain the ocean liner tradition of building attractive ships with well-appointed interiors.

How Ships Move

Ships are pushed through the water with the turning of propellers, two of which are usually used on cruise ships. A propeller is like a screw threading its way through the sea, pushing water away from its pitched blades. Props can be 15 to 20 feet in diameter on large cruise ships and normally turn at 100 to 150 revolutions per minute. It takes a lot of horsepower – about 30,000 on a large ship – to make these propellers push a ship along and almost all cruise ships use diesel engines to do the work. It's the job of the chief engineer and his crew to keep these engines running efficiently. In addition to propelling the ship, the engines generate electrical power for the rest of the ship. Gauges, meters and control panels monitor the various systems that keep hot and cold water flowing to your cabin, lights working, the radio and television playing, and the heat and air conditioning functioning. Computer technology has transformed the workings of a ship's engine room

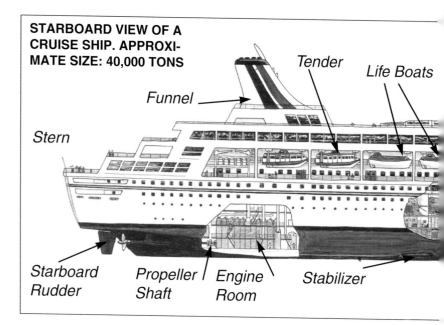

STARBOARD VIEW OF A CRUISE SHIP. APPROXIMATE SIZE: 40,000 TONS

Funnel

Tender

Life Boats

Stern

Starboard Rudder

Propeller Shaft

Engine Room

Stabilizer

which, in addition to improving engine efficiency, also gives more control and information to the crew on the bridge. The bridge crew can tap into any amount of engine power by moving small levers which adjust the angle (or pitch) of the propeller blades. The angle at which the blades are set determines the speed of the ship.

The amount of soot smoke from today's ships is a fraction of that produced by ships earlier in the century. Up to the end of the First World War, most ships used vast amounts of coal to heat large boilers along the length of the lower part of the ship. As a result, ocean liners of the past usually had two and sometimes three funnels to dispel the exhaust. More efficient steam turbine engines, introduced after the Second World War, replaced coal with diesel oil to generate the needed steam. Normally only one large funnel near the middle of the ship was needed to collect and disperse the gases. Diesel engines on modern ships transmit the power either directly through a transmission, which can result in some vibration felt throughout the ship, or by supplying electricity to motors that smoothly turn the prop shafts. Steam-driven ships, a few of which are still in operation, also run very smoothly.

One or two rudders are used to turn a ship in much the same way a paddle is held at an angle in the water to turn a canoe. A hydraulic arm connects the ship's rudder(s) to the helm – a small steering wheel located on the bridge. The bridge, positioned near the bow (the front of the ship) is where the captain and his officers oversee the safe operation of the ship.

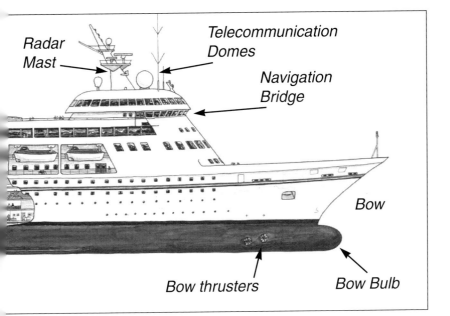

A modern ship's underwater appendages include stabilizers, which are small wings located near the middle of the ship about 10 feet below the water's surface. The angle of the wings is constantly adjusted to minimize any rolling motion of the ship. Another innovation is the use of bow and stern thrusters, which have almost entirely replaced the need for tugboats when a ship is being maneuvered. In most situations, a captain can dock his ship using one of three unidirectional joysticks located on the bridge and both bridge wings. These link the propellers and thrusters to one control center. A symbol (which looks like an upside-down question mark with two small circles inside) is painted on the hull near the bow to indicate the location of the bow thrusters in relation to the bow bulb. The bow bulb reduces the bow wave, allowing a ship's hull to move more efficiently through the water.

Ship Size and Registry

A ship's size is determined by measurements that result in a figure called tonnage. There are approximately 100 cubic feet to a measured ton. Cruise ships used to be called large if they exceeded 30,000 tons and, while that's still a big ship, most new ships are over 50,000 tons.

At the stern of every ship, below its name, is the ship's country of registry. It may be surprising to note that your ship is registered in Monrovia, Liberia, Panama or the Bahamas. Certain countries grant registry to ships for a flat fee, without restrictions or onerous charges and ships often fly these 'flags of convenience' for tax reasons.

Officers on the bridge plot a course in the Caribbean. A senior officer and two junior officers are on the bridge whenever the ship is underway, and an officer remains on duty when the ship is docked.

The Ship's Officers and Crew

The captain, the highest-ranking officer on a ship, is ultimately responsible for the overall running of the ship. He also acts as host to the passengers. Reporting directly to the captain are his officers (ranked 1st to 4th), with the chief officer overseeing the physical condition of the ship. In charge of all technical operations is the chief engineer.

The captain, chief engineer, and their officers and crew, make up only a small portion of total staff on board a ship. The majority of employees are engaged in transforming the ship into a floating resort hotel. This extensive service staff is overseen by a Hotel Manager (sometimes called the chief purser), who is second in rank only to the ship's captain. Reporting to the hotel manager are various managers in charge of departments ranging from food service to housekeeping. Most visible is the cruise director, who oversees the ship's entertainment and on-board passenger events. He or she usually has a background in show business.

Dining, of course, is a very important aspect of cruising, and the quality and preparation of meals receives a great deal of attention. Quality control begins on the dock as various food managers inspect shipments before they are delivered on board. Inspection continues on a daily basis to ensure kitchen staff can prepare meals to the standard most passengers expect on a cruise. If a problem with a particular item occurs, a fresh supply will be purchased locally or flown to the ship.

While passengers are enjoying their evening meal in the dining room, their cabin stewards are busy tidying and cleaning their staterooms for the second time that day. No wonder some people don't want to disembark at the end of their cruise. It's always a bit of a shock to step back into the real world, where you no longer enjoy the special status that comes with being a cruise passenger.

Navigational Challenges in the Caribbean

The Caribbean poses a number of challenges for cruise ship officers, not the least of which are hurricanes from June to November. However, weather information has become very accurate in the last few decades and officers are aware of approaching storms well in advance. If necessary, cruise ships will take evasive action and alter course for other ports. Ships are usually safer at sea than near land, where wind strengths can increase dramatically and there is the danger of a ship being blown onto a reef or suffering damage while moored to a dock.

Pinpoint navigation is lesson number one for all junior officers on a cruise ship, who must always be aware of local hazards such as reefs or strong ocean currents. Specifically, currents are strong in the Straits of Florida (between Florida and Cuba) where the Gulf Stream flows north at speeds up to five miles per hour. Old Bahama Channel and the Windward Passage (between Haiti and Cuba) also have north-flowing currents, as does Cozumel Channel where currents can reach four m.p.h. If undetected, a strong current can slowly push a ship off course and lead to danger. During the days of the Spanish Main in the Caribbean, a number of galleons came to ruin when pushed by currents onto sandbars or reefs.

The Caribbean is now well charted and the numerous reefs and submerged hazards are known and indicated on nautical charts. Ships also use sophisticated depth sounders which look ahead to ensure there is ample water below the keel. A pilot is usually on board to guide a ship into and out of each port, drawing on his local knowledge to advise the captain .

A few Caribbean ports present special challenges during docking. The most difficult ports are: Cozumel for strong currents and afternoon wind, Ocho Rios for strong winds which start early in the evening, and Barbados for the port's twisting narrow entrance and strong afternoon winds. Grand Cayman also gets a mention by various captains for the swell which rolls into the bay where cruise ships anchor. Curacao is also a challenge with its narrow entrance and cross winds which develop in the evening. Tampa is a beautiful harbor to depart from or arrive at, with a long entrance to Hillsboro Bay and narrow channels leading to Garrison Seaport, but it can be a navigational challenge during bouts of fog which occur from January to April.

The history of the West Indies is one of the richest stories ever to unfold. In less than a century, the islands ringing the Caribbean Sea went from tropical paradises to prizes of European imperialism, their fates determined by battles and revolutions staged on both sides of the Atlantic. Yet, the Caribbean was once an unimaginable place to Europeans, including Christopher Columbus who, to his dying day, believed he had found the Far East.

The Early Natives

The Caribbean Islands were initially inhabited by three major Amerindian native groups – the Ciboney (the oldest and most primitive tribe), the Arawak and the Carib. All came from around the Amazon basin and migrated to the north coast of South America before travelling by canoe to the Caribbean. The Ciboney were first to ride winds and currents north along the island chain, followed by the Arawaks who settled first on the Lesser Antilles and then, pushed from these small islands by the warlike Caribs, moved to the Greater Antilles.

By the time Columbus arrived in 1492, the aggressive and proud Caribs had settled most areas of the Caribbean, their largest populations located on the Lesser Antilles. The Ciboneys had been reduced to settlements on the northwest coasts of Cuba and Hispaniola where they lived in small shelters and caves, surviving on shellfish, wild fruits, herbs and small game. They wore little clothing, painted their bodies and their only implements were stone tools.

Well ventillated, easy to rebuild after hurricanes and providing good shelter from sun and rain, Arawak houses were well suited for the Caribbean.

More is known about the Arawaks, who lived in simple houses of brush and practiced *conuco,* a unique agricultural method of growing root plants by placing their cuttings in large mounds of ash and earth. Columbus described Arawak homes as '...simple and clean, very high with good chimneys.' Arawaks also rested on woven nets strung between trees and called these *hammocks,* an Arawak word.

A surplus of leisure time allowed them to develop skills for making pottery, baskets, woven cotton clothing, stone tools and jewelry such as rings, necklaces and masks which were shaped from small amounts of gold found in local riverbeds. They also enjoyed games, including a form of soccer, and built rectangular playing courts similar to those of the Maya whose influence was widespread.

The peaceful Arawaks, content with their simple housing needs and easily obtainable food, enjoyed a tropical paradise. Politically, they were organized as loose federations of provinces within an island with the local village headman holding the greatest sway over his people. Women were equal to men in most areas.

Equality of the sexes was not the case with the Caribs. Tasks between genders were strictly defined and men treated their wives as servants. The Carib men excelled at boat building and navigation, useful skills for fishing and raiding other islands. The Caribs, who had little difficulty pushing the Arawaks from desirable islands, were fearless in battle. They were one of the few native groups in the Caribbean region to defeat Europeans in battle and, unlike the Arawaks who welcomed the first Spaniards with open arms, the Caribs consistently resisted attempts to conquer or enslave them.

They also developed a reputation for cannibalism, a word derived from the Spanish word *caribal*, but human flesh was not part of their regular diet. They did occasionally eat parts of warriors taken in battle, and Columbus, who witnessed this ritualistic act, used it as a pretext for enslavement.

Carib petroglyphs have been discovered on a number of Caribbean islands such as this one on St. Vincent.

Columbus Discovers the Caribbean

Europe's discovery of the New World came as a result of the ambition and persistence of one man – Christopher Columbus. Born in Genoa, Italy in 1451, Columbus's first sea adventure took place in 1476 when he was sailing with a small fleet of cargo ships that was attacked by pirates. Over 500 men were killed, but Columbus managed to escape by swimming six miles to the Portugese shore. He married a Portugese woman of high birth whose father was governor of the Madeira Islands and, while living there, Columbus formulated his audacious plan of reaching the Far East by sailing due west.

Finding no support in Portugal, Columbus turned to Spain. In 1486, he presented his plan to King Ferdinand and Queen Isabella who were interested but preoccupied with driving the Moors from their country. For five years Columbus stayed near the court and campaigned the Queen for financial support. Finally, in January 1492, upon Spain's defeat of the Moors, an agreement in principle was reached.

With three ships, the *Nina*, the *Pinta* and the flagship *Santa Maria*, Columbus set out from Spain on August 3, 1492. This first voyage across the Atlantic was completed in 33 days when he arrived at an island at the south end of the Bahamas island group which he named San Salvador (also know as Watling Island). Columbus promptly met some friendly local Arawaks (also known as Tainos) who saw the newcomers as protection against the Caribs. Columbus convinced a few to guide him further west and sailed on to discover Cuba, then Hispaniola where he left the crew from the wrecked *Santa Maria*. After a few more adventures, and finding a small amount of gold, Columbus returned home to a hero's welcome. He completed three more voyages to the Caribbean, each less successful than the last. On his third voyage, Columbus and his brother were sent home in chains by the Governor of Hispaniola on charges of misrule.

Columbus's favorite ship was the Nina. A replica of this ship is shown above.

By this point, relations with the natives had deteriorated dramatically and Columbus now saw Indians simply as a labor force for mining gold and gathering food. He introduced the dreaded system of *encomiendas* which allotted Spanish settlers the lands and lives of natives. Historians trace the beginning of slavery in the New World to this act and attribute it to Columbus's years of exposure to Portugese culture which, at that time, tolerated the trade of slaves. As Columbus continued his explorations he came in contact with other native villages and on his second voyage had a skirmish with some Caribs at Salt River on St. Croix. This is thought to be the first fight between Europeans and natives, and it was a victory for the Spanish.

Columbus's last voyage (1502-04), with four ships, was along Panama and Central America in search of a strait leading to the Indian Ocean. He found no strait, no gold and lost all four ships. He returned to Spain near collapse and died in 1506 in obscurity. In the end, Columbus received some gold and an estate, but he was denied the trade commissions promised in his contract with the Spanish crown. A year after his death, he failed to receive another honor when a German mapmaker labeled the new continent 'America' after an Italian pilot named Amerigo Vespucci whose reports had recently been published in Europe.

The Extermination of the Arawaks

The impact of Spanish commerce and culture on the indigenous population was rapid and devastating. Population estimates for the Caribbean at the time of Columbus's arrival range from half a million to as high as six million. Many scholars now think it possible the Caribbean did indeed support millions of native people but, whatever the number, it was soon reduced to zero for the Arawaks.

By the end of 16th century the friendly Arawaks, of whom Columbus said 'there is no better nor gentler people in the world', were extinct. This unprecedented genocide was denounced by outspoken religious leaders living in the Caribbean. One of the most influential was a Dominican priest, Bartolome de Las Casas, who wrote a scathing critique of the Spanish conquerors in his book called *A Short Account of the Destruction of the Indies*. Spanish native policy, according to Las Casas, was one of enslavement and genocide and not in keeping with Christian teachings.

One of the most famous passages from Las Casas's book is a quote by the Arawak leader Hatuey who had fled from Hispaniola to Cuba. Moments before he was to be burned alive he was offered last rites by a Franciscan friar. On being told of a choice between Heaven or Hell, Hatuey asked if there were any Christians in Heaven. When he was assured there were, he retorted he would choose Hell where he would not be subject to their cruelty.

Las Casa's disturbing firsthand account of Spanish atrocities had a profound and lasting impact on European politics. Printed in 1552, it became a best-seller throughout Europe and was translated into every major language. For 300 years it upheld an image of the cruel Spanish conquest of America. Protestant countries regarded the book as proof of the unholy greed of Catholic Spain and used it in support of an ongoing campaign to attack and plunder treasure ships returning to Seville.

Eventually Spain introduced laws to curb the abuses inflicted on the natives. In 1512 King Ferdinand assented to limiting working hours and guaranteeing food rations for the Arawaks, and in 1542, Charles V ended new grants of *encomiendas*, but it was too little too late. So many Amerindians had been killed that settlers were already using African slaves bought from Portugese traders. Many natives perished from overwork and murder, but even more died from various European diseases such as influenza and small pox. Isolated for thousands of years, the Arawak simply did not have the natural immunities needed to fight off even the common cold. The tranquil, gentle Arawaks lost their tropical paradise to the jaws of Spanish conquest.

Spanish Settlements

Soon after Columbus's last voyage, thousands of Spanish settlers arrived in the Greater Antilles eager to find gold. After the conquest of Mexico and Peru, many moved on, leaving the exhausted island mines to seek fortunes on the mainland. Almost all of the Lesser Antilles were abandoned once it was determined they were 'useless' for lack of gold. The natives were carted off as slaves and by 1570 the islands were empty and forgotten. All that remained was wild Spanish livestock which, ironically, sustained Dutch, English and French privateers while they preyed on Spanish fleets.

Although the Caribbean islands suffered a dramatic population loss, cities were established at Havana, Santo Domingo and San Juan. South and Central America were the core of Spain's great wealth and sustained an empire which lasted well into the 19th century. Important ports were established at key points along the mainland coast, at Cartagena, Portobelo, Veracruz and Panama.

Spanish Monopoly System

A cumbersome system of regulations was enacted by Spain to control and monopolize trade with the New World. From about 1550 to 1750, two armadas would leave Spain annually for the New World. The *New Spain* flotilla, bound for Mexico, sailed in April for Veracruz to load silver from Central Mexico. The *Tierra Firme* fleet would sail in August to Cartagena and wait for the gold and silver to arrive from Portobelo. Both fleets would rendezvous in Havana to reprovision for the long trip home through the Florida Straits and past the Bahamas.

Although many vessels fell prey to pirates, storms and reefs, most ships made the journey safely back to Seville. It is estimated that from 1500 to 1750 about $10 billion (current dollars) worth of cargo was brought back to Spain. While gold and silver was the main cargo, numerous plants were introduced to Europe including tobacco, corn, potatoes, tomatoes and peppers. But it was sugarcane, a grass plant Columbus brought from Europe on his second voyage in 1493, which would eventually turn the Caribbean islands into coveted colonial holdings for centuries to come.

The Dutch Caribbean Empire

By the late 16th century, English, French and Dutch interlopers had spent more than 50 years harassing Spanish treasure fleets. Exploits of various captains, most notably Sir Francis Drake, made pirating a romantic career option for young men (see Pirates and Plunder). However, it was the Dutch who first turned the West Indies into a viable trading zone when a Spanish embargo in 1598 forced them to look elsewhere for salt and tobacco. By 1630, the Dutch West India Company, operating as a commercial venture with shareholders in Amsterdam, had settled on St. Maarten, Curacao and Bonaire. The Dutch reached their stride during this period, developing trade with Spanish

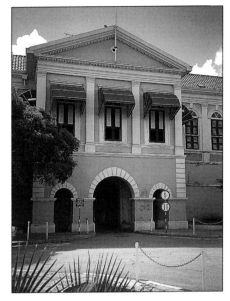

Fort Amsterdam was the center of the fortified town of Willemstad, Curacao, capital of the Dutch West Indies.

and other European settlements. Citizens of the tiny Netherlands owned half of the world's merchant fleet and Amsterdam was the center of international trade. Dutch aggression against the Spanish reached its zenith in the 1620s and 1630s when, for a brief period, they took control of eastern Brazil and monopolized the slave and sugar trade in the Caribbean. The greatest victory against the Spanish came in 1628 when Piet Heyn captured the entire Mexican treasure fleet near Cuba.

England and France Gain Caribbean Colonies

Dutch attempts to usurp Spanish control in the Caribbean and South America eventually failed but the net gainers were adventurers from France and England who, encouraged by high tobacco prices, looked around the Lesser Antilles for suitable land. On January 28th, 1624, Thomas Warner, with 20 fellow adventurers from Guyana, landed on the beautiful island of St. Christopher (St. Kitts) and founded the first British settlement in the Caribbean. Some French sailors arrived about the same time and the two groups divided the island, with local Caribs their mutual enemy. St. Kitts became the Caribbean mother colony for further settlements by the British and French.

Second largest fortress in the Caribbean, the British citadel and surrounding fortifications of Brimstone Hill on St. Kitts were known as the 'Gibraltar of the West Indies'.

Warner's tobacco plantation was a huge success and news of the fortunes being made in tobacco prompted rapid settlement of other islands – Barbados, Montserrat, Nevis, Antigua and the British Virgin Islands by English farmers; Martinique, Guadeloupe and the western half of Hispaniola (Haiti) by French farmers. The Carib natives, after being pushed off St. Kitts, retained strongholds on Dominica, Grenada and St. Vincent.

Tobacco was still the crop of choice for settlers arriving at new islands, but it was soon observed tobacco, like most weeds, will grow almost anywhere. Supply soon outstripped demand, prices fell and the tobacco boom burst. Then settlers on Barbados began planting sugarcane after visiting Brazil to learn of Dutch innovations in planting and harvesting. The first successful crop on Barbados set off a frenzied boom and by 1647 most planters had switched to sugar, a luxury commodity with far greater staying power than tobacco. Demand for labor soared and the population grew from 10,000 in 1640 to 43,000 by 1655. Sugar became the new gold of the Caribbean and thousands of English peasants signed themselves into years of indentured work.

The French colonies grew at a slower pace until the early 18th century when sugar production finally lifted their prospects. Like the British, the French crown tried to enact laws to keep its colonies under exclusive control by restricting their trade. The effort was unpopular and Caribbean planters – both British and French – soon got their own way in commercial matters as well as control of their local governments.

The Struggle for Caribbean Control

During the 17th century, Spain's influence declined significantly and the Dutch, with the greatest number of ships and least amount of regulatory baggage, succeeded in controlling trade. To the Dutch, free trade was almost a religion, and Dutch merchants provided the best service and highest profits for Caribbean farmers. But, during a determined effort in the latter half of the 17th century, England and France finally wrenched control from the Dutch who were left with six small islands – Sint Maarten, Sint Eustatius, Saba and the ABC's – Aruba, Bonaire and Curacao.

By this point, both English and French merchants had increased their Caribbean possessions. In 1655, a fleet under Cromwell's government took Jamaica while the French solidified their hold on Martinique, Guadeloupe and Saint-Domingue (later renamed Haiti), and took possession of St. Barts, St. Croix and Grenada. The Caribs continued to suffer at the hands of Europeans. A massacre of natives was organized by the French on Grenada in 1653 where 40 desperate Caribs jumped to their deaths from a cliff known as *Morne des Sauteurs* (Leapers' Bluff). In 1654, the French failed to eliminate the Caribs on St. Lucia and St. Vincent but did slaughter those remaining on Martinique. Finally, in 1660, a treaty was signed reserving Dominica and St. Vincent for the Caribs.

One other European country got into the act of taking and settling Caribbean islands. The Danish West India Company was the first to permanently settle St. Thomas when its sponsors, encouraged by the

Christiansted, on the prosperous island of St. Croix, was Denmark's colonial capital, its harbor protected by Fort Christiansvaern.

***At Fort-de-France on Martinique, the French built Fort Saint-Louis
on a point of land overlooking the harbor where it stands surrounded on three sides by water.***

Dutch, believed they could make large profits by carrying slaves from Africa to St. Thomas for resale in the West Indies. The Company went on to acquire St. John and St. Croix. However, like its Dutch and French rivals, the Danish West India Company rarely made a profit and went out of business in 1754, when the Danish crown purchased the islands. The Company had given up its monopoly rights at St. Thomas in 1724 and permitted ships of all nations to trade, charging only small customs taxes. Since then, St. Thomas has been known as a 'free port'.

Throughout the 18th century, France and England engaged in a series of wars of which the Caribbean was a major theatre with islands changing hands several times. St. Lucia, only 25 miles from Martinique, may hold the record for different owners as both governments viewed this mountainous island as an important strategic base.

Impressive forts were erected to protect the islands from enemy attack, but the battles were fought mainly by each country's navy. Britain permanently stationed squadrons of warships in the West Indies while France sent over fleets in response to specific issues or conflicts.

The first of these conflicts was the War of Jenkins Ear from 1739 to 1748 which ended inconclusively with both sides returning their conquests. The next war was the Seven Years War from 1756 to 1763, which resulted in a huge gain for Britain in North America when they received Canada in exchange for Guadeloupe. The years from 1776 to 1783 proved to be one of the most historic periods throughout the Caribbean when American colonists threw off the yoke of colonial rule and confronted Britain's oppressive trade laws.

Sugar was an important factor leading to the American War of Independence. Shown above, slaves push hogshead barrels of sugar out to a tender for loading onto ships.

In a direct way, Caribbean sugar pushed the United States to revolution. American merchants were buying sugar from a number of Caribbean sources and, to stem this illicit trade, Britain's Parliament in 1733 placed high duties on all sugar products imported from non-British islands. American merchants openly violated this act until the 1760s when Britain prohibited the American colonies from importing any foreign rum and molasses. Such restrictions infuriated American merchants and became a major grievance leading to revolution in 1776.

The American Revolution received support throughout the Caribbean where the same conflict of interest between home countries and colonies existed. Troops from Saint-Domingue fought for George Washington under Lafayette. The Jamaica Assembly demanded equality with England, the Bahamas openly supported the mainland colonies and, it seemed, without the British Navy to stop them, the islands of the British West Indies would have joined the Revolution. The Dutch island of St. Eustatius became the first territory in the New World to recognize the independence of the United States.

The sugar industry also gave the United States the very symbol of its independence, the Capitol. It was designed by a planter from Jost Van Dyke in the British Virgin Islands, Dr. William Thornton, a Quaker interested in architecture. After seeing an advertisement for a competition to design the Capitol, he presented his winning design to President Washington.

The effect of American independence was devastating for the Caribbean islands. Britain blockaded the mainland ports from West

Indies trade and, with exports and imports suddenly cut off, food became a scarce commodity. Between 1780 and 1787, 15,000 slaves died of famine on Jamaica alone. In 1778, 300 white planters fled St. Kitts to escape court action for recovery of debts. And yet, England continued to enforce the archaic Navigation Act. Economist Adam Smith pleaded with the British government to allow resumption of trade between the United States and the British West Indies, and warned that continued interruption would hurt the islands more than America. Slowly, Britain reopened trade and relaxed the embargo.

In the meantime, however, the French West Indies enjoyed boom times as the main supplier of rum and sugar to America. But the sweet life was not to last for effects of the French Revolution eventually spread to the Caribbean. Saint-Domingue convulsed in a terrible civil war led by slaves yearning for freedom. Guadeloupe and Martinique were also caught in the struggle, enduring battles and a reign of terror after Jacobin republicans arrived to take control. In 1793, planters sought protection from the British crown which quickly took advantage of the chaos in the islands to capture almost all French possessions. This was overturned in the fall of 1794 when Victor Hugues led a squadron of troops and retook Guadeloupe. More than 1,200 white planters went to the guillotine at his order. Hugues went on to stir up rebellion on other islands and successfully expelled the British from St. Lucia. On Grenada, the British just managed to hang on to their main fort while fighting an insurrection led by the colored planter Julien Fedon. In Saint-Domingue Britain endured its most serious losses when the government decided to invade the war-torn country at the urging of local white planters. In a disaster which dragged on until 1798, Britain lost vast sums of money and thousands of men – almost all to disease which was the main killer during Caribbean battles. A creole slave named Toussaint L'Ouverture successfully repelled the British from Haiti.

Abolitionist leader William Wilberforce at the age of 29.

Abolition and the Road to Freedom

In the latter part of the18th century, the Age of Enlightenment resulted in new ideas about freedom and equality. Confidence in human reason and progress lent credibility to radical beliefs, and people were open to change. During this time, anti-slavery movements throughout Britain gained momentum and, led by a number of powerful parliamentarians, they won the support of the prime minister, William Pitt. The chief spokesman for abolitionists, William Wilberforce, initiated a series of parliamentary inquiries publicizing the horrors of the Middle Passage – from Africa to the colonies. Armed with information to reveal the slave trade as a vast graveyard for African slaves and British sailors who died from various tropical diseases, the abolitionists spread their campaign across the country and found a receptive public

Cover of abolitionist pamphlet in late 18th century. Millions of similar tracts were circulated in England before emancipation.

willing to sign petitions. The result was a success and the British Parliament scheduled an abolition bill for 1796. However, revolutionary France's Reign of Terror discredited radical ideas and not until May 1806 did the British government pass the Foreign Slave Bill prohibiting the shipping of slaves to foreign colonies. Two years later, it abolished the importing of slaves into British colonies.

Convincing planters to accept abolition was a different matter and transitional steps were attempted, with slave registration introduced in 1815 to prevent illegal importing of slaves and provide evidence of their maltreatment. Resistance from planters only stiffened the resolve of abolitionists who were convinced stronger measures were needed to free Caribbean slaves.

While planters and politicians fretted about the method and consequences of changing the status of slaves, the slaves took matters in their own hands. The frequency of revolts increased dramatically from the end of the 18th century to emancipation and in 1816 a revolt ravaged Barbados which had not known a slave conspiracy since 1701. Ironically, the very measures enacted to end slavery made the situation worse. The labor force dwindled at the cessation of the slave trade in 1808 and masters forced their slaves to work harder, moving women, children and older domestic servants out to the fields to work.

By 1830, Caribbean slaves and British abolitionists were losing patience with the slow progress towards freedom. A large slave rebellion in Jamaica led by a Baptist lay preacher named Sam Sharpe brought events to a head when more than 60,000 slaves revolted by burning 200 sugar estates in the northwestern parishes. Over 500 slaves and 14 whites died. News of the revolt and its repression galvanized British abolitionist groups to organize a final drive to end slavery. More than one and a half million people signed petitions which were presented to Parliament early in 1833. The Abolition Act was passed in August ordering the end of slavery by the following year, making Britain the first European power to abolish slavery. Parliament voted to pay planters about £25 per slave which went a long way toward encouraging passage of the Emancipation Bill in the colonial assemblies.

France, during its revolution, abolished slavery on Saint-Domingue in 1793 but, under Napoleon, slavery was restored in 1802. Britain forced the French government to outlaw the trade in 1818 but it was not until 1848, when French abolitionists gained power, that an emancipation decree was passed. The Dutch and Spanish islands were slow to free their slaves. The Netherlands ended slavery in the Caribbean in 1863 while the Spanish colonies, which were enjoying a boom in sugar production in the 19th century, took longer, eventually abolishing slavery on Puerto Rico in 1873 and Cuba in 1886.

The Danish Virgin Islands had many ties to the British colonies and were prompted to introduce slavery reforms by 1839. A slave rebellion on St. Croix in 1848 speeded up the process when their leader Buddhoe demanded immediate emancipation or the town of Frederiksted would be burned to the ground. The governor quickly wrote out an emancipation decree which was confirmed a few months later. As revenue on the island fell, the Danish government began negotiations to sell the islands to the United States in 1865 and these were finally concluded during the First World War in 1917.

Although most Caribbean islands suffered for a number of years after emancipation, the population of the islands soared, nearly doubling from 1841 to 1891. On some islands, freed slaves moved off plantations to form 'free villages' and grow their own food on small plots of land. New schools, hospitals and jails, which did not exist in 1838, had to be built by island governments. Sugar prices fell while labor costs climbed as former slaves fled from the harsh routines of field labor. Markets for Caribbean cane sugar were undermined by beet sugar, successfully grown in large quantities in Europe, and by Asian countries which were exporting cane sugar, as were Cuba and Brazil using slave labor. Jamaica, once the biggest producer of sugar in the Caribbean, saw its output plummet. Other islands thrived, however, as black laborers – now earning wages – continued to work on the estates.

Caribbean Politics in the 19th and 20th centuries: British Islands

After emancipation, the Caribbean islands all beat to a different drum. Most British colonies utilized representative governments which proved unsatisfactory and, by 1860, many were seriously in debt. A rebellion in 1865 by black peasants on Jamaica prompted the British Government to place the island under the Colonial Office as a Crown colony. This system was adopted for the remaining British islands and stayed in place, virtually unchanged, until after the Second World War. In the late 1930s, economic hardship gave rise to powerful labor movements with accompanying strikes and riots .

Populist leaders emerged, urging full autonomy from Britain. Jamaica, Barbados and Trinidad were led by forceful leaders with socialist leanings who borrowed ideals and slogans of the British Labour party. The 1940 Moyne Report recommended self government for the islands and, although the British government agreed, it wanted to hand over the reigns of power to moderate political leaders who enjoyed popular support. Jamaica and Trinidad were the first colonies to gain independence in 1962, followed by Barbados in 1966 and most of the other colonies by the 1980s. A number of the smaller islands have remained colonies, these being Anguilla, the British Virgin Islands, the Cayman Islands, and Montserrat.

French and Dutch Islands

Following a plebiscite in 1945, the French Antilles chose assimilation and political union with France, of which they remain overseas departments. Like provinces within a state, their political evolution runs parallel with France. Each island has its own governor who controls the island's armed forces and has some say over local funds. The connection has generally worked and the islands were protected from the worst effects of the 1930s depression.

The Netherlands Antilles have also retained links with their home country, with all of the original six islands remaining part of the Kingdom of the Netherlands. In 1986 Aruba separated from the Netherlands Antilles but remains part of the Kingdom. Curacao enjoyed good years during the oil boom of the 1960s and 1970s but refining capacity has been cut since the 1980s and the state has taken over ownership. St. Maarten leads the Dutch islands in attracting tourism dollars.

Haiti has perhaps suffered the most, with a series of repressive and corrupt governments plundering the country's treasury and resources. Haiti, once very prosperous and the site of the first successful slave revolution, continues to seek political stability and economic recovery.

After emancipation, many former slaves settled into a new life tending small plots of land growing food for themselves and local markets. Shown above is a scene in Christensted, St. Croix, about 1910.

Spanish Islands and American Influence

Finally unburdened of trade restrictions in the late 18th century, the economies of Spain's colonies improved. Cuba became a huge sugar producer but resentment against Spanish rule and taxes continued, leading to civil wars in the latter part of the century. A separatist movement, with strong support in the United States, resulted in an open conflict between Spain and America which lasted for 10 weeks in 1898. After two naval losses to the American fleet, Madrid surrendered. Cuba was granted independence, and Puerto Rico and other possessions were ceded to the United States.

The United States became the main economic and political force in the Caribbean. American capital provided the means to rebuild sugar, banana and coffee industries in the Greater Antilles and, by the 1920s, American-owned companies were producing most of the world's cane sugar. The United States also began to intervene directly in the politics of various Caribbean states, occupying Cuba, Haiti and Dominican Republic for brief periods of time. The presence of the United States was generally beneficial to the islands as roads were built, institutions established and communications improved.

The Caribbean Today

Any island, with its limited resources, is challenged to meet the economic needs of its citizens and this is especially true in the Caribbean. Tourism has been a bright spot for many islands and the cruise ship industry has created over 82,000 full-time jobs in the Caribbean region with a total economic impact estimated at $4 billion annually.

Notwithstanding Cuba, the Caribbean region's political determination is adherence to democracy. The acid test of this occurred in 1983 when countries of the Caribbean refused to tolerate the murder of Grenada's prime minister, Maurice Bishop, by an unelected military regime and backed intervention by the United States. Grenada has enjoyed democratic elections ever since. The Caribbean remains fragmented politically, each island retaining its own character and culture, but with democracy a valued institution, peace and stability have been achieved.

SLAVERY

I n the early years of sugar planting, white indentured laborers, serving terms of three to five years, were far more common in the islands than black slaves. An important boost for planters came when Cromwell sent thousands of Scottish and Irish people to Barbados in the 1650s. However, Barbados was a death sentence for white laborers and as many as three out of four white workers perished soon after arrival. Many died from tropical diseases, introduced by Dutch-sold African slaves in the 1640s. Black workers generally fared better at adjusting to the climate with one out of three dying in the first two years. But survival meant a constant routine of hard work and it was a

West African tribes, sometimes hundreds of miles from the coast, were under continual onslaught by slave traders who would march whole villages to a slave depot.

toss up which was the worse job – cutting the cane or working in the sugar mill where temperatures reached 120 degrees.

By 1650 it was clear a massive labor force was needed to grow sugar. Africa was already supplying slaves to Asia, the Middle East and Europe, and slave traders were quick to satisfy the labor needs of Caribbean planters. Trade in human cargo was underway and about to take place on a scale never before seen.

Europe's acceptance of slave labor in the Americas for over 300 years is, today, difficult to understand. Slavery had virtually disappeared in Europe by the Middle Ages and had been replaced with the notion of semi-freedom under which most serfs labored. However, from the beginning of slavery's rebirth, Europeans expressed ambivalence to the trading of human beings. In 1610 a Jesuit named Alonso de Sandoval wrote words that were in stark contrast to what was soon to be common practise: 'Among human possessions, none is more valuable and beautiful than liberty...All the gold in the world and all the goods of the earth are not a sufficient price for human liberty. Slavery is not only exile but also subjection, hunger, sorrow, nakedness, insult, prison, perpetual persecution and, in short, a Pandora's box of all that is evil.'

It was the Portugese who first began the lucrative trade of transporting black labor from the west coast of Africa in the 15th century. Catholic blacks were shipped from Spain to Hispaniola in 1505 to work in copper mines and within two decades, colonists were buying thousands of slaves from many sources. By the middle of the 17th century,

Cutting cane was backbreaking work and field laborers toiled from sunup to sundown during harvest from January to June. Women often outnumbered men in the fields.

French, English and Dutch slavers were actively buying and selling from warlords along the African slave coast. From Senegal to Angola, forts were built to protect slave companies, and cities such as Luanda, Accra and Lagos existed for centuries as human warehouses.

The Atlantic triangle brought manufactured goods from Europe to Africa, slaves from Africa to the Caribbean, and sugar, cotton and tobacco back to Europe. It was a system that suited accepted economic dogma of the time and was so profitable it seemed providential. The triangle made the West Indies among the most valuable colonies the world has ever known. Scholars estimate over 15 million people were taken from Africa in the transatlantic slave trade. This massive depopulation had far-reaching negative effects on Africa, from the wrenching of families and communities to long-standing tribal animosities.

England's Liverpool was transformed from a fishing village into a center of international commerce and became one of the largest ports in Europe devoted to the slave trade. The city's red brick Customs House, blazoned with Negro heads, bore mute testimony to the origins of the city's rise in the world. (Britain's first permanent gallery examining the transatlantic slave trade recently opened in Liverpool.)

After South America, the Caribbean was the most active buyer of black labor, importing over four million Africans from 1601 to 1870. (The United States, by comparison, imported about half a million slaves.) The biggest buyers of slaves in the Caribbean in the 18th century were Saint-Domingue (Haiti), Jamaica and Barbados. The appalling rate of mortality, both on the plantations and on the slave ships, kept the death rate far in excess of the birth rate and new slaves for the islands were always in demand. For every 100 slaves put on a ship bound for the Caribbean, only 56 would be alive after three years.

Planters had complete control over their slaves who had little recourse against injustices, although some – called Free Coloreds – earned their freedom through faithful service or bought it with money raised by selling handicrafts or garden produce. Desperate slaves simply ran away and on most islands were quickly captured and severely punished. Runaway slaves stood a better chance on the Greater Antilles where they hid in the dense rainforests and rugged mountain areas. Jamaica was home to the best known and most successful group of runaways who became known as the Maroons. They successfully raided frontier plantations, established towns, and beat off numerous attacks by British troops. Eventually the Maroons won two homelands of more than 2,500 acres. This semi-independent status lasted until 1962.

Sugar played an important role in the development of international trade but, as other world sources for sugar were found, the importance of the Caribbean diminished and slavery became an odious anachronism in the new era of enlightenment.

The immense wealth brought back to Spain from Mexico and Peru was a constant source of envy for other European countries, and resentment grew when Spanish claims were confirmed by papal decree. Without the resources to attack the Spanish empire directly, northern European nations relied on piracy to tap into the New World's gold supply.

Piracy was called privateering when it received tacit approval from British, French and Dutch crowns in the form of licensing or commissions. This subtle distinction gave captains latitude to pursue innocuous activities, such as collecting livestock on Caribbean islands, when the real purpose was to pillage Spanish towns and ships. The captains would return home to divide their spoils with the crown while receiving the royal pardon.

France, almost continuously at war with Spain until 1559, was the first to attack Spain's source of wealth. When news that French privateer Jean d'Ango seized four Spanish ships laden with treasure near the Azores in 1523, men throughout France boarded ships bound for the Caribbean to prey on Spanish vessels. As many as 30 French ships raided the West Indies annually, the climax of these efforts coming in 1555 when corsair Jacques de Sores captured Havana and burned it to the ground.

The exploits of Sir Francis Drake fired the imagination of all of Europe when he captured an entire year's production of Peruvian silver in 1572. With only two ships and 73 men he took the city of Nombre de Dios (near today's location of the Panama Canal) and captured three mule trains transporting 30 tons of silver. This voyage brought Drake wealth and fame, and inspired generations of adventurers to seek their fortune in the Caribbean.

Sir Francis Drake (1540-1595)

Drake made a number of sorties to the Caribbean and is also credited with being instrumental in the defeat of the Spanish Armada in 1588. Drake met his end during a siege of the newly-built El Morro fortress in San Juan, Puerto Rico. After failing to penetrate the settlement, he sailed to other ports looking, without success, for treasure. Returning to his old haunt of

The El Morro fortress in San Juan, Puerto Rico was Drake's undoing. The Spanish, unlike earlier days, were ready for the much feared privateer in 1595.

Nombre de Dios, he met his fate when a mosquito bite brought on the dreaded yellow fever. Drake died off Portobelo and was buried at sea.

The struggling Spanish colonies, limited by crown decree to trade only with Spanish ships, were themselves participants in piracy. When ships from Seville were captured by pirates, the motley crew would sell the prized cargo to Spanish merchants in the Caribbean at prices well below the official tariffs.

The term buccaneer derives from French colonists who, hiding out on Hispaniola, sold the meat and hides of cattle left by the Spanish. These buccaneers began setting up camps on various islands to repair their vessels and rest before venturing back onto the high seas. One of the first such camps was on Isla Tortuga off the north coast of Haiti. Established in the late 16th century, this multinational settlement was perhaps the earliest independent European community in the New World, owing allegiance to no crown and trading with every nation. The Bahamas, Turks and Virgin Islands were also excellent pirate hideouts for they were windward of Spanish bases in the Greater Antilles and difficult for the lumbering galleons to approach.

One of the best harbors was Charlotte Amalie on St. Thomas, which proved a haven for pirates who brought booty to sell to local merchants. Collusion with pirates was most blatant during the 1680s when they were chased from Jamaica by governor Henry Morgan, a reformed pirate. The warmth of the welcome extended by the new governor of St.

Thomas, Adolph Esmit, resulted in an international incident when he refused to hand over a pirate ship to a British man-of-war in 1683. The notorious Blackbeard made St. Thomas his base for several years.

However it was Jamaica which had the most infamous reputation as a pirate enclave in the 17th century and for 30 years, from 1643, it offered hospitality to thousands of pirates drawn from Europe and the Caribbean. The most celebrated of all pirates at Port Royal was Henry Morgan. A bold captain who knew the coasts of the Spanish Main well, Morgan's first great success was taking the rich city of Portobelo in 1666. This astounding achievement garnered Morgan a pardon from the Jamaican governor and earned Morgan a reputation throughout the Caribbean as a shrewd and fearless leader.

More exploits followed, climaxed by the spectacular capture of Panama in 1671. When the pirates marched back across the isthmus, they took a string of 200 pack mules laden with gold, silver and other valuables plus a large number of captives. While the crew quarreled over their share of the loot, Morgan slipped away in his ship with the greater part of the booty, leaving his followers without food or ships. Although Morgan was sent to England to stand trial (England and Spain had recently signed a treaty) he was exonerated as a hero, knighted by the king, and sent back to Jamaica not as a prisoner, but as Deputy Governor of the island. Sir Henry finished his days on his sugar planta-

Sir Henry Morgan's (1635-1688) life as a pirate was the exception rather than the rule, living in luxury to his dying day. After being knighted by Charles II, he was sent back to Jamaica as Deputy Governor to rid Port Royal of pirates. Morgan's Lookout, his famous retreat, is located near Ochos Rios on Noward Coward's Firefly estate.

tion and, unlike others of his kind, died in his bed in 1688.

Pirates were an unpredictable and contradictory bunch. Many a notorious captain would, upon sinking a ship and killing the survivors, call his crew together for prayer service. Some skippers forbade swearing, drinking and gambling, and some even displayed empathy for their hapless victims.

Two female pirates, Anne Bonny and Mary Read, made the annals of pirate history early in the 18th century for their exploits and method of escaping the hangman's noose. Convicted of piracy in Jamaica, Bonny and Read successfully pleaded for their lives claiming they were pregnant. On the day that Bonny's lover 'Calico' Jack Rackam was hanged, he obtained permission to see Anne for a farewell interview in which she apparently told him '...she was sorry to see him there, but if he had fought like a Man, he need not have been hang'd like a Dog.'

Piratess Anne Bonny was a tough pirate who fought bravely against being captured.

One of the most interesting pirates was Major Thomas Bonnet. He was not raised for a seafaring life and, before taking to piracy, he had settled into retirement on his large estate in Barbados. A married man, he lived in a fine house and was much respected by his neighbors and other gentry of the island.

But one day, something snapped. Bonnet decided to fit out a ship armed with ten guns and a crew of 70 men. To satisfy the curious, he said he intended to trade between the islands. Without so much as a word of good-bye to his wife, Bonnet slipped out of Bridgetown harbor at night and began looking for victims off the coast of Virginia, capturing half a dozen small ships.

Captain Thomas Bonnet is the only pirate actually known to make his victims walk the plank.

His undoing was meeting the infamous Captain Teach (better known as Blackbeard) who had terrorized the Bahamas and American mainland for years. Teach attracted warships like flies to molasses and both he and Bonnet were finally captured by armed sloops. Bonnet was found guilty and hanged in November 1718. When news of Bonnet's exploits and demise reached Barbados, his neighbors were shocked and found it difficult to imagine what had caused this sudden change in one of their own. It was suggested his mind had become unbalanced from the unbridled nagging of Mrs. Bonnet, whose husband was one of few known pirates, other than those in fiction, who made his prisoners walk the plank.

The archetypical pirate was Blackbeard. Notorious for his cruelty, torturing victims and crew with equal enthusiasm, he was successful for many years in the Caribbean and the U.S. eastern seaboard before being killed near Bath in North Carolina. A physical giant with an enormous appetite, he was reputed to have 14 wives. He wore 12 pistols and several cutlasses when heading into battle and once, after blowing out the candle in his cabin, he fired at his guests in the darkness, severely wounding one. He said afterwards that if he didn't shoot one or two, they would forget who he was.

Pirate activity had been virtually eliminated by the early 18th century by various governors determined to clean up their islands. Some, like Henry Morgan and Nassau's Captain Woodes Rogers, were former pirates who knew where in the 'faggot heap to search for the ferret.' An

extraordinary navigator (he found Alexander Selkirk, a.k.a. Robinson Crusoe, on a small island in the Pacific) and a natural leader, Woodes Rogers rounded up 2,000 pirates in the Bahamas and convinced most to give up pirating. Although sporadic outbreaks of piracy occurred into the 19th century, the game was over for most by the 1740s when Britain began stationing naval ships in the Caribbean. The age of pirating and plunder had come to an end.

Bluebeard's Castle in Charlotte Amalie was typical of pirate homes with a watchtower as the main structure.

SUGAR REIGNS SUPREME

Sugar had a tremendous impact on the world in the 17th and 18th centuries because it was one of the first products to go from strictly elite use to being a luxury item of the masses. The result was prolonged high prices and huge profits for owners at the top of the industry. What the sugar producing islands were then, the oil producing countries are now. Highly prized, the Caribbean 'sugar islands' were often bargaining chips at peace conferences between warring powers.

Although there were cyclical periods of boom and bust, sugar prices generally rose until the 19th century when production of beet sugar began in Europe. British consumption in particular soared. In 1700 the average Briton ate four pounds of sugar per year and by 1800 this figure had increased to 18 pounds, peaking in the early 1960s when the average Briton ate more than 110 pounds of sugar annually.

Although sugar had its start with Spanish cultivation on Hispaniola, production there died out in 1540 after Spain began obtaining cheaper sugar produced in Brazil and Mexico. Sugar cultivation really caught on in the Lesser Antilles about 1650 after the success on Barbados. The cane grew so well in the Caribbean, and such huge profits were being made that almost all the islands turned themselves completely over to cultivation of sugar cane. As a result, until the 19th century most food for the islands had to be imported. Sugar production in the 17th century

The production of sugar began with the harvesting of cane which was brought to the mill for crushing. Wind-powered mills were more common on low-lying islands such as Barbados and St. Croix.

Cane juice was boiled and impurities removed before workers ladled the juice into cooling troughs.

required large investments of capital for buildings, machinery, land and the purchase of slaves. Planters contended with drought, hurricanes and fluctuating market conditions to survive a business loaded with risk.

Cane cultivation usually took place from June to December, during the rainy season, when slaves planted cane cuttings and nurtured the growing plants. After 18 months, the cane was eight to 10 feet tall and ready for harvesting during the dry season from January to June. Early methods of extracting juice required an enormous amount of cane; about 20 pounds were needed to produce a pound of sugar. Heavy bales of cane stalks were brought from the fields to the mills where the juice was extracted. The cane was run through the mill's rollers at least twice to squeeze as much juice out of the stalk as possible. The juice would run by trough to the boiling house where it was boiled and clarified in a series of copper vats to remove excess water and impurities. Workers would skim off gross matter and strain the juice before finally allowing it to flow into cooling troughs. The resulting raw sugar, called muscovado or unfinished sugar, was put in huge barrels called hogsheads which weighed 1,600 pounds. The hogsheads were placed on racks and left to stand for 12 to 16 hours when a plug at the bottom was removed and the molasses drained off. The barrels were then topped up with sugar and ready for export.

The refining of this raw sugar product was normally completed in Europe or North America although the production of rum, at least for domestic consumption, was usually carried out on the individual islands. Early rum was made by fermenting a mixture of water and molasses (five parts to one) in a vat with a measure of skimmings, oranges and herbs to taste. After fermentation, the mix was heated in a still through condensing coils, emerging as rum of 120 proof or stronger. It was sometimes rough, usually uneven, but it was rum.

RUM

Known as *ron* in Spanish and *rhum* in French, no matter how it's spelled, rum is a versatile spirit with a range of taste and characteristics unique to each producing island. The history of rum runs parallel with that of the Caribbean. Sir Henry Morgan glowingly described rum as, 'A friend and brother to one alone in the dark, a warm blanket on a chilly night, an excitement in the cheek and an inspirer of bold and brave deeds.' In the tropics, rum has long been the preferred drink, and not just for its taste. Alcohol dilates the peripheral blood vessels and actually has a cooling effect on the body, which makes rum more refreshing than ice water.

Rum can be produced from two different raw materials – molasses or cane juice. Rum is unique in that it retains more natural taste factors from its product of origin than any other spirit. Starch-derived spirits, such as vodka (made from potatoes) or whisky (from grain), must be cooked or malted to produce a sugar for fermentation. Since rum is derived from sugar, it doesn't have to go through a cooking process, nor does it have to be distilled at very high proofs, so it receives the minimum of chemical treatment.

A distillery on St. Croix with pot stills shown at left . Workers roll hogshead barrel filled with raw sugar along the loading dock.

Rum production begins with the fermentation of either cane juice or molasses to make the originating product for the start of distillation. Rum's natural color is water-white but it will pick up some color if it is aged in charred casks (which also adds aroma) or, more usually, if sugar caramel is added.

Rum differs according to the strain of yeast used, the method of distillation and aging, and the type and amount of caramel used in coloring. Rum, like whiskey and brandy, needs to mature, and each rum-producing island ages the product for different lengths of time to achieve the desired taste. For example, full bodied Jamaican rum is normally aged three years or more while drier, lighter rums from Puerto Rico are aged only one year or more. Distillation methods also vary and include the traditional pot still (also known as batch production) and the more modern method of using continuous column stills. Some rums are a blend of both methods.

Different Types of Rum

Most of the popular rum distilleries in the Caribbean hold regular tours for visitors and are well worth the visit for rum aficionados. Most Caribbean rum is produced from local sugar cane products although imports from Mexico and Central America are sometimes used. Here is a quick overview of various island rums.

Puerto Rico: The rums produced here are dry and light-bodied. The molasses is fermented in gigantic vats using mash from a previous fermentation. If the rum is matured for only a year in uncharred oak casks, it is light-bodied, neutral in flavor and white in color. Two years in charred barrels and the addition of caramel produces a somewhat darker rum with more body and a stronger aroma. Puerto Rico's best-known rum of course is Bacardi – biggest selling rum in the world. Bacardi, using continuous stills which impart a remarkable consistency in taste, has a range of rums aged one to six years including an excellent reserve rum (six years old) best savored neat. The bat on the logo comes from the company's beginnings in 1862 when Don Facundo bought the distillery which was then home to a colony of fruit bats. The bat symbol was, at that time, an easily recognized trademark for illiterate customers.

Jamaica: The traditional Jamaican rum, full bodied with a pungent aroma, has in recent decades been blended lighter with taste and aroma toned down. However, most Jamaican rum is still made using pot or batch stills and aged (for rum) a lengthy three to five years. The molasses is allowed to ferment naturally which can take up to three weeks but allows for greater saturation of cane flavor. A number of fine rums are produced on Jamaica and the major producer is Appleton which makes an excellent range of rums from its own sugar cane, blending pot-still and continuous-still rums to make its popular brands. Appleton produces a 12-year old rum, one of the oldest and finest available.

Barbados: Rums from this island are softer, with an almost smoky flavor, and are semi-light in body and color. Distillation methods include pot and continuous stills and most Bajan rums are a blend of the two. Cockspur, Mount Gay and Doorly's are popular brands. The world's oldest rum is claimed by Mount Gay, its production traced prior to 1703. Mount Gay rums are distilled from molasses using natural spring water from the island. Different aged rums are blended to make its final smooth-tasting Eclipse product.

French West Indies: A considerable amount of full-bodied rum is made on Martinique and Guadeloupe. There are nearly a hundred cane growers on Martinique and about 14 large distillers. French West Indies rum is different from other islands in that the product is distilled from the concentrated juice of sugar cane rather than from molasses. It is produced by pot still and takes on a darker color.

Other Islands: The Virgin Islands produce a light-bodied rum with Cruzan on St. Croix enjoying a very good reputation. Antigua produces a decent and inexpensive rum called Cavilier, and Westerhall distillers on Grenada produce a limited pot-still rum from sugar cane juice aged in oak. Each bottle is numbered, which somehow makes the sipping of this rum all the more delightful.

The Caribbean is a showcase of West Indian colonial architecture, its variations reflecting the Spanish, Dutch, Danish, French and British styles. Forts and other structures were built using brick brought from Europe as ship's ballast, or of volcanic rock and limestone quarried on the island. (Left) Built of red brick and rubble, Fort Christian on St. Thomas was begun about 1666, its crenelated clock tower added in 1874.

(Above) The West Indian neo-classical style is preserved in Christiansted on St. Croix. Features include rows of arches running the length of arcaded sidewalks and upper-floor galleries designed to provide shade from the tropical sun and catch the breezes. (Left) The Dutch colonial architecture in Willemstad, Curacao, is baroque in style with gabled roofs and rich golden hues reminiscent of the colorful tulips grown in Holland.

(Above) The Frederick Lutheran Church in Danish-colonized Charlotte Amalie was built in 1793, gutted by fire in 1826 and damaged by hurricane in 1870, after which the tower was added. (Below) Martinique's Saint-Louis Cathedral was designed in the late 1800s by French architect Henri Pick (a contemporary of Gustave Eiffel) to resist fire, hurricanes and earthquakes.

(Above) European planters lived in 'great houses', their outer walls often built of thick limestone blocks up to 20" thick which absorbed the sun's heat. St. Nicholas Abbey in Barbados, one of the oldest great houses in the West Indies, was built by a British colonel around 1650 in the Jacobean style with Dutch gables and corner fireplaces – an unlikely feature for the tropics.

The sturdy West Indian house is both functional and visually pleasing. Its steep, gabled roof withstands strong winds, sheds rain quickly and, vented at both ends, allows hot air to escape. Hoods and louvered wooden blinds keep out the hot sun and driving rain while admitting light and fresh air. Solid wood shutters are another feature on islands where hurricanes are an annual threat. Gingerbread fretwork, in a variety of patterns, is often added as decoration.

(Above) A Marigot street in St. Martin is lined with French West Indies buildings, their fretwork balconies built over the sidewalk where they provide shade. (Left) In the walled city of Old San Juan, a narrow cobblestone street of Spanish townhouses leads to the Church of San Jose which, built in 1532, is a beautiful example of late-Gothic architecture. (Below) A British West Indies building in Road Town, Tortola, stays cool inside with its ground floor arcade, upstairs gallery and louvered windows with their hurricane shutters swung open.

T he Caribbean is a sea of cultures, its people as diverse as the world itself. Their official languages include English, French, Spanish and Dutch, yet it's a Creole dialect, based on a French vocabulary and African grammar, which is used on many of the islands and incomprehensible to most outsiders. Local customs and cuisine also vary from island to island, but what does prevail throughout the Caribbean is exuberance, especially during each island's Carnival.

Carnival is a celebration of life and no where is it displayed with more fervor than in Trinidad where the music of Carnival – calypso and steel band – was born. Pulsating Afro-Caribbean rhythms provide the beat and the brilliant costumes worn by dancing paraders provide the color. A year of preparation produces elaborate, three-dimensional costumes, some up to 10 feet tall and weighing 300 pounds. Competition for prizes is fierce – not for the money but for the honor.

Mocko jumbie stilt walkers – the traditional symbol of Carnival – originate from the traditions of West Africa. They parade atop 10-to-20-foot stilts, dressed in bright colors and covered in mirrors because these 'elevated spirits' are said to be invisible and onlookers see only themselves. Carnival celebrations vary from island to island, and not all are held in the days prior to Lent. In the Bahamas, a festival called Junkanoo is held right after Christmas with people flocking to Nassau to participate in the parades. In Puerto Rico, fiestas honoring patron saints are held in central plazas and include religious and costumed processions. In the U.S. Virgin Islands, Carnival is celebrated on St. Thomas in April, on St. John over July 4th, and on St. Croix in December. Crop Over Festival on Barbados – a revival of the traditional celebration of the end of the sugar harvest – is held each summer, as is Antigua's annual festival celebrating the abolition of slavery.

Whether it's called a 'jump-up' or a 'mas' (masquerade), the celebration is uninhibited and the mood joyful, with spontaneous street parties, reggae concerts, calypso competitions, food fairs and the crowning of a Carnival queen.

A girl on St. Vincent partici-
pates in the children's parade,
a popular event at Carnival.

Business is brisk at the harborfront market in Point-a-Pitre, Guadeloupe, where both locals and visitors can shop.

Each port has a bustling marketplace, located in a central square, where fresh produce is sold along with other wares. Traditionally a social gathering place as well as the town's commercial hub, with island farmers, fishermen and traders bringing their goods here to sell, the market reflects traditions long rooted in Africa. Matriarchs called 'market women' often control, through mutual understanding, a specific spot in the square and acquire goods to sell either by purchase or on consignment.

The fresh fruits, vegetables and spices on colorful display at the market are the mainstays of creole cooking. Ground vegetables, including yams and sweet potatoes, are commonly used, as are breadfruits, tomatoes, peppers and ackee which, when removed from its ripened pod and cooked, resembles scrambled eggs. Rice, peas, beans and fried plantains are served alongside a main dish of saltfish (salted cod), curried goat or conch fritters. Stews are also popular, such as *kalaloo* which consists of okra, spinach, goat, crab, fish and West Indian spices.

The flavorful dishes created in West Indian kitchens incorporate a number of local spices. Allspice, chives, curry, ginger, nutmeg, turmeric (the 'poor man's saffron') and thyme are all favored. Rum is another important ingredient, used widely in deserts featuring bananas and coconut. A typical Caribbean fruit punch, with or without rum, consists of orange and pineapple juice with grenadine syrup and nutmeg added. Limes, mangos, pineapples and papayas are just some of the delicious fruits grown locally and served up Caribbean style.

In a region where self expression and creativity are evident in the dancing, singing and easygoing nature of the people, it's easy to forget there's a more serious side to Caribbean culture, one which has produced a number of critically acclaimed writers and poets. Nobel-winning writer Derek Walcott, born of mixed-race ancestry on St. Lucia in 1930, was educated in Jamaica where he immersed himself in classical literature. His poems draw both on the folklore of a West Indian childhood and the teachings of a higher education, a dichotomy that once caused him to complain he felt more at ease describing an English cherry tree than the breadfruit tree under which he sat while writing.

Other famous Caribbean writers include V.S. Naipaul, born in Trinidad in 1932, knighted in 1990, and considered a contender for a Nobel Prize. Also making her mark on the world is Antigua-born Jamaica Kincaid, who ran away to New York City at age 17 to escape an unhappy childhood which, along with the bitter realities of her homeland, are frequent subjects of her writing.

Caribbean artists have been widely influenced by Haiti's primitive art which developed in isolation among the peasantry until discovered by the outside world in the 1940s. Colorful and vivid, Haitian art often depicts voodoo images based on African tribal practises. African motifs – animal patterns and geometric designs – are often incorporated in Caribbean works, both fine art and folk art, and the works of local painters and artisans are widely displayed in island shops and galleries.

Prominent singers and songwriters who hail from the Caribbean include the late reggae superstar Bob Marley of Jamaica and Cuban-born songstress Gloria Estefan. The actor Sidney Poitier was born on Cat Island in the Bahamas, and fashion designer Oscar de la Renta was born in Dominican Republic, his namesake perfume inspired by his mother's garden in Santo Domingo.

West Indian men and women are leaders in many fields. St. Lucian-born Sir Arthur Lewis won a Nobel prize for economics in 1979, and Dominican prime minister Eugenia Charles, dubbed the 'Iron Lady of the Caribbean' for her outspoken personality and political strength, has led her country since 1980. Famous Caribbean athletes include Puerto Rico's baseball legend Roberto Clemente, and two of the world's fastest 100-metre sprinters – Donovan Bailey (winning Olympic gold for Canada in 1996) and Linford Christie (Britain's gold medalist in 1992) – are from Jamaica.

Fame and fortune come to few, however, and most Caribbean people are employed in less glamorous pursuits. Tourism is a growing source of employment on many of the islands, and cruise passengers are welcomed the moment they step ashore. Crafts tables are often set up near the cruise pier and some terminals contain shopping malls with a selection of duty-free goods and locally made arts, crafts and clothing.

(LEFT) Caribbean taxi/tour opera-tors, their vehicles hired by ship-organized groups and individual pas-sengers, are usually excellent guides and proud of the service they provide. Taxis and vans are maintained in good condition with drivers providing customers with a running commen-tary on the island's sights.

(ABOVE) Islanders who fish for a liv-ing keep their boats brightly painted and can be seen mending their nets on the beaches of seaside villages.
(LEFT) Local vendors include this young woman on Dominica, selling chilled soft drinks at Trafalgar Falls.

(ABOVE) Children are often seen heading to or from school, such as these Grenada school girls smiling shyly at some visitors.
(BELOW) Wearing her prep school uniform, a Jamaican child beams for the camera.

Caribbean children are doted on, the little girls often wearing party dresses and ribbons in their braided hair. ABOVE: Pretty in pink is a young girl of Willemstad, Curacao.

Cricket, along with soccer and baseball, is popular on the islands where casual games are often played on local beaches. (ABOVE) Young boys play in a square of Old San Juan. (LEFT) A Dominican woman walks with easy grace and swaying hips while balancing a basket on her head. Languid scenes of island life include tethered goats grazing at the edge of schoolyards and dogs lying dormant in doorways.

(RIGHT) Their truck loaded, workers relax on the ride through St. George's, Grenada.

C aribbean music is drum laden, rooted in Africa, and always danceable. Many songs are lyrically linked to the experience of slavery, in style and subject matter, for although slaves could not speak to each other in the fields, they *could* sing. After emancipation in 1838, former slaves maintained their musical heritage at social events and church services, passing on rhythms, techniques and lyrical motifs to successive generations.

The roots of modern Caribbean music have been a focus of academics for over 70 years. Researchers studying Jamaican music in 1924 found direct connections to music produced in West Africa. The main rhythm of reggae – in which the accent is put on the second and fourth beat of a four/four time signature – has been traced directly to the Yela rhythm created by women in southern Senegal by alternating hand claps with the pounding of grain.

Scholars also trace Caribbean music to the Gankogui (or double African bell) which provides a steady repeating pattern and is the rhythmic basis to West African music. This 12-count rhythm evolved into the eight-count 'clave' rhythm which is the foundation for most Caribbean music. Wooden concussion sticks called claves produce a beat which guides all other instruments in their rhythmic variations. The clave sticks may or may not be used in a particular piece of music, but their underlying rhythm is always present.

In addition to its African wellspring, Caribbean music has been influenced by other musical forms. European waltzes, quadrilles and mazurkas are blended with Latin styles such as the Cuban rumba, as well as rock, rhythm-and-blues and jazz, to form an evolving tapestry of sounds.

The following is a compilation of the different styles you will hear when walking through the ports of the Caribbean.

Calypso and Soca

Originally from Trinidad, calypso is popular throughout the Caribbean. The beauty of Calypso is twofold: sophisticated lyrics with clever word play and driving rhythms for a festive unwinding. The music is thought to have progressed from field songs of slaves employing allegory to pass along information and gossip. This interest in subtle lyrics, to hide meaning from slave masters, was turned into a source of entertainment and art. The game evolved with work crews fighting mock battles in song and the number of 'bon mot' lyrical strikes determining the winner. Instruments were added to the sound in the 19th century when calypso was first recorded. Today, driven by syncopated bass rhythm, calypso is filled in with drums, guitars and occasionally tenor and alto steel drums. Calypso, like its offspring soca, is a favorite at Carnival

Carnival time in Trinidad is an important musical event for all calypso and soca artists competing for the Calypso Monarch Crown and Road March King titles.

time in Trinidad where there are competitions for lyrical quality and party-pleasing rhythms. Current artists include Chalk Dust, Mighty Sparrow, David Rudder, Roaring Lion (who is over 80 years of age) and Eddy Grant. A major record label for calypso (and soca) is Ice Records which has a dazzling array of artists and releases a selection of Carnival competitors each year.

Soca: A blend of soul and calypso, soca is jumped-up calypso with bawdier lyrics. The music of choice on Trinidad, soca is popular throughout the Caribbean and played non-stop at Carnival time when famous calypso and soca artists perform at competitions. Well-known artists include the versatile Mighty Sparrow (who has the longest straight number of wins at the Road March King competition in Trinidad) as well as Superblue, Fab 5 and ring bang artist Viking Tundah. Cuban percussionist Changuito, often referred to as the father of modern soca, developed the soca rhythm while playing with the group Los Van Van.

Goombay

Unique Bahamian music with a fast-paced tempo driven by a range of skin drums, goombay is directly linked with West African dances and drums. Nassau holds an annual Goombay Summer Festival featuring this and other Afro-Caribbean music.

Reggae

Perhaps the biggest revolution in Caribbean music, reggae literally lifted Jamaica from a post-colonial funk in the late 1960s to an era of new confidence and hope. Born in the slums of Kingston, reggae quickly became popular around the world as mainstream artists such as Eric Clapton, Paul Simon and the Rolling Stones produced hits using the reggae beat. Evolved from earlier ska music (speeded up R&B) and the slower rock-steady beat, reggae was slower still with a greater emphasis on bass and, traditionally performed outdoors, was played loudly. Reggae's early lyrics were social, political and spiritual, exerting a real impact on Jamaican politics in the early 1970s. Its main artist was the late Bob Marley whose songs of redemption, salvation and prophecy made him a leader for poor Jamaicans (see profile in Jamaica chapter). Bob Marley and the Wailers produced a string of reggae hits with best-selling albums such as *Catch a Fire* and *Natty Dread* and became the leading reggae group of the 1970s. *Get Up, Stand Up; I Shot The Sheriff,* and *One Love* are some of Marley's well known songs.

Although local DJ's gave reggae its big push in the mid-to-late 60s, it was record producer Chris Blackwell's early support that gave reggae an audience in the markets of Europe and the United States. One of the first albums to become an international hit, now a classic, was Jimmy

Cliff's *The Harder They Come* which was actually a soundtrack to a movie about the hardships of attaining success as a musician in Jamaica. Other reggae artists from this era include the Maytals, Desmond Dekker and Burning Spear. Marley's son Ziggy and wife Rita continue to record, and current popular artists include Beres Hammond and 'dancehall' artists Buju Banton, Shabba Ranks and Maxi Priest.

Beres Hammond, a leading Jamaican artist, has returned to the roots of reggae with lyrics reflecting social conscience.

Salsa

Hot, sensuous dance music with a distinct call-and-response singing style, salsa is popular in Puerto Rico. Its strong emphasis on brass and percussion is derived from the

Steel band music is still one of the strongest images of the Caribbean.
Tunes selected are often calypso numbers.

Cuban salsa which uses timbales, bongos and congas to carry the rhythm. Popular artists include Eddie Palmieri and Bobby Valentin.

Steel Band

The steel pan, the only contemporary instrument created in the Caribbean, is made from a 55-gallon oil drum. The base of the drum is heated and stretched into a concave shape and the surface is then pounded out in graduating rectangles to create different notes. Steel bands normally arrange popular calypso songs for their drums. The Rising Stars of St. Thomas are a popular steel pan band. Cruise lines often arrange for steel bands to play their music during arrival or departure of their ships.

Merengue / Cadence/ Zouk

Created during the 19th century in the rural townships of Dominican Republic, merengue is experiencing a comeback in its country of origin and in Puerto Rico. Merengue utilizes the cylindrical, double-headed tambora drums and brass instruments. Cadence is popular on Martinique, Guadeloupe and Dominica, and first evolved as a sort of Caribbean jazz fusion (featuring clarinet and trombone) which has synthesized various Caribbean musical forms, including soca and reggae, with exuberant driving drum rhythms.

Zouk: Popular French Caribbean music which grew from cadence, zouk is very fast with lots of Latin influences. Vocal harmonies are featured in zouk music, which was originally used to describe parties on Martinique and Guadeloupe.

The Caribbean's plant and animal life is unsurpassed in diversity and beauty. Flowers, both indigenous and exotic, flourish here amid the verdant greenery of palm trees and tropical forests. Nearly 300 species of butterflies inhabit the West Indies along with hundreds of species of birds. An abundance of life also thrives in the surrounding waters where coral reefs fringe islands and support schools of tropical fish and other aquatic creatures.

Plant Life

The vegetation on a single island can vary considerably, with a jungle-like growth of dense foliage proliferating on its windward side, and stunted plants which tolerate arid soil growing on its leeward side. The

vegetation zones occurring on mountainous islands are well defined. At the summits of the higher peaks is an **elfin woodland** of matted mosses, lichens and ferns which can survive in wet and windy conditions. A **montane forest** grows on the mountains' upper slopes and ridges, and consists of small trees and ground vegetation of grasses and ferns.

The Caribbean's lush and scenic rain forests are also important watersheds.
(ABOVE) Trafalgar Falls, Dominica
(RIGHT) El Yunque National Forest, Puerto Rico

Tropical blossoms provide splashes of color amid lush vegetation. The hibiscus, shown here, is one of many exquisite flowers found in the West Indies.

At lower elevations is the **rain forest**, its tall trees and interlaced foliage forming a dense canopy through which little sunlight can penetrate. Bromeliads (air plants) sprout from massive tree trunks and ferns grow at their bases. A **secondary forest** will grow in areas previously cleared through natural disaster or cultivation for crops, its open canopy allowing the growth of shrubs and small plants at ground level. Often intermingled with secondary forests are **seasonal formations** which contain many of the flowering trees that blossom during the dry season.

In addition to being sources of food and material for handicrafts and construction, a number of island plants and trees are also used for bush medicines and herbal remedies, their leaves boiled to make therapeutic teas and soothing baths for treating such ailments as rheumatism and the common cold. Children use young green fruits for playing marble games and a broad leaf on a stick can serve as a parasol.

Many of the trees found in tropical forests are deciduous but are considered evergreen because, rather

The massive trunks of some rain forest trees are supported by buttress roots.

Caribbean palm trees shade sandy beaches and line country lanes.

than shed all their leaves at once, they do so sporadically throughout the year. In addition to supplying oxygen, tropical trees support vines and air plants, an example being the banyan tree which sprouts roots that hang between the tallest branches and the ground. Tree roots supply nutrients to the soil and prevent soil erosion during heavy rains.

Forests are important watersheds, with almost all fresh water originating in forest rivers and lakes. The widespread cutting of tropical rain forests has become a controversial practise due to its destruction of fresh water sources as well as its destabilization of the earth's temperature, humidity and carbon dioxide levels. Island rain forests, being self-contained ecosytems, are much more susceptible to extinction than those on a continental land mass. On some Caribbean islands, the removal of vegetation around watersheds has caused rivers to dry up and fresh water must be imported or produced by desalinization plants.

The importance of forest preservation is recognised by a growing number of Caribbean nations which are countering development with the establishment of national parks, nature reserves and wildlife sanctuaries. Guided tours are offered throughout the islands and these allow visitors to see first hand such species of tree as the mahogany, soapberry, fig and maho, its bark used for making rope. Limes, bananas, papayas and other fruits can be seen hanging from tree branches, as can cocao tree pods containing cocoa beans. Many species, such as the nutmeg tree, were introduced to the West Indies for cultivation. Beautiful flowers blossom everywhere. These include bougainvillea, hibiscus, orchid, frangipani, flamboyant (royal poinciana) and the trumpet-shaped yellow cedar.

Palm trees grow throughout the Caribbean, their flowing crowns of frond leaves swaying in the breeze. Palms grow to heights of 100 feet or more, their smooth cylindrical stems marked by ringlike scars left by former leaves. The towering royal palms, often seen lining avenues, reach heights of up to 120 feet and were traditionally used as boundary markers for sugarcane plantations.

The coco palm, from 60 to 100 feet tall, easily establishes itself on shorelines and small islands because its seeds, enclosed in a large buoyant pod, can float. Its fruit is the coconut, a hard woody shell encased in a brown fibrous husk, and a single coco palm can bear more than 200 nuts annually. A coconut has three round scars at one end, its embryo lying against the largest which is easily punctured to drain the nutritious juice inside. Copra, from which oil is extracted to make soaps, cooking oil and suntan lotion, is produced when a ripened coconut is broken open and dried.

Every part of a coco palm has value, its leaves used for making fans, baskets and thatch, its coarse coconut husks turned into cordage, mats and stuffing, its nutshells polished and carved to make attractive cups and bowls. Even the fibrous center of old trunks can be used for rope. In addition to its fruit being a staple food, the young head of its tender leaves – called palm cabbage – is cooked as a vegetable.

Animal Life

Over the centuries various animal species have been introduced to the West Indies, such as the mongoose, a ferret-sized mammal imported to hunt rats and snakes. The **iguana**, a herbivorous lizard, is common on Mexico's Yucatan peninsula and a number of Caribbean islands. Being cold blooded, it derives body heat from the sun and basks on rocks and tree tops for much of the day to maintain a body temperature high enough to digest the leaves and fruits it consumes. Peaceful and harmless, iguanas grow to three feet in length and can weigh over 400 pounds. The larger males are gray with a tall crest on the back, while the females retain the bright green body of a young iguana. The female burrows a

The iguana must bask in the sun to maintain its body temperature.

nest in sandy soil, laying her eggs at the end of a tunnel which she then refills for concealment. When the young iguanas hatch, they dig their way to the surface where they are vulnerable to predators.

The Caribbean's abundant bird life ranges from tiny hummingbirds to the high-flying frigate bird. Because the West Indies are close to both South and North America, there is some crossover of range between tropical birds and those commonly seen in the United States.

The magnificent **frigate bird**, also called man-o'-war bird, is the most aerial of the water birds with a wingspread of 7 1/2 feet – the largest in proportion to its body of any bird. Highly skilled fliers, frigate birds can be seen riding thermal updrafts along coastlines for extended periods of time. They feed mainly on fish they spot while in flight and they will harass other birds, such as pelicans, until they drop their catch which is then snatched in midair or retrieved from the water or beach. Its long tail, deeply forked and scissor-like, is opened only while maneuvering in flight. Although classed as a sea bird, it is awkward in the water.

The **brown pelican**, in contrast to the frigate bird, is heavy bodied with a long neck and large, flat bill. It too is a graceful flier as well as a skilled swimmer, and it will glide in circles in the air before suddenly diving straight into the water to scoop a fish into the large, expandable pouch hanging from its lower jaw. Brown pelicans nest on shore and the young feed from their parent's pouch.

The **flamingo** is a tall, pink-colored wading bird related to the stork and heron.

The frigate bird, an aerial acrobat, soon becomes waterlogged if its feathers get wet, unlike the brown pelican (RIGHT) which is equally adept at flying and swimming.

An infrequent visitor to southern Florida, the flamingo's main habitats are the Greater Antilles, the Bahamas and Bonaire with its large colonies. The flamingo feeds in the shallow water of marshes and lagoons where its scoops water into its large bill, the serrated edges of which strain algae and shellfish from the water. Flamingos build conical mud nests, one to two feet high and one foot across, with mates taking turns incubating the one or two eggs.

Flocks of flamingos nest on the island of Bonaire near the South American coast.

Many of the world's **parrot** species are endangered, including those found in the Caribbean, such as Dominica's imperial amazon. Amazons, with their brilliant plumage and ability to mimic the human voice, fetch a high price on the black market and are vulnerable to poaching.

The **Great Egret** (also called Common Egret) is a type of heron that feeds in shallow water on small aquatic life. Threatened at the turn of the century when its white, silky plumage was used to adorn ladies hats, the egret is now a protected species.

The St. Vincent amazon is a colorful example of a Caribbean parrot.

Over 50 types of hard corals are found in Caribbean waters. They grow in various shapes and sizes, including the aptly named brain coral.

Coral Reefs

Some of the Caribbean's most unusual animal life is found beneath the water's surface where coral reefs, formed by living organisms, are home to a fascinating variety of fish and other sea creatures.

These underwater habitats are formed by soft, saclike animals called polyps. Smaller than a pea, each polyp secretes an exoskeleton of limestone which is cemented by blue-green algae to the skeletons of other polyps to form a coral colony. These tiny polyps, each living inside its own limestone cavity, feed on floating plankton which they trap with their extended tentacles. When a polyp dies, a new polyp forms on top of it, and these layers of skeletal material gradually accumulate over time to form a massive but fragile formation called a coral reef.

Although corals live in temperate as well as tropical waters, coral reefs are found only in tropical waters, within 30 degrees of the equator, where the water temperature remains above 70 degrees Fahrenheit year round. Coral reefs that extend from shore are called fringing reefs and those separated from shore by a wide lagoon are called barrier reefs. Barrier reefs rise like fortress walls from the sea floor and are habitat for tropical fish and large ocean-going predators which feed here on the smaller fish. Fringe reefs, often within a few yards of the water's surface, enjoy optimum growth and serve as nurseries for hundreds of small tropical fish.

Many of these slow-growing reefs are now protected in the Caribbean, where environmental pressures in the form of coastal development, water pollution and increased recreational use have threatened their survival. Preservation measures include the installation of mooring buoys so that no anchors are dropped from boats, and prohibiting

Growing on top of the hard corals are various soft corals, including sea fans and gorgonians, as well as sponges and sea anemones.

snorkelers and divers from touching and taking pieces of coral. A number of marine parks contain sign-posted underwater trails guiding visitors past the colorful corals while providing an appreciation of their delicate environment.

Most reef-forming corals belong to the stony or hard group of corals. There are many different types of hard corals, some branch-like, others rounded, their distinctive shapes determined by the growth pattern of the various polyp species. Corals are often named for their appearance and some common hard corals include elkhorn, with its thick stocky branches, and staghorn, which has smaller branches. Other branching colonies include flower, finger, pencil and ivory corals. Pillar and ribbon corals grow upright in clusters, and brain corals grow in rounded shapes. Soft corals also help build the reefs, their feathery forms including sea fans and gorgonians in a variety of vivid colors. Sea anemones, unlike the corals, do not have a skeleton and often look like flowers when their feeding end is open and tentacles are fully extended. Brilliantly-colored sponges, another aquatic animal, attach themselves to coral reefs, often in colonies. They vary in shape and size, and show little movement.

The shimmering tropical fish found along coral reefs come in an assortment of shapes, sizes, colors and markings which often change as the juvenile fish matures. Angelfishes are among the most beautiful of the small fish which inhabit shallow reefs, their flattened disc-like shapes allowing them to slip through nooks and crannies. Their elabo-

The Queen Angelfish is one of many brilliantly colored reef fish found in Caribbean waters.

rate markings are often blue and yellow, or black with yellow stripes. They feed on sponges and the ectoparasites of other fishes. Butterflyfishes are similar to angelfishes with yellow their dominant color. They travel in pairs, feeding on coral polyps, sea anemones, tube-worms and algae.

Blue tangs are another disc-like fish which live on the algae that grows on or among the coral. The juveniles are a lemon-yellow color, pre-adults are often part yellow/part blue, and adults are a blue to pur-plish gray. The size of reef fish can vary, the butterflyfishes growing to about 6 inches, the angelfishes ranging from one to two feet in length, and the tiny cherubfish, which prefers deepwater reefs, reaching only 2 3/4" in size.

Parrotfishes begin life as drably colored females then turn into males with gaudy green and blue scales. They have molarlike teeth with which they grind algae off the corals, producing sand in the process. Other members of the coral reef community include the spiny lobster which hides in crevices by day and feeds at night, and the sea horse – only a few inches long – which uses its tail to hold onto the coral.

In addition to tropical fish and other reef-feeding creatures, Caribbean waters contain a range of ocean-going animals including species of shark, dolphin and whale. From the deck of a cruise ship sightings of the fast acrobatic Bottlenosed Dolphin are common. This dolphin grows to 12 feet and is particularly adept at locating prey using echolocation by projecting a sound beam and listening to the echo. Dolphins often ride the bow waves of ships. Schools of flyingfish are also spotted from the ship's rail as they glide (they don't actually fly) a few feet above the water's surface on their pectoral fins. Depending on sea and wind conditions, flyingfish can glide up to a quarter of a mile.

The green sea turtle, an air breathing reptile, belongs to one of the world's oldest surviving species which has been in existence since the time of the early dinosaurs.

Turtles

Once a source of food for sailors, endangered green sea turtles are now protected by law, as are the hawksbill (hunted nearly to extinction for its beautiful tortoiseshell) and leatherback, the largest of all turtles reaching lengths of eight feet and weighing up to 1,100 pounds. These three marine turtles are found in the Caribbean, sleeping under reef ledges or feeding on sponges and seagrasses. With their toeless, oar-like legs they can swim at speeds approaching 20 miles per hour, and some will travel thousands of ocean miles to reach their nesting sites.

The female nests on beaches where the warm sand incubates her eggs. She drags herself onto shore in the night, selects a site and digs a hole in which 100 or more eggs are laid. After covering them, she returns to the sea having spent one to three hours on shore under cover of darkness. The two-inch-long hatchlings emerge two months later, again in the cool of the night, and crawl into the water. For years, the catching of females while they laid their eggs was a major factor in the marine turtle's decline, for as few as one in a thousand hatchlings survive to adulthood and it can take up to 20 years or more for some turtles to reach sexual maturity.

Rays

A ray is a flat-bodied fish related to the shark. Shaped like a kite with winglike pectoral fins which propel it through the water, a ray also has a long whiplike tail. There are three basic groups of ray: mantas, eagles and stingrays. Mantas are the largest, up to 22 feet in width and 3,000 pounds in weight. Mantas and eagles are active rays whereas stingrays are bottom dwellers, lying like rugs on the sea floor as they dredge up shellfish and other small animals. Its eyes and spiracles (breathing orifices) are on top of the head, its mouth and gill slits on the underside. Southern stingrays are common along Caribbean reefs, the female growing up to six feet in width. They have rows of spines along their tail which contain a poison that can inflict pain and be fatal to humans. Stingrays defend themselves against sharks by lashing with their tails but they rarely attack humans unless provoked or stepped on. Stingrays can be viewed daily in a shallow feeding area at Grand Cayman Island.

Manatees

Also called sea cows, these large aquatic mammals spend their entire life in the water. From seven to 12 feet in length and weighing 500 pounds (the males often much larger), the manatee's thick, heavy body is covered with hairless grey-brown skin. Sluggish, nocturnal bottom feeders, they propel themselves with two weak flippers and a beaver-like tail. Shy and reclusive, they live in warm, shallow and sheltered waters where they consume up to 100 pounds of vegetation daily. The female gives birth to one calf every two to five years and uses her flippers to hold the nursing calf to her chest. Both parents care for their young, one holding it while the other dives for food. The Florida manatee is found in the coastal waters of Central America, the West Indies and Florida where it's protected by law.

Tectonic Beginnings

In geological terms, the Caribbean is an active part of the world. The earth's surface is divided into crustal plates, and most of the Caribbean islands lie close to the boundaries of one of these plates. Called the Caribbean Plate, it roughly coincides with Central America and the Caribbean Sea. The slow movement of this plate has, over millions of years, formed the West Indies. Volcanic eruptions, massive uplifting, fluctuating sea levels and large-scale erosion have all played a part in shaping the islands. Today, the Caribbean Plate's eastern boundary is marked by an arc of volcanoes, some of which are still active, and earthquakes have damaged or destroyed various coastal towns over the last few centuries.

Some 70 million years ago, the Caribbean Plate began pushing against the much larger American Plate, which encompasses the western half of the Atlantic Ocean. These tectonic pressures produced three volcanic mountain ranges which now comprise the Greater Antilles and some of the Lesser Antilles, including the Virgin Islands, St. Maarten and Antigua. Meanwhile, volcanic forces were also forming the Andes Mountains of South America, branches of which extend to the north coast of South America where their partially submerged peaks are now islands, including the Dutch islands of Aruba, Bonaire and Curacao, and, to the east, the islands of Trinidad and Tobago.

All of this volcanic activity was followed by an era in which the sea temporarily covered the newly-formed islands. Sediments of sandstone

The Pitons of St. Lucia are dramatic examples of the West Indies' volcanic origins.

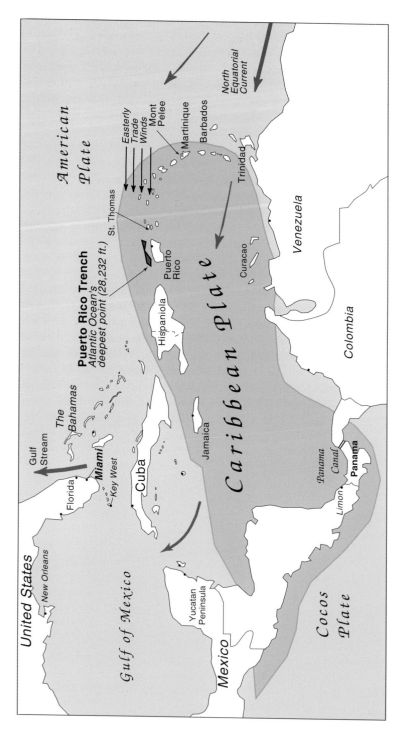

and limestone built up as the bodies of marine animals decayed, and some of the islands were flattened. Uplifting returned these islands to the sea's surface, and the Caribbean Plate began to move slowly eastward, creating a deep-sea subduction zone between it and the American Plate. A new chain of volcanoes erupted along this boundary, their conical peaks now comprising an arc of mountainous islands that extends from Saba, at the top, to Grenada, at the bottom. Sea mounts (underwater volcanoes) also lie along this boundary.

Not all of the islands are volcanic in origin. Barbados began to form about 700,000 years ago, when tectonic forces slowly pushed a section of seabed to the surface. The eastern half of Guadeloupe also formed in a similar manner, whereas its western half is volcanic in origin. The Bahamas, some of which stand only a few feet above sea level, are elevated areas of the Bahamas Bank. These islands were likely part of a large land mass in the ancient past, before rising sea levels submerged all but the highest points.

Volcanic Eruptions

Volcanoes form around an aperture in the earth's crust, through which gases, lava (molten rock) and solid fragments are ejected. A volcano's crater, its floor often covered with steam vents, is formed when the cone collapses during an eruption. Bays and harbors of the West Indies are often flooded craters. A dormant volcano quickly loses its conical shape to erosion, so any mountain that is cone-shaped can be considered a potentially active volcano. Numerous volcanoes in the Lesser Antilles are active, including St. Vincent's La Soufriere which erupted in 1979. Montserrat's Chance's Peak recently rumbled back to life, its lava dome threatening to flow down its eastern slopes, and plans were in place to evacuate the island's entire population to neighboring Antigua in the event of an eruption.

The most violent eruption in recent times was that of Martinique's Mount Pelee on May 8, 1902. Gases within the volcano reached such a critical pressure that masses of solid and liquid rock erupted into the air and a superheated cloud of burning gas and fine ash swept down the mountainside, blanketing the nearby town of St. Pierre and destroying all life in its path. Torrential rain, caused by the condensation of steam, often accompanies such an explosion.

There had been warnings that Mount Pelee would erupt, but the 30,000 residents of St. Pierre chose to ignore the earth tremors, the rumbling sounds within the volcano, and its emissions of steam and light ash. The local wildlife, however, followed their instincts and evacuated the area. When the volcano finally erupted, all but one of St. Pierre's residents – a prisoner protected by the walls of his jail cell – died in the massive explosion.

Earthquakes

Earthquakes have also plagued the West Indies. The Caribbean Plate is no longer moving north, so volcanic activity has ceased in the Greater Antilles, but there is faulting and fracturing due to the plate's moving eastward. In 1693, Port Royal on the south coast of Jamaica was completely destroyed by an earthquake. The Lesser Antilles have also experienced earthquakes in historic times with a number of ports suffering damage over the centuries, including Basseterre on St. Kitts where a quake occurred in 1974.

Earthquakes are generated by blocks of rock passing one another along fault lines (fractures in the earth's crust). Their relative movements can be vertical, horizontal or oblique, and are usually measured in inches per year, except when a sudden release of stress along a fault triggers an earthquake. An earthquake begins with tremors, followed by more violent shocks which gradually diminish. The origin (focus of a quake) is underground or underwater, and the epicenter is a point on the surface directly above the focus. The magnitude and intensity of an earthquake is determined by the Richter scale, which measures ground motion to determine the amount of energy released at the quake's origin. A reading of 4.5 on the Richter scale indicates an earthquake causing light damage; a reading of 8.5 indicates an earthquake of devastating force.

Hurricanes

Of the natural phenomena affecting the Caribbean, hurricanes have been the most feared, causing widespread loss of life and billions of dollars in property damage. Leaves are ripped from trees, palms are toppled, roofs are peeled off buildings and flying debris is scattered island-wide. For the people huddled inside boarded-up homes, the noise is deafening. A storm surge – a wall of water pushed by the hurricane – may form and crash onto shore, and reefs lying offshore are often damaged by the pounding action of waves. Even if an island is spared the winds, torrential rains from the tail of a hurricane often cause floods that wash out roads and swell rivers to dangerous levels. In a hurricane's wake, tens of thousands of residents are without electricity, running water or telephones. Some are missing a roof, or even an entire house if poorly built.

The word *hurricane* originated from the Arawak language and meant "evil spirits and big winds". The word was adopted by the Spaniards when they arrived in the Caribbean. In other parts of the world, terms such as *typhoon* and *cyclone* apply to the same sort of intense storm. Meteorologists in North America describe an intense tropical storm with winds exceeding 74 miles per hour as a hurricane.

The Caribbean islands and coastal areas of the eastern United States are vulnerable to the devastating winds and wave action of hurricanes. The National Hurricane Center in Miami keeps a constant watch on disturbances in the Atlantic Ocean in an effort to provide ample warning and reduce both loss of life and property damage.

Hurricane season for the Caribbean and the eastern seaboard of the United States starts in June and lasts through November. The northward shift of the sun increases the temperatures of the Atlantic Ocean and the air mass lying between Africa and North America. In an average year, more than 100 disturbances (low-pressure systems) with hurricane potential are observed in the Atlantic Ocean, Gulf of Mexico and Caribbean Sea; on average only 10 of these reach the tropical-storm stage and about six mature into hurricanes. The 1950s and 1960s were active years for hurricanes in the Caribbean, and meteorologists think hurricane frequency may be related to rainfall over Africa's western Sahel where hurricane seedlings originate. Rainfall in this area was above normal from 1949 to 1967, but since then has been generally below normal. A recent trend, however, seems to be one of normal rainfall and there is concern that hurricane activity may increase.

All storms in the northern hemisphere spin in a counter-clockwise direction and hurricanes are no exception. The wind speed is caused by heavy, cool air rushing to fill a low-pressure area where the warmer, lighter air is rising. If the low-pressure area is large and the pressure gradient (the rate of pressure change over distance) between it and adjacent pools of air is steep, it will attract larger amounts of cooler air. As the cooler air spins around the eye of the low-pressure system, it can begin to tighten the eye, making it smaller in diameter. This begins a

Photo University of Virgin Islands

Hurricane Marilyn was especially damaging to the Virgin Islands.
When it hit St. Thomas on September 15th, 1995, its winds exceeded
100 mph. Hundreds of yachts were sunk or severely damaged.

cycle of increasing winds and an increase of air flowing upward. The warm, rising air loses heat and, as a result, water is condensed to form massive nimbostratus clouds. Heavy torrential rain is always a precursor of an approaching hurricane.

Although a hurricane's greatest wind strength (usually between 100 and 200 mph) is at the wall or edge of its eye, where the winds cause very heavy seas and spray that reduces visbtility to almost nil, the eye itself is very calm with little wind and a warmer air temperature. A hurricane can have a diameter of 500 miles or more, and the greatest wind strength is always to the right of the hurricane's eye.

The strength or intensity of a hurricane is unrelated to its overall size and very strong hurricanes usually have relatively small eyes – less than 10 miles in diameter. Other factors come into play, such as the proximity of large high-pressure systems and whether the storm track is over warm, shallow water. Hurricanes often create large tidal surges which are perhaps the biggest concern for coastal communities. These surges are sometimes referred to as *domes* and are caused by the low pressure of the hurricane lifting the ocean's water into a mound one-to-three feet higher than the surrounding surface. This mound can result in coastal surges, with the sea level rising 20 feet or more. Swells from a storm can pulse out along the water's surface for thousands of miles and Pacific surfers often ride the oceanic memory of distant typhoons.

Hurricanes are assigned different categories depending on their storm surge, wind speed and other factors that provide a measure of the storm's destructive power. The United States National Oceanic and Atmospheric Administration (NOAA) uses five categories, beginning with category one. A hurricane of this strength will produce winds of 75 to 95 mph and, although no real damage is done to fixed building structures, damage is still significant to unanchored mobile homes and vegetation. A category-five hurricane packs winds exceeding 155 mph. Such winds inflict complete roof failures on most buildings, and some may be completely blown away. Massive evacuation of residential areas within 10 miles of the shoreline is required.

In this century, there have been just two category-five hurricanes – one in 1935 which hit the Florida Keys especially hard, and Hurricane Camille in 1969. Andrew was the third-strongest storm in history to hit the Carribbean and United States. With sustained winds of 145 mph and gusts over 175 mph, Andrew annihilated homes and businesses along a 30-mile swath through Dade County in Florida. When it was over, more than 60,000 homes were destroyed and 200,000 people left homeless. Insurance pay-outs and government recovery expenditures topped $29 billion – the costliest hurricane on record. Eleven insurance companies failed and 40 companies pulled out or curtailed underwriting property in Florida after Andrew. But it could have been even worse. The National Hurricane Center in Miami estimates that if Andrew had tracked only 20 miles further north when it hit Florida, losses would have topped $75 billion.

In the Caribbean, Hurricanes Gilbert and Hugo caused major destruction. In 1988, Hurricane Gilbert – a category-three hurricane –

Photo NASA

This spectacular view of the eye of Hurricane Diana in 1984, shot by NASA, shows the intense center of the storm.

pounded Jamaica, with the eye of the storm passing right over the capital of Kingston. More recently, in mid-September 1995, Hurricane Marilyn was especially destructive among the Lesser Antilles as it passed north of Martinique and across Dominica. When Marilyn hit the U.S. Virgin Islands, it was a strengthening category-two, nearly category-three, hurricane. The strongest part of the hurricane, the eyewall to the east and northeast of the center, passed over St. Thomas and surface winds of 110 mph were recorded. Five people were killed and property damage was widespread. The island has since recovered and cruise ships returned to Charlotte Amalie within a few months of Marilyn.

Fortunately for the residents of the Caribbean, and for cruise ship passengers, the prediction and surveillance of hurricanes has improved dramatically in the last 30 years. The National Hurricane Center in Miami successfully provided accurate advance warnings for Hurricanes Gilbert, Andrew and Marilyn, resulting in a relatively small loss of life. In addition to hurricane forecast centers in the United States, warning stations have been established throughout the West Indies.

Weather systems in the Atlantic are monitored 24 hours a day with highly advanced radar and satellites to give hurricane forecasters the ability to detect and track storms long before they hit land. Island residents are warned of an approaching hurricane up to three days in advance – time enough to nail plywood over the windows or bolt the hurricane shutters. They also make sure they have survival kits which include flashlights, batteries, extra food and other essential items. Many retreat to public shelters, built of solid concrete, to wait out the storm.

The officers of cruise ships receive hurricane information from the National Hurricane Center and from NOAA. A cruise ship will sometimes forego a port if the captain decides conditions warrant such avoidance. The ship will either head to another port, or spend a day at sea, keeping well away from the track of the hurricane.

A beach on Antigua was missing some sand following Hurricane Luis, which struck in September of 1995.

PART II

The Voyage and the Ports

(Top) *A Little Inn By The Sea, near Fort Lauderdale*

(Middle) *Anna Maria Island, south of Tampa*

(Bottom) *Bayside Marketplace, across the water from Miami's cruise port*

(Top) Nassau, capital of the Bahamas, is a popular cruise port.
(Middle) Government House in Nassau is one of numerous colonial buildings reflecting the city's British past.
(Bottom) A turquoise sea laps ashore in the Bahamas.

FLORIDA

Atlantic Ocean

Jacksonville

•*St. Augustine*

•*Daytona Beach*

■*Orlando*

Port Canaveral

Clearwater •
■**Tampa**

St. Petersburg•

•*Sarasota*

•*Venice*

Charlotte Harbor

Lake Okeechobee

Palm Beach

Fort Meyers •

Fort Lauderdale

Gulf of Mexico

Naples •

🚢 **Cruise Ports**

Everglades National Park

Miami

0   30   60

Statute miles

Florida Bay   • Key Largo

Key West

Straits of Florida

CHAPTER ONE

FLORIDA

The Caribbean Connection

Florida is America's answer to the Caribbean. Warmed by subtropical waters, cooled by trade winds, this southern state of swaying palms and coral cays has much in common with the history, culture and natural habitat of the West Indies. An international tourist destination, Florida is also a gateway to the Caribbean and its cruise ports are among the busiest in the world.

Florida counts its visitors, and cruise passengers, in the millions. Every conceivable 'fun in the sun' attraction is here – palm-shaded swimming pools, championship golf courses, tennis camps, shopping malls, sporting events and theme parks galore, including one of the world's most popular – Walt Disney World ® near Orlando. Yet, it is water more than anything that defines Florida. The sea is readily accessible from any point in the state and some of the best beaches lie on barrier cays that line much of the splendid coastline. And the water doesn't stop at the seashore. Rivers and canals meander past cypress stands and waterfront homes, linking many of the lakes, lagoons and wetlands that make Florida an angler's paradise.

Lake Okeechobee is the largest of these lakes and is a chief source of water (along with Big Cypress Swamp) for the Everglades – a marshy, tropical savanna extending southward to Florida Bay. Covering more than 4,000 square miles, the Everglades is a unique wilderness region of slow-flowing water. Sawgrass and hammocks (island-like masses of vegetation) grow here in the solidly packed black muck which has

Beautiful beaches line the coasts of Florida, including this stretch of sand at Lauderdale-By-The-Sea.

formed over millions of years as vegetation decays in the nearly stagnant water. Everglades National Park includes Florida Bay and its many islets and islands, and contains a great variety of flora and fauna, including palms, pines and mangrove forests, and such endangered species as the crocodile, alligator, egret and bald eagle.

Birdlife abounds in Florida, where critical wetlands are now protected as wildlife refuges. A shoreline of seemingly endless beaches and holiday resorts has become dotted with parks, preserves and recreation areas. These conservation measures follow a century of unbridled development in which men with a passion for building – be it hotels, railroads, planned communities or theme parks – were attracted to Florida's broad, untouched landscapes.

The first 'developer' to arrive on Florida's shores was Spanish explorer Ponce de Leon. Seeking the fabled Fountain of Youth, he landed near the site of St. Augustine in 1513 during the Easter season (Pascua Florida) and mistook the long peninsula for an island, which he claimed for Spain. Turning south, he explored the coast to Key West, then headed up the west side to Cape Romano before retracing his route to Miami Bay and returning to his settlement in Puerto Rico where gold and slave labor had made him a wealthy man. The next year the Spanish king commissioned Ponce de Leon to colonize the 'isle of Florida' but it wasn't until 1521 that he returned with 200 men, farm implements and domestic animals, his two vessels landing in the vicinity of Charlotte Harbor.

The development-minded conquistador's plans were, however, thwarted by the Native Americans already living in the area. Called Caloosas, they built their dwellings on high rectangular mounds surrounded by waterways and boat basins. These terraced mounds were interconnected with ramps and shell-covered causeways and canals, some of which led to burial mounds and other midden mounds where waste was discarded. Temples, storehouses and leaders' homes were built on the tallest mounds. These people, their urban culture over 2,000 years old, did not take kindly to the sight of strangers attempting to subdivide their land, and they attacked the Spanish party, fatally wounding Ponce de Leon with a poisoned arrow. The Spaniards retreated, sailing immediately for Cuba where their leader died.

Spain abandoned any further plans to colonize Florida until the French began encroaching upon the area. St. Augustine was founded in 1565 to protect Spain's shipping route through the Straits of Florida. England, intent on expanding her American colonial holdings, was the next European country to threaten Spain's hold on Florida. At the end of the Seven Years War, England acquired Florida in the Treaty of Paris (1763), then returned it to Spain in 1783 at the conclusion of the American Revolution. But Spain's hold on Florida remained tenuous and in 1819 Florida was reluctantly ceded to the United States, with

'Old Florida' endures in grand seaside hotels, complete with Florentine fountains, many of which were built by the New York financier Henry Flagler in the late 1800s when he invested millions to develop the state as a winter playground.

Photo Carnival Cruise Line

Miami, a former trading post, is today the busiest cruise port in the world, with luxury ships departing its harbor year-round on cruises to the Bahamas and Caribbean.

official U.S. occupation taking place in 1821. Andrew Jackson was appointed military governor and the next year Florida became a territory, with settlers from other states soon establishing cotton and tobacco plantations around the new capital of Tallahassee. The resident Native Americans – the Seminoles – resisted being displaced and a small band fled to the Everglades where their descendants live today on reservations near Lake Okeechobee.

Florida, a slave-holding state, was admitted to the state of the Union in 1845, but seceded from the Union in 1861 to join the Confederacy. After the war, Florida's new constitution provided for black suffrage and the state was readmitted to the Union in 1868. A decade later, New York financier Henry Flagler paid a visit to Florida's east coast. He envisioned the state as the perfect winter playground and proceeded to build a business empire of railroads, steamships and palatial hotels, while anonymously donating to the construction of schools, churches and hospitals. Another industrial tycoon, Henry Plant, built railroads and hotels on Florida's west coast. Sections of the Everglades were drained, starting in 1906, and land booms caused real estate prices to soar one year and plummet the next.

Following World War II, sustained growth came in the form of manufacturing, especially in aeronautics after the opening of the John F. Kennedy Space Center at Cape Canaveral. Florida's population, now over 13 million, continues to grow with thousands of retired persons moving here. Nations of the Caribbean, most notably Cuba, are also a source of immigrants. In 1980, when Fidel Castro briefly opened the port of Mariel, more than 100,000 Cuban refugees were boat-lifted to Florida.

Florida's resources are diverse. A leading grower of citrus fruits, as well as vegetables, sugarcane and tobacco, the state also supports cattle and dairy farming, and the sea is a source of crab, lobster and shrimp. The state's timber is yellow pine, from which lumber and wood products are produced, and its mineral resources include phosphate rock, gravel and sand. Florida is not without problems, however. Most pressing, many would say, is the degradation of the natural environment, with south Florida containing one of the most threatened wildlife habitats in the country.

In the 1920s a ring dike was built around Lake Okeechobee to prevent water from blowing off the lake during hurricanes. This diking, along with land development in Big Cypress Swamp, disrupted the natural flow of water into the Everglades, and damaged plant and animal life. In the 1980s Florida instigated a massive conservation project which called for the reflooding of drained swampland and restoring to their natural state those areas previously cleared for agriculture and development. Then, in 1992, a natural disaster in the form of Hurricane Andrew again disrupted these sensitive ecosystems, and their recovery is expected to take several years.

Tourism, which has contributed to Florida's environmental problems, may prove to be beneficial in the long run as areas of natural and historical significance are preserved for the enjoyment of visitors, residents and, most importantly, for posterity.

MIAMI

Named for an American Indian tribe, Miami was a trading post when Henry Flagler, having built grand hotels at St. Augustine and Palm Beach, set his sights on this southern port. He made Miami a railroad terminus in 1896, the year it was incorporated, then proceeded to dredge the harbor to accommodate his fleet of steamships. Set on a low ridge overlooking Biscayne Bay, Miami is now the transportation and business hub of south Florida. It is also the busiest cruise port in the world with ships based here year-round for sailings to the Bahamas and the Caribbean.

Greater Miami encompasses the City of Miami, Miami Beach, Coral Gables, Hialeah and many smaller communities. About half of the City of Miami's population is Hispanic, many of Cuban descent, with hundreds of thousands of Cuban refugees moving here from the late '50s to early '70s, settling in the city's **Little Havana** section. Calle Ocho

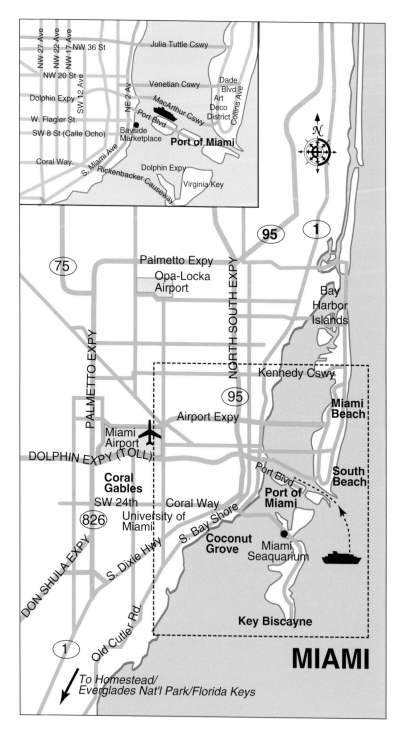

(Southwest Eighth Street) is the main thoroughfare and scene of an annual Hispanic festival that's held in March and stretches the length of 23 lively blocks of music and dancing.

Miami Beach, located on a barrier island in Biscayne Bay, was a mangrove swamp until connected to the mainland by a wooden bridge in 1913. Opulent hotels and huge estates were soon built here, while the South Beach area was sub-divided into smaller lots and developed as a middle-class resort of modest hotels and apartments. Many of these buildings went up during the Depression, when visitors came to Miami Beach to temporarily escape their worries. The area suffered a decline following World War II. Then, in 1979, South Beach's square mile area of Art Deco structures, built between the two world wars, was declared a national historic district – the first containing registered buildings less than 50 years old. Their style, sometimes referred to as Tropical Deco, consists of smooth lines and white exteriors trimmed with hot colors. During South Beach's revitalization in the late '80s and early '90s, many of the run-down hotels were refurbished and repainted in pastel colors. Today the area is one of the trendiest in America, where the steady stream of pedestrian and car traffic along Ocean Drive includes movie stars and fashion models frequenting the stylish eateries. The Art Deco Welcome Center at 1001 Ocean Drive is a good place to start a tour of South Beach. Points of interest include the Cardozo Hotel at 1300 Ocean Drive, which was featured in the 1959 film *A Hole in the Head,* starring Frank Sinatra.

Miami Beach's revitalized Art Deco District is one of the trendiest hotel-and-restaurant strips in America.

Coral Gables, situated four miles south of downtown Miami, was founded in 1925 at the height of the Florida land boom which sparked an explosion of growth in the Miami area. A planned city designed by George Merrick, its Mediterranean architecture includes such highlights as the Venetian Pool – a huge municipal pool set in a coral quarry with caves, waterfalls and arched bridges. Merrick's boyhood home, a gabled plantation house on Coral Way, is open to the public. His dream city of canals, plazas and tree-shaded streets is also home to the University of Miami, where the Lowe Art Museum houses a permanent collection of Renaissance and Baroque art as well as Spanish and American paintings and artwork by North American Indians. The Orange Bowl Classic & Festival has been a major annual event in Miami since 1933 when the University of Miami played the Manhattan University.

Coconut Grove, on the waterfront east of Coral Gables, was settled in the late 19th century by New England intellectuals and Bahamian seamen. The conical home of founding father Ralph Munroe, a New York yacht designer, is called the Barnacle and is open to the public at 3485 Main Highway. Also in Coconut Grove is the Vizcaya Museum and Gardens (3251 S. Miami Avenue), a restored Italian Renaissance-style villa built in 1916 as a winter residence for industrialist John Deering. The 34-room mansion, set in grounds of formal gardens and fountains overlooking Biscayne Bay, contains 15th- through 19th-century antiques and artwork.

A toll causeway links the mainland with **Virginia Key,** location of the Miami Seaquarium, and **Key Biscayne,** where the late Richard Nixon had a presidential retreat. Both islands contain parks, with a golf course and tennis stadium located on Key Biscayne.

Getting Around

The Port of Miami's cruise port is a two-island complex in Biscayne Bay adjacent to downtown Miami. The port, consisting of a dozen passenger terminals, is located eight miles from Miami International Airport. Most cruise lines provide passenger and baggage transfer services between the airport and cruise terminal.

It's a short taxi ride from the cruise terminals to Bayside Marketplace, a bustling waterfront development of shops, restaurants and open-air entertainment. Tour boats depart daily from Bayside on 90-minute narrated tours of the port, affording passengers a view of the Miami skyline, waterfront mansions and other sights. Trolley tours of Miami and Miami Beach also depart regularly from Bayside, as do water taxis which ply the waters of Biscayne Bay, stopping at various waterfront attractions. The elevated Metromover links downtown Miami's major hotels and shopping areas.

SHOPPING & DINING: The Bayside Marketplace is a popular spot for cruise passengers with a good selection of waterfront restaurants and shops. Other areas that offer a combination of shopping and dining are bohemian-flavored **Coconut Grove**, with its interesting shops, open-air bistros and sidewalk cafes along CocoWalk on Grand Avenue, and **Coral Gables** where its Miracle Mile – the main shopping thoroughfare on Coral Way between Southwest 42nd Avenue and Douglas Road – is lined with some of Miami's best restaurants. For a taste of Latin America and Miami's famous Cuban coffee, try one of the eateries on Calle Ocho in Little Havana.

Whether your taste in cuisine is Continental or Cuban, French or family fare, Miami has a restaurant to suit your preference. The city offers not only a multicultural spectrum of dining choices, its finer restaurants feature chefs who excel in creating innovative dishes that accentuate the region's abundance of fresh seafood, fruit and vegetables, blending these ingredients with a spicy mix of Caribbean and Latin American influences. The result: a main dish such as grilled yellow-fin tuna with pineapple papaya salsa and rum coconut butter and, for dessert, the ever popular Key Lime Pie.

For seafood lovers seeking a refined ambiance, **The Fish Market** (on Biscayne Boulevard at 16th Street) is recommended. Highly popular is the family-run **Joe's Stone Crab Restaurant**, a Miami Beach favorite since opening in 1913. **The South Pointe Seafood House** in Miami Beach is a good spot to watch the cruise ships come and go, and for a sunset view of the Miami skyline, try **The Rusty Pelican** on Key Biscayne.

GOLF: There are hundreds of golf courses in Florida, and the Greater Miami area has a diverse selection of courses designed by top names in golf course architecture. The **Doral Resort** (592-2000), near the Miami International Airport, has four 18-hole courses including one of the most challenging courses in the Miami area. The **Links at Key Biscayne** (361-9129), one of the top-ranked municipal courses in the U.S., is built around lagoons and contains four waterside holes with views of the Miami skyline. The city-owned **Biltmore Golf Course** (460-5364) in Coral Gables opened in 1925 and was recently refurbished, and the **Golf Club of Miami** (821-0111) offers three different courses.

WHERE TO STAY: Greater Miami has more than 500 hotels and motels providing over 50,000 rooms. The selection is extensive and covers everything from traditional to hip.

Yesteryear's elegance can be enjoyed at the Biltmore Hotel, built in 1926 as the centerpiece of Coral Gables. In a lovely setting of waterways, tennis courts and golf links, this is a classic grand hotel with a vaulted lobby and an opulent swimming pool/bar area.

Nearby in Coconut Grove, is the modern **Grand Bay Hotel** overlooking Biscayne Bay. Luciano Pavarotti's two-level suite, which contains a baby grand piano and circular staircase, can be rented when he's not there.

In downtown Miami, the **Hotel Inter-Continental Miami** contains a stunning lobby that features a massive marble sculpture by Henry Moore. Across the bay, in Miami Beach, the choices of accommodation range from luxury resorts and hotels, such as the highly-touted **Casa Grande**, to small, stylish establishments in the Art Deco District of South Beach.

FORT LAUDERDALE

The 'Venice of America', Fort Lauderdale is interwoven with more than 270 miles of natural and artificial waterways, including a navigable canal that connects with Lake Okeechobee. In neighborhoods crisscrossed with canals, both cars and yachts can be seen parked outside the palm-shaded homes.

Situated on the New River, this retirement and resort city of some 150,000 residents was settled around a fort built by Major William Lauderdale in 1837-38, during the Seminole War. Fort Lauderdale was incorporated in 1911 and the city grew rapidly during the Florida land boom of the 1920s. Its suburbs continue to expand, and today close to 4.5 million people live in the metro area. Fort Lauderdale has one of the most popular beaches in the country, one of the largest marinas in North

Recreational sailors enjoy a fresh Atlantic breeze at the entrance to Port Everglades, just south of Fort Lauderdale.

Photo Norwegian Cruise Line

A cruise ship returns to Port Everglades, where the nearby beaches of Fort Lauderdale stretch northward as far as the eye can see.

America, and a cruise port that is fast becoming one of the busiest in the world, second only to Miami.

Fort Lauderdale's seaport was originally a small lake used by recreational boaters. Locally known as Bay Mabel Harbor, it came to the attention of a developer and businessman named Joseph Young who moved to the area in the early 1920s, purchased 1,440 acres adjacent to the lake, and created the Hollywood Harbor Development Company. On February 28, 1927, expectant spectators gathered to watch an explosion that would remove the lake's rock barrier to the ocean. At the appointed time, President Calvin Coolidge pressed a detonator in the White House, but nothing happened. Nonetheless, the harbor was officially opened that day and the rock barrier was removed a short while later. In 1930, the new seaport was named Port Everglades – chosen from submissions to a naming contest.

The port is located opposite the John U. Lloyd Beach State Recreation Area, situated on 251 acres of barrier island separating the Intracoastal Waterway from the Atlantic Ocean. The park is named in memory of a local attorney whose efforts helped bring about its creation. The park is entered at its south end via Dania Beach Boulevard, and its broad flat beach – popular for swimming and sunning – is also one of Broward County's most important sea turtle nesting beaches. A jetty at the north end is excellent for fishing and watching the comings and goings of cruise ships and small sailing craft.

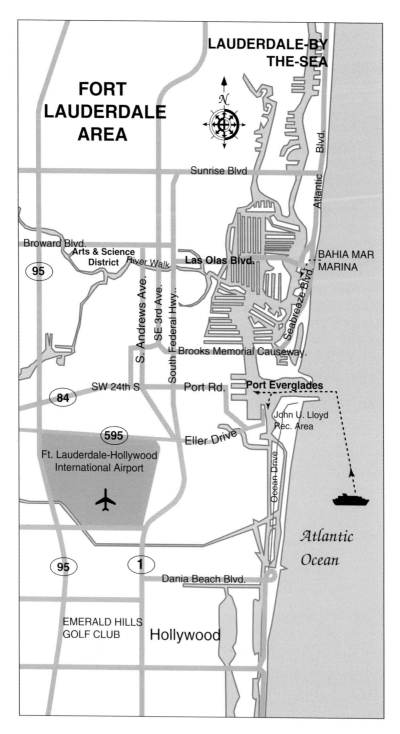

The park also contains an open-air Environmental Education Facility. This timber structure and adjoining waterfront boardwalk were built by Port Everglades in 1991 as part of a wildlife protection/awareness project which includes a comprehensive Manatee Protection Program. The Florida manatee is a protected species and in winter months these sluggish sea mammals frequent the Port where they are attracted to the heated effluent from the Florida Power & Light plant. When calving mothers were found to be utilizing the FPL discharge canal, a section of it became designated a 'Manatee Nursery' and access to it was restricted. Manatees and other marine life also frequent the mangrove-lined tidal waterway that runs down the middle of the John Lloyd park.

Getting Around

Located south of downtown, Port Everglades is an artificial deepsea port with a short, straight entrance channel. Its passenger terminals are modern and efficient, with long-term parking available in nearby self-parking garages. Less than two miles from Fort Lauderdale/Hollywood International Airport (and 30 minutes from Miami International Airport via I-95), Port Everglades is serviced by a fleet of taxis and by several car rental companies that provide shuttle service between the Port and their rental lots.

Water taxis and tour boats are a popular way to explore Fort Lauderdale's waterways. Water Taxi picks up at most waterfront hotels

The John U. Lloyd Recreation Area, with manatees and sea turtles among the protected species sighted here, lies across the channel from Port Everglades.

A passing pageantry of river vessels can be enjoyed along the pleasant pathways of Fort Lauderdale's Riverwalk.

and restaurants north of the Brooks Memorial Causeway. Call 467-6677 for a pick-up; the one-way fare between two points is $7.00 and the round-trip fare is $12. The Jungle Queen operates two sightseeing vessels out of Bahia Mar Yacht Center. Another sightseeing vessel, the *Carrie B.*, offers narrated, 90-minute tours departing Riverwalk at SE 5th Avenue. The cruise lines also offer sightseeing tours for disembarking passengers and these often include a boat ride along the city's scenic waterways.

LOCAL SIGHTS: Las Olas Boulevard is an upscale shopping street of boutiques and restaurants. The Greater Fort Lauderdale Convention & Visitors Bureau is located at 200 E. Las Olas Boulevard

At the western end of Las Olas is **Riverwalk**, a lovely promenade on the north bank of the New River. Attractions in the Riverwalk area – also known as the **Arts and Science District** – include Esplanade Park which features outdoor exhibits on astronomy and navigation; the Museum of Art; a complex housing the Museum of Discovery and Science, and Blockbuster IMAX Theater; the Broward Center for the Performing Arts; and the Fort Lauderdale Historical Society Museum.

The eastern half of Las Olas runs through an exclusive residential area of canal-lined streets called **The Isles**. Nearby is the Bahia Mar Marina and the International Swimming Hall of Fame. To the east lies Fort Lauderdale's famous beach which used to attract crowds of college students on spring break. They go elsewhere now, and the beach has been given a multi-million-dollar facelift. A wave-themed beachfront promenade consists of wide walkways, crested gateways and neon lamp posts. Across the road from the beach is the Hugh Taylor Birch State Recreation Area with nature trails, picnic facilities and a museum. With more than 50 **golf courses** in the Fort Lauderdale area, there's plenty to choose from. The Emerald Hills Golf Club in Hollywood, about two miles south of the airport, is one of many open to the public.

SHOPPING AND DINING: A good selection of restaurants is found along Las Olas Boulevard and in Lauderdale-By-The-Sea where the **Sea Watch**, serving superb seafood, is popular for lunch and dinner. American cuisine can be enjoyed at **Burt & Jack's**, co-owned by movie star Burt Reynolds and situated on a scenic lookout near the passenger terminals of Port Everglades. Window shoppers will want to take a stroll along **Las Olas Boulevard**, the 'Rodeo Drive' of Fort Lauderdale. Serious shoppers should head to the huge **Sawgrass Mills Mall** on Sunrise Boulevard, where more than a mile of shops are located in the 'World's Largest Outlet Mall'.

The oceanfront boulevard proceeds north to **Lauderdale-by-the-Sea**, an inviting stretch of sand, restaurants and motels. Beyond is Pompano Beach, Hillsboro Beach and Deerfield Beach, and south of Fort Lauderdale are the beaches of John U. Lloyd State Recreation Area, Dania and Hollywood. There are 23 miles of beach in the Fort Lauderdale area, the shoreline punctuated by fishing piers.

WHERE TO STAY: Whether it's a waterfront resort hotel in downtown Fort Lauderdale or a more modest, low-rise motel in Lauderdale-by-the-Sea, the selection of accommodation is diverse both in character and cost. The beachfront **Lago Mar Resort Hotel & Club** has an elegant atmosphere with its bougainvillea-bordered swimming lagoon and luxurious lobby. Four restaurants, two swimming pools, tennis courts and miniature golf are among its extensive facilities.

The **Riverside Hotel** on Las Olas Boulevard, built in 1936, is distinctly decorated with tropical murals and finely appointed rooms, the best ones overlooking the New River. North of downtown, in Lauderdale-by-the-Sea, the wide array of comfortable motels includes **A Little Inn By The Sea** with its bright and airy rooms overlooking a beach-side swimming pool. Guest facilities include a tennis court, and breakfast is served daily in the tiled lobby area.

TAMPA

Tampa's impressive harbor is one of the city's greatest assets. Located on Tampa Bay, an inlet of the Gulf of Mexico, Tampa is the third largest city in Florida and one of the largest ports in the U.S. Incorporated in 1855, Tampa has long been a shipping and manufacturing hub on the Gulf Coast.

Tampa Bay was visited by Panfilo de Narvaez in 1528, and the sole survivor of this Spanish expedition was rescued in 1539 by Hernando De Soto. He also negotiated a peace treaty with the Native Americans, on the present site of the University of Tampa, but they remained hostile and for almost two centuries Europeans avoided the area.

The first white settlement began in 1823 and Fort Brooke was built the next year. A farming and fishing town grew around the fort which was taken by Union troops during the Civil War. The late 1800s brought a surge in development with the construction of railroads, the discovery of phosphate, an expanding fishing industry and the introduction of cigar making in Ybor City, the center of Tampa's Hispanic population. During the Spanish-American War, Tampa became a military base with Theodore Roosevelt training his Rough Riders there.

A commercial center, Tampa also has a thriving arts-and-culture scene which includes the Florida Symphony Orchestra and the Tampa Ballet. It's also a sports-oriented city, and several major league baseball teams have spring training camps in area. Tampa Stadium, home to the Tampa Bay Buccaneers of the NFL, is the locale of an annual mock invasion by the legendary pirate Jose Gasparilla.

Tampa shares the shores of Tampa Bay with neighboring St. Petersburg and Clearwater. **St. Petersburg** is a popular resort and retirement community, its places of interest including a municipal pier, the Salvador Dali Museum and a Museum of Fine Arts, all located on

Photo Florida Division of Tourism

Caribbean-bound cruise ships pass beneath the 11-mile Sunshine Skyway Bridge, spanning the entrance to Tampa Bay.

the bay waterfront. **Clearwater**,with a thriving tourist industry dating back to 1896 when railroad baron Henry Plant built a luxury resort called The Belleview on a bluff overlooking the water, includes a long island of white sand beaches connected to the mainland by a causeway.

The most impressive bridge in the area, however, is the one spanning the mouth of Tampa Bay. Completed in 1987, the Sunshine Skyway Bridge is a dramatic sight for both motorists and passengers on board Caribbean-bound cruise ships that pass beneath this 11-mile-long span when heading to and from the Gulf of Mexico.

Getting Around

Tampa International Airport, one of the top-rated airports in the U.S., is located 12 miles from downtown and the Garrison Seaport Center where the cruise ships dock. The Tampa-Ybor Trolley offers daily service around downtown Tampa, Ybor City and Garrison Seaport Center. A Visitor Information Center is located downtown at the corner of Ashley and Madison streets.

The fascinating Florida Aquarium, open daily from 9 a.m. to 6:00 p.m., is located right beside Tampa's cruise passenger terminal at Garrison Seaport Center.

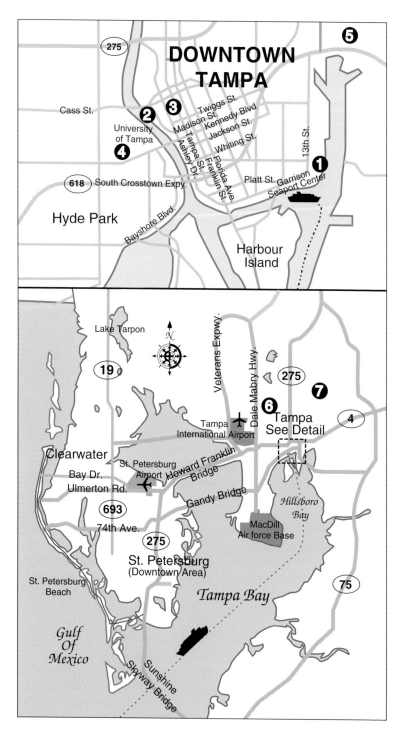

BEACHES: The Bay Area's beaches are concentrated on the barrier islands of Clearwater and St. Petersburg, a popular one being Indian Rocks Beach on Sand Key.

GOLF: There are over 90 courses in the Tampa Bay area, many of which are open to the public. Babe Zaharias Golf Course (932-8932), Rogers Park Golf Course (234-1911) and USF Golf Course (632-6893) are all located north of downtown Tampa; the Rocky Point Golf Course (884-5141) is just west of the Tampa International Airport.

TAMPA ATTRACTIONS: The **(1) Florida Aquarium** is located right beside the passenger terminals at Garrison Seaport Center. It features sea creatures in near-natural habitats as well as a fascinating exhibit in which visitors follow the path of a water drop from its underground source to the open sea, viewing aquatic animals and plants native to Florida along the way.

The **(2) Tampa Bay Performing Arts Center** and **Tampa Museum of Art** are located downtown overlooking the Hillsborough River. East on Franklin Street is the Spanish-Mediterranean-style **(3) Tampa Theatre**, a restored 1926 movie palace.

Across the Hillsborough River, on the University of Tampa campus, is the **(4) Henry B. Plant Museum**, housed in a wing of an opulent building originally built as the Tampa Bay Hotel by Henry Plant in 1891. It's a striking example of Moorish-Revival architecture and is a city landmark with its domed spires.

Northeast of the downtown core is historic **(5) Ybor City.** Settled by Cubans, Spaniards and other Europeans, this designated national landmark district features Mediterranean-style buildings housing art galleries, cafes and antique stores. Popular attractions here include the Tampa Rico Cigar Company (a retail store with cigar-rolling demonstrations) and tours of the Ybor City Brewing Company, located in a 100-year-old cigar factory.

Animals in their natural habitats can be seen at **(6) Lowry Park Zoological Garden** which also operates a manatee research and rehabilitation center. The **(7) Busch Gardens** theme park is famous for its large African zoo, tropical garden and big rides such as the inverted roller coaster.

SHOPPING & DINING: Old Hyde Park Village in the historic Hyde Park area of Tampa contains more than 60 shops as well as restaurants and movie theatres. **Ybor Square** is another historic marketplace, consisting of three large brick buildings converted into shops and ethnic restaurants. **Brandon Town Center Mall**, east of downtown Tampa, is the Bay Area's newest shopping attraction, with more than 100 stores and numerous eateries. For unusal gifts, the Tampa Museum of Art in downtown Tampa and the Salvador Dali Museum in downtown St. Petersburg are worth visiting.

The Belleview Mido Resort Hotel, built in 1897 by the railroad baron Henry B. Plant, was a popular retreat for industrial tycoons who arrived by private rail car, more than dozen of which were sometimes parked on the grounds of this palatial resort.

WHERE TO STAY: Accommodation in Tampa ranges from luxury hotels to family-oriented motor inns. Some of the Tampa area's best hotels are situated on Tampa Bay, such as the Hyatt Regency Westshore and the Stouffer Renaissance Vinoy Resort. Pink and palatial, the resort's **Vinoy Park Hotel** was built in 1925 and is listed on the National Register of Historic Places. Nearby on the bay front is the more modest **Grayl's Lantern Lane**, built in the Spanish style in 1922. Clearwater's best known heritage hotel is the Victorian-style **Belleview Mido Resort Hotel**, also listed in the National Registry of Historic Places. The largest occupied wooden structure in the world, this gracious hotel with four restaurants is surrounded by beautiful grounds containing swimming pools, red clay tennis courts and an 18-hole golf course.

PORT CANAVERAL

Cape Canaveral is better known as a spaceport than a seaport, but Port Canaveral is increasingly busy as a staging area for cruise ships. Only 50 miles east of Orlando, Port Canaveral is ideally situated for passengers looking to combine a Caribbean-style cruise with a visit to Walt Disney World. And those fascinated with space travel can begin or end their cruise with a visit to Kennedy Space Center and the Cape Canaveral Air Force Station.

Since 1947, the low sandy promontory of Cape Canaveral has been the principal U.S. launching site for long-range missiles, earth satellites, manned space flights and space shuttle missions. John Glenn, the first American to orbit the earth in 1963, and Neil Armstrong, the first man on the moon in 1969, were launched from this cape. In 1982, operational flights of the space shuttles began here. Missile launches can be watched from Jetty Park right in Port Canaveral. Other popular viewing spots include Cocoa Beach and the Merritt Island National Wildlife Refuge, location of Spaceport USA which features multimedia displays on the U.S. space program, including a moon rock and an actual spacecraft. In its IMAX theatre you can watch footage of astronauts in space on a 5-1/2-storey screen. Bus tours of the Kennedy Space Center and Cape Canaveral Air Force Station begin at Spaceport USA. Nearby is the U.S. Astronaut Hall of Fame.

The Canaveral National Seashore, north of the Kennedy Space Center, contains 25 miles of unspoiled barrier beaches and grassy dunes, with swimming beaches at either end. The community of Cocoa Beach, south of Port Canaveral, features a downtown section called Olde Cocoa Village in which restaurants and specialty shops are housed in heritage buildings along cobblestone lanes.

Seeing More of Florida

By rental car is the best way to tour Florida, which has implemented policies to make touring safer for visiting motorists. Company stickers no longer identify rental cars as such, and sunburst logo highway signs help visitors find their way to destinations. Tourists are advised to take certain precautions, such as driving with the car doors locked and not stopping if flagged down by a stranger or bumped from behind. Other common sense advice includes keeping valuables locked in the trunk of your rental car and parking in well-lit areas at night. Millions of visitors tour Florida each year and, of these, the number who become victims of crime is very small.

Homestead: The gateway to Everglades National Park, Biscayne National Park and the Florida Keys, this small city is the center of Florida's fruit and nursery production. One of its major attractions is **Coral Castle** (two miles north on US 1) which was built from massive blocks of coral by a Latvian immigrant who labored alone from 1920 to 1940.

Biscayne National Park: Located south of Miami, this undeveloped wilderness park is 95% underwater and contains miles of coral reefs. Its shallow waters are very clear and warm – a natural habitat for sponges, crabs, manatees and more than 500 different kinds of fish, including colorful parrotfish and angelfish. The park is primarily accessible by boat, with tour boats operating out of park headquarters at

Convoy Point, nine miles east of Homestead on SW 328 Street. Glass-bottom boat rides depart mid-morning; snorkeling/scuba excursions depart in the early afternoon.

Everglades National Park: The Everglades, a slow-moving river about 50 miles wide and only a few inches deep, contains mangrove forests, sawgrass marshes, pinelands and hammocks. The tropical and sub-tropical foliage also includes six species of palm, and the park is a sanctuary for manatees, crocodiles, sea turtles and nearly 300 kinds of land and wading birds. Mosquitoes proliferate from May to November, and insect repellent is recommended year-round.

Parachute Key Visitor Center is located at the park's southeast entrance and another, the Royal Palm Visitor Center, is just inside the park. A road leads through the southern half of the Everglades to the Flamingo Ranger Station and Visitor Center on Florida Bay. In addition to canoe trails, boardwalks and nature trails in the Flamingo area, tours can be taken of Florida Bay and the backcountry for possible sightings of manatees, alligators and many varieties of birds, as well as the opportunity to disembark at a hammock to see Indian open-air dwellings. The Flamingo area has restaurants, accommodations, charter fishing boats and canoe rentals.

The 99-mile Wilderness Waterway winds between Flamingo and Everglades City, situated on the northwest side of the park, where airboat tours can be taken to the Ten Thousand Islands – a mangrove wilderness of islets, oyster bars and shell beaches.

Boating is a popular pastime in Florida where miles of waterways meander past coastal communities such as Venice on the Gulf Coast.

Gulf Coast: A drive south of Tampa takes in historic Bradenton and nearby Anna Maria Island with its public pier and numerous white sand beaches. Next is Sarasota, a cultural center of Florida, its bay protected by a string of keys connected by bridges. One of Sarasota's noted attractions is the Ringling Museum of Art, located on the circus baron's winter estate which was built in the Italian Renaissance style with fountains, courtyards and gardens. The art museum's huge galleries are lined with priceless paintings, including one of America's largest Baroque art collections.

Venice, to the south of Sarasota, is another upscale community of palm-lined streets and waterfront restaurants. Fort Myers, about 50 miles south of Venice, is where you'll find Sanibel Island – famous for sea shells by the seashore. Fort Myers was once a resort getaway for the wealthy, and the winter estates of Thomas Edison and Henry Ford are now museums. A wide range of accommodations can be found along the scenic Gulf Coast. In **Bradenton**, the Spanish-style Holiday Inn Riverfront on the Manatee River is a good choice. The Crow's Nest Marina Restaurant & Tavern on **Venice's** waterfront is recommended for lunch or dinner.

Boca Raton/Palm Beach: The coastal drive north of Fort Lauderdale to Palm Beach follows a scenic highway, bordered by the Atlantic Ocean to the east and the Intracoastal Waterway to the west. Spanish River Park, in Boca Raton, provides access to an ocean beach and contains a lagoon, nature trails and picnic sites.

Palm Beach is where you'll see some of Florida's most palatial estates along Ocean Boulevard. For a taste of Old Florida, visit The Breakers (on County Road) – a luxury grand hotel originally built by tycoon Henry Flagler in the late 1800s. Rebuilt in 1926, the resort's Italian Renaissance architecture includes vaulted ceilings, frescoes and Florentine fountains outside the main entrance. Nearby, on Cocoanut Row, is Whitehall – a mansion built by Flagler in 1901 which is now a museum containing original furnishings and railroad exhibits.

Orlando: Orlando is a real city, incorporated in 1875, but its world-famous tourist attractions are pure fantasy. Since opening in 1971, Walt Disney World has drawn millions of visitors to its theme parks and resorts. Self-contained with its own transportation system of trams, buses, launches and a monorail, Walt Disney World is home to the Magic Kingdom (similar to California's Disneyland), EPCOT Center (an educational theme park) and Disney-MGM Studios (a 'Hollywood' theme park). It also contains 13 family-oriented theme resorts and five championship golf courses. Providing stiff competition to Disney-MGM Studios is Universal Studios, a movie studio/theme park featuring dozens of rides, shows and attractions.

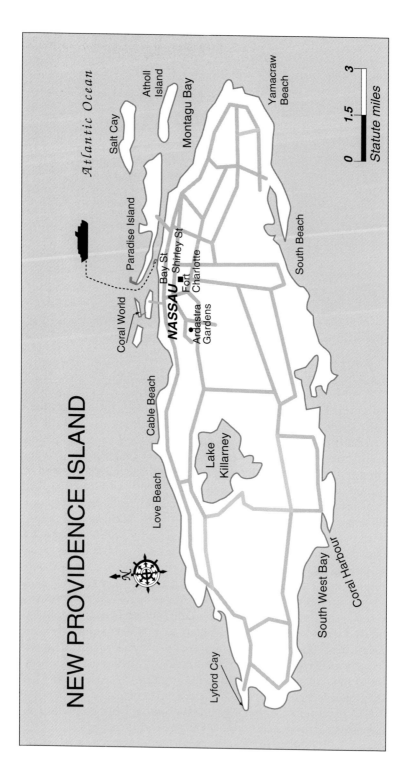

NEW PROVIDENCE ISLAND

Atlantic Ocean

Salt Cay

Atholl Island

Montagu Bay

Yamacraw Beach

Paradise Island

Bay St

Shirley St

Fort Charlotte

South Beach

Coral World

NASSAU

Ardastra Gardens

Cable Beach

Love Beach

Lake Killarney

South West Bay

Coral Harbour

Lyford Cay

0   1.5   3
Statute miles

CHAPTER TWO

THE BAHAMAS

Shallow Seas and Coral Cays

The Bahamas form a labyrinth of islands and islets, cays and coral reefs, which bounds the northern edge of the Caribbean Sea. Small and snakelike in shape, these limestone islands lie low on the horizon and are surrounded by beautiful turquoise seas filled with coral gardens and sunken wrecks. A diver's delight, they were treacherous waterways in the days of piracy when buccaneers, intent on pillage, would lure passing ships into these shallow reef-strewn waters.

An archipelago of some 700 islands and islets, the Bahamas start about 50 miles off southeast Florida and extend 600 miles in a south-easterly direction toward Haiti. Spanish galleons laden with gold and silver had to pass through the Straits of Florida and around the top end of the Bahamas on their way back to Spain, so they became easy prey for pirates like the notorious Blackbeard who would escape Spanish convoys by retreating to the port of Nassau on New Providence Island.

Two centuries earlier these far-flung islands were home to a much different breed of seafaring people – a tribe of Arawaks called Lucayans who lived here in fishing villages. Travelling by canoe, the Lucayans had migrated from South America to these remote and river-less islands to avoid the aggressive Carib tribes. Their solitude was shattered in 1492 by the arrival of an unexpected visitor.

The Bahamian island of Guanahani was where Christopher Columbus first stepped ashore in the New World after crossing the Atlantic into the unknown. Relieved to have reached what he assumed

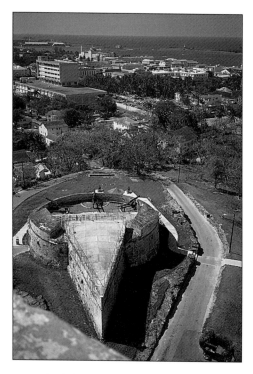

To protect its crown colony from Spanish invasion, the British built Fort Fincastle overlooking Nassau Harbour.

were the islands of Asia, Columbus called the island San Salvador and claimed it for Spain. The Spanish, whose goal was to find gold and other treasures, were not interested in colonizing these islands situated in what Columbus called a *baja mar* (shallow sea). They did, however, enslave the Lucayans to work in the gold mines on Hispaniola, and the first inhabitants of the Bahamas were soon exterminated.

The islands remained deserted until the mid-17th century when a group of English Puritans arrived from Bermuda. They settled at Preacher's Cave on Eleuthera and tried to scratch out an existence, but conditions were harsh. The Bahamas rise from a vast submarine plateau, their brackish lakes connected with the ocean by underground passages, and rainfall or desalinization are the main sources of fresh water. The settlers on Eleuthera slowly cultivated the thin soil for growing cotton, tobacco and vegetables. Meanwhile, another settlement was established on New Providence Island. Originally called Charles Towne, it was renamed in 1695 for England's King William III, a member of Europe's Orange-Nassau dynasty. The settlement quickly grew and Fort Nassau was built in 1697 to ward off Spanish invasions.

A period of lawlessness prevailed in the Bahamas, which had become a rendezvous for pirates. The British did little to discourage the plundering of Spanish ships until the Bahamas were made a crown colony and Captain Woodes Rogers was dispatched to Nassau in 1718 to restore order. The town was so squalid he chose to live on board his ship while overseeing the cleaning of its streets and wells. Its forts were improved and regular garrisons were stationed there. Woodes Rogers also restructured the island government and issued a proclamation guaranteeing freedom for slaves from Bermuda and the American colonies, with which the islanders had close trading ties. Many a settler, disappointed with their meagre livelihoods, moved to Carolina or Virginia rather than return to England. Runaway slaves fleeing the American colonies would stow away on board Bahama-bound merchant ships, and when the American Revolutionary War broke out in 1776, hundreds of loyalists also fled to the Bahamas.

American revolutionists captured and held Nassau for three days – long enough to raid the port for arms and ammunition. Then, in 1781, Spain captured Nassau and took possession of the whole colony which was returned to Great Britain in the Treaty of Paris (1783). The British built two more forts (Charlotte and Fincastle) to protect Nassau from any future invasions but the islands were largely ignored. Many of the loyalists, their plantation farms failing, returned to England.

During the American Civil War, the islanders profited from blockade running into Southern ports. The islands also became a base for rum-running during the prohibition era that followed World War I. However, the islands remained in relative isolation, their inhabitants developing a unique culture of Goombay music, Junkanoo dance and straw crafts. Yet the influence of British colonialism was still strong with English nobility maintaining beautiful homes and gardens on New Providence Island. Wealthy Americans also began vacationing in the Bahamas in the 1860s, arriving by steamship from New York.

In 1900 the Florida railroad baron Henry Flagler built the huge Colonial Hotel in Nassau and offered steamship service from Miami. But it wasn't until after World War II that tourism flourished, as did social activism. Black Bahamians began to challenge the ruling white party and in 1967 the Progressive Liberal Party, led by Bahamian-born and London-educated Lynden Oscar Pindling, won control of the government with a close but surprising victory. His party, campaigning for independence, won an overwhelming majority in 1972 and began negotiations with Britain. The following year, Britain's Prince Charles presented the new Constitution of the Bahamas to Prime Minister Pindling and a former crown colony of Britain became the Commonwealth of the Bahamas.

Pindling, in power for 25 years, was defeated in 1992 amid accusations of mismanagement. Offshore banking has grown in the major centers of Nassau and Freeport on Grand Bahama Island, but tourism remains the number one industry.

About a quarter million people live on the islands, and Nassau on New Providence Island is the capital and principal city. Other main islands, called 'out islands' or 'family islands', include Grand Bahama, Great and Little Abaco, Andros, Eleuthera, Cat Island, San Salvador, and Great and Little Inagua. The Turks and Caicos Islands, lying southeast of the Bahamas, are geographically part of the archipelago but have been separately administered by Great Britain since 1848.

The Bahamas are blessed with beautiful beaches, crystal clear waters, coral gardens, exotic birds and an ideal climate. Their proximity to Florida and the enticement of casinos also add to their appeal. Still, many of the islets and cays remain uninhabited and undeveloped, just as they were when Christopher Columbus first set eyes on the New World.

NASSAU

Nassau, one of the busiest cruise ports in the world, is a vibrant city with a population of about 150,000. Its pink buildings and white gloved bobbies are part of the British colonial charm of this bustling port.

Getting Around

Nassau is fairly compact and the major historical sights can be seen on foot, although there is some uphill walking. Another option is to see the local sights by horse-drawn buggy. These can be hired in Rawson Square and the usual fare is $10 for a half-hour ride, but settle on a price before climbing in.

Jitney buses to Cable Beach leave from the British Colonial Hotel every 10 or 15 minutes and the fare is 75¢ per person. A cab to Coral Beach costs $4.00 per person. A one-hour island tour costs about $25.

The water taxi to Paradise Island is $2.00 each way and takes about half an hour (plus a ten-minute walk if you're heading to the Atlantis Resort). A cab ride, which is much faster, costs $3.00 per person each way, plus a $2.00 bridge toll.

Rental cars and scooters are available in Nassau. Driving is on the left and helmets are mandatory for people on scooters.

SHOPPING: Nassau and Hong Kong have been touted as the two best places in the world to buy watches. Other duty-free items to look for in Nassau include jewelry, crystal, china, leather and liquor. Bay Street (from East Street to the British Colonial Hotel) is where the majority of shops are located, as is the famous Straw Market where handcrafted baskets and other items are sold. For quality handicrafts and artwork, Caripelago (a block east of Rawson Square on Bay Street) has a good selection.

The Bahamian Dollar is on par with the U.S. dollar and the two currencies are used interchangeably. When paying with American money, ask for your change in the same currency or you'll receive Bahamian currency. Travellers cheques and credit cards are widely accepted.

GOLF: There are plenty of golf courses to choose from in the Nassau area, a popular one for cruise passengers being the par-72 course at the Paradise Island Golf & Country Club.

BEACHES: The best beaches in the Nassau area are Cable Beach, west of downtown, and those on Paradise Island. Access at both locations is through the many hotels located there. A beach within walking distance of the cruise pier fronts the British Colonial Hotel.

SNORKELING & DIVING: Excellent snorkeling and diving can be enjoyed in the waters off Nassau, and several dive operators are located on Paradise Island and in Nassau at the foot the Paradise Island bridge. Local snorkeling sites include the reefs at Silver Cay (see Coral World) and Athol Island. Divers can explore numerous wrecks immediately north of Paradise Island and, about 10 miles east of Nassau, the famous Lost Blue Hole – a massive oceanic hole which begins at 45 feet and contains coral heads, moray eels and other creatures.

The southwest coast also has great snorkeling and diving, and many a filmmaker has shot underwater footage here. The shallow reef areas at Goulding Cay contain magnificent elkhorn coral – featured in such movies as *20,000 Leagues Under the Sea* and *Splash*. A number of James Bond flicks have also been filmed in these waters, including *Thunderball*, *For Your Eyes Only* and *Never Say Never Again*. Their sunken props include the Vulcan Bomber and Tears of Allah freighter, both of which are popular dive sites. Natural attractions include Tunnel

By horse-drawn buggy is a popular way to tour the colonial streets of Nassau.

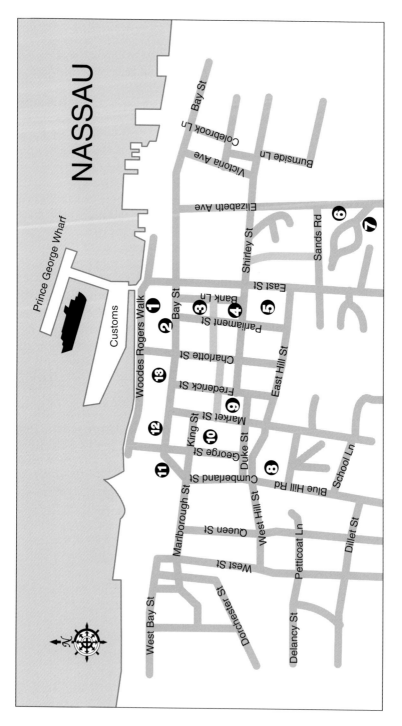

Wall, Southwest Reef and Shark Wall, a drop-off along the edge of a deep-water abyss called Tongue of the Ocean.

LOCAL SIGHTS: The **(1) Tourist Office** is located right beside the cruise pier on the edge of **(2) Rawson Square**, named for a former governor. Horse-drawn buggies wait here for hire.

Clustered around a statue of Queen Victoria in **(3) Parliament Square** are the Houses of Parliament, built from 1805 to 1813. When facing Queen Victoria's statue, the House of Assembly is to the right, the Senate Building is straight ahead and the old Colonial Secretary's Office and Treasury is to the left. South of these buildings are the Supreme Court and Garden of Remembrance with a cenotaph.

The octagonal-shaped **(4) Public Library**, once used as a prison and complete with dungeons, stands at the corner of Parliament and Shirley Streets.

(5) The Royal Victorian Gardens offer a shady spot to rest before tackling the **(6) Queen's Staircase** where 66 steps, cut into a limestone gorge by slave laborers in the 18th century, lead up the hill to **(7) Fort Fincastle**. The fort was built in 1793 to ward off Spanish invasions. Nearby is a water tower where visitors can take the stairs or an elevator (for a small charge) to the top for a commanding view of the fort and harbor beyond.

Informal tour guides can be engaged at the base of the Queen's Staircase, which was cut from a limestone gorge and leads to Fort Fincastle.

A sentry stands at the entrance to the grounds of Government House, the official residence of the Governor of the Bahamas.

(8) Government House is one of Nassau's most photographed buildings with a statue of Columbus standing on the steps leading to its front entrance. The building isn't open to the public and sentry guards man the gates on either side of the grounds, but they will allow visitors to walk through. Edward, Duke of Windsor, resided here when he was governor of the Bahamas from 1940 to 1945. A former King of England who renounced his throne to marry American divorcee Wallis Warfield Simpson, the Duke was suspected of either inadvertently or intentionally leaking Allied secrets to the Nazis. To keep him a safe distance from the war raging in Europe, the British government sent him to the Bahamas in July, 1940.

(9) St. Andrew's Presbyterian Church, begun in 1810, stands at the corner of Duke and Market streets, and **(10) Christ Church Cathedral** at the corner of George and King streets was built in 1837. Dominating the waterfront, the **(11) British Colonial Hotel** stands on the former site of Fort Nassau.

(12) Vendue House, which stands on the site of a former slave market, dates back to 1769 and was rebuilt in the early 1900s. It now houses the Pompey Museum of Slavery and Emancipation, opened in 1992 as part of the Columbus Quincentennial. The museum is named after a slave and Bahamian hero who lived on Exuma.

The **(13) Straw Market**, in the heart of Nassau's shopping district, is a traditional Bahamian market where shoppers bargain with the ven-

Vendue House on Bay Street, standing on the site of a former slave market, is now a museum devoted to the story of slavery and emancipation.

dors for items which include jewelry, t-shirts, carvings and, of course, an array of straw woven products.

Area Attractions

The turquoise waters of the Bahamas are a major attraction, whether for swimming, snorkeling, diving or simply observing the colorful marine world that thrives just below the sea's surface. Glass-bottom boats, catamarans and other excursion vessels depart from the cruise pier on harbor tours and trips to nearby beaches and coral gardens.

Coral World Marine Park – Located on Silver Cay in Nassau Harbor, this attraction is connected by a bridge to the mainland or can be reached by a short ferry boat ride from the cruise pier. Its admission fee includes access to various tanks holding sharks, stingrays and turtles, in addition to an underwater observatory for viewing coral reefs and tropical fish. Also located here is a white sand beach, snorkel trail, equipment rental, change facilities, bars and a restaurant.

Paradise Island – Beach-lined Paradise Island was once a playground for the wealthy, and the Astors, Rockefellers and Vanderbilts all built winter residences here in the 1920s. Called Hog Island, its name was changed to Paradise Island when Huntington Hartford bought the island and developed it into a holiday resort. A unique attraction is the Versailles Gardens and French Cloister, a ruined 14th-century Augustinian monastery transported from France. The island's modern resorts include the Atlantis, a huge Sun International Resort and Casino (formerly owned under a different name by Merv Griffin) which features a spectacular water park of pools, waterfalls, underground grottos and various lagoons, one containing sharks, barracudas and stingrays.

Athol Island – The waters surrounding Athol Island, lying east of Paradise Island, are referred to as the Sea Gardens, for they are filled with shipwrecks, coral colonies and schools of tropical fish. Seaworld Explorer's tours begin at Captain Nemo's Dock (just east of the cruise pier) with a 20-minute boat tour of Nassau Harbor en route to Athol Island, where passengers transfer to an observatory vessel in which they sit five feet beneath the water's surface for a submarine-like viewing experience.

Atlantis Submarine – Based at the west end of New Providence Island, this recreational submarine departs from West Bay near Lyford Cay for deep-water viewing of the area's renowned reefs and wrecks.

Fort Charlotte – Built from 1787-94, this imposing fort features a moat and dungeons. Nearby are the beautiful **Botanical Gardens**.

Ardastra Gardens and Zoo – Located one mile west of downtown, this 5-1/2 acre nature park is home to nearly 300 animals in a tropical garden setting. Amid the lush foliage there live peacocks, parrots, monkeys and some famous marching flamingos.

FREEPORT

The cruise port of Freeport/Lucaya, located on Grand Bahama Island, was developed as a tourist destination and world-class dive resort in the 1950s and '60s. The island, 75 miles long by 15 miles wide, is an exposed portion of the Little Bahama Bank, where a combination of shallow waters and deep chasms create a diver's paradise of shallow, medium depth and deep reefs as well as dramatic drop-offs.

Beaches, nature parks, golf courses, gambling casinos, duty-free shopping and every conceivable water sport await visitors to Freeport. Cars, mopeds and bicycles can be rented, and metered taxis are available at the cruise terminal which is about five miles from town. Local attractions include the **Garden of the Groves**, an 11-acre botanical garden containing the Grand Bahama Museum, and the **Rand Memorial Nature Center**, 100 acres of natural woodland containing trails and a bird sanctuary. **Lucayan National Park**, 20 miles east of Freeport, contains an underground system of limestone caverns, shady trails, pine forests, a mangrove creek and ocean beach.

Shopping can be enjoyed at the International Bazaar & Strawmarket and at the Port Lucaya Marketplace & Marina. At the Perfume Factory, a restored 18th-century Bahamian mansion located next to the

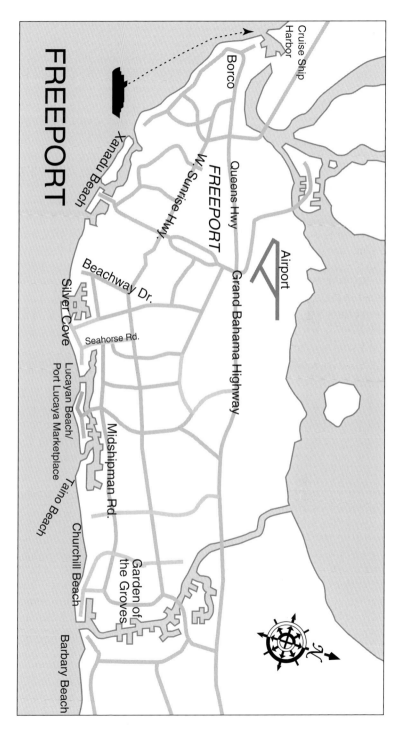

International Bazaar, shoppers can mix, bottle, label and name their own fragrance.

Beaches abound on Grand Bahama and they line the shores of Freeport and Lucaya. Those with hotels and facilities include Xanadu Beach (about five miles from the cruise pier) and Lucaya Beach, located across the street from the Port Lucaya Marketplace.

Golfers can choose from three PGA-rated courses – Princess Ruby Golf Course, Princess Emerald Golf Course and Lucaya Golf & Country Club.

The Underwater Explorers Society (UNEXSO), a famous scuba diving school, is located at Port Lucaya. Their organized dives include a daily trip to Shark Junction, where a dozen or more Caribbean Reef Sharks often appear and feed on bait. Also popular is The Dolphin Experience at Sanctuary Bay, the world's largest dolphin sanctuary, where Atlantic Bottlenose dolphins swim with divers both in a sheltered lagoon and in open water along an offshore coral reef. For wild dolphin encounters, White Sand Ridge off the northwest point of the island is a good place to interact with a resident pod of Spotted Dolphins that frequent these waters. A number of local dive boats offer snorkel trips to this area.

An abundance of marine life is found in the waters off Freeport on Grand Bahama Island.

Top) The shady streets of Key West contain colonial homes associated with famous artists. (Middle) In New Orleans, the Riverfront Streetcar runs between the the cruise pier and the historic French Quarter where St. Louis Cathedral (bottom) overlooks Jackson Square.

Photo Michael Terranova

Photo Mariano Advertising

(Top) A Jamaican hostess greets visitors to Firefly, the late Noel Coward's beloved home.

(Middle) Jamaica's north coast is one of lush vegetation and beautiful beaches, including the one at the mouth of Dunn's River (bottom).

Photo Raymond Norris Jones

Photo Gordon Persson

*(Top) Mexico's magnificent
Mayan ruins include Tulum,
located across the channel
from Cozumel.
(Middle and Bottom) Grand
Cayman Island, with its
clear waters and extensive
coral reefs, is considered
one of the best dive locations
in the world.*

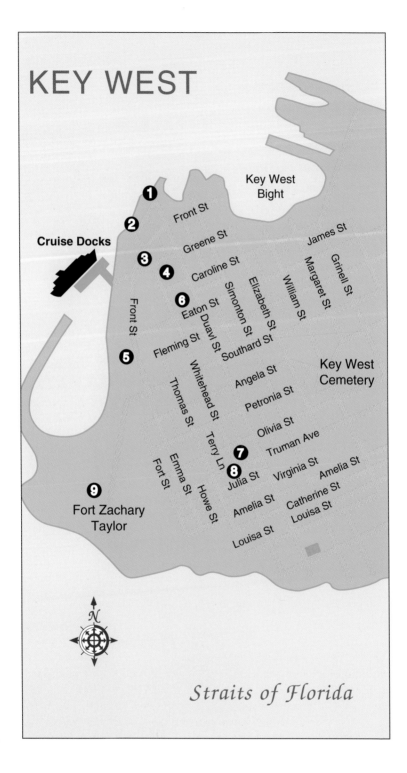

KEY WEST

Key West Bight

Cruise Docks

Front St

Greene St

James St

Front St

Caroline St

Grinell St

Margaret St

William St

Eaton St

Elizabeth St

Simonton St

Duavl St

Southard St

Fleming St

Angela St

Key West Cemetery

Whitehead St

Petronia St

Thomas St

Olivia St

Terry Ln

Truman Ave

Julia St

Virginia St

Amelia St

Fort St

Emma St

Amelia St

Catherine St

Fort Zachary Taylor

Howe St

Louisa St

Louisa St

Straits of Florida

N

CHAPTER THREE

KEY WEST & NEW ORLEANS

Southern Variations of Charm

T he Florida Keys are both exotic and all-American. Their tropical vegetation, steady trade winds and coral reefs are quintessentially Caribbean, while Key West's clapboard houses and white picket fences are reminiscent of a New England coastal town.

A chain of small coral islands extending 110 miles from the southern tip of Florida, the Keys' reef-riddled waters once supported a thriving salvage industry in the mid-19th century. These same reefs have made the Keys a popular tourist destination, with excellent scuba diving and beachside resorts. Key Largo, the largest of the islands at the 'top' of the Keys, is famous both as the setting for the '40s film classic *Key Largo*, starring Humphrey Bogart and Lauren Bacall, and as the location of John Pennekamp Coral Reef State Park – America's first underwater park containing some 78 square miles of living coral and a variety of marine life which can be viewed by glass-bottom boat and snorkel or scuba tours.

Key West, the southernmost point of the continental United States, and only 90 miles from Cuba, is the largest center in the Keys with about 25,000 residents. Incorporated in 1828, Key West was once a base of operation against pirates who preyed on Spanish treasure ships as they sailed from Cuba to Spain via the Straits of Florida. When Florida was ceded by Spain to the United States in 1819, Key West became a haven for exiled Cubans, including revolutionary leaders trying to rid their country of Spanish rule. The sinking of the battleship

Scenes from the forties film Key Largo, starring Bogart and Bacall, were shot inside the Caribbean Club at Key Largo.

Maine in Havana harbor in 1898 led the U.S. to declare war on Spain, and some of the 266 men who died in that incident are buried in the Key West Cemetery.

Key West has long been an enclave for writers and artists drawn to the tiny island's exotic locale. In 1912 the Keys became linked with the mainland with completion of Henry Flagler's railroad. The rail line was abandoned after sustaining hurricane damage in 1935 and replaced a few years later with the 123-mile Overseas Highway which includes 42 bridges. Despite this tangible and well-travelled connection to the rest of Florida, the Keys retained an island ambiance and sense of seclusion.

As a port of call, Key West holds many attractions. The cruise ship dock is located close to downtown with its shady streets of shops, restaurants and colonial homes, a number of which are listed on the National Register of Historic Places and have been lived in by some of the world's finest creative talents.

Of Key West's famous former residents, the one whose presence is most pervasive is Ernest Hemingway. His memory lives on in the home he once occupied on Whitehead Street, in his favorite bar on Duval Street and in his stories, such as *To Have and Have Not,* which is set in Key West and Cuba. Key West celebrates this great American writer with an annual Hemingway Days Festival, which includes a writers' workshop, short-story contest, Caribbean street fair and a concert on the grounds of his former home. Other illustrious names associated with Key West are John James Audubon, Winslow Homer, Robert Frost and Tennessee Williams, all of whom spent time here, as did Harry Truman whose presidential retreat is located in Key West.

A warm trade wind luffs the sail of a sightseeing schooner returning to Key West.

Haitian-born and French-educated John James Audubon, for whom one of the oldest and best-known U.S. environmental organizations is named, visited Key West in 1832 to study and sketch the native birds. Born in 1785 in Haiti, the son of a French naval officer and Creole woman, Audubon was educated in France before moving to the family estate near Philadelphia in 1803, where he spent time observing birds. He began painting and taught for a while before finding a publisher for his bird drawings.

Another famous artist to spend time in Key West was Winslow Homer, a 19th-century painter best known for his watercolor depictions of the sea. Robert Frost, one of the most popular 20th-century poets, and Tennessee Williams, one of America's foremost playwrights, also sought their muse in Key West.

Getting Around

The cruise ships dock near (**1**) **Mallory Square**, a bustling waterfront which attracts artists, entertainers and sunset watchers. Most major sights are within walking distance of the cruise pier but another option is to board either the Conch Tour Train at Mallory Square, or the Old Town Trolley at one of numerous stops, for a 90-minute, narrated tour of Key West.

WATER SPORTS: Local scuba diving, snorkeling and sailing excursions are available. Departing just north of Mallory Square are glass-bottom boat rides to the nearby coral reef. The beach at Fort Zachary Taylor is popular for swimming and snorkeling along its artificial reef.

SHOPPING: Clinton Square Market on Front Street contains a number of shops selling handcrafted jewelry and Caribbean clothing. Key West Hand Print Fashions, located in the Historic Curry Warehouse at 201 Simonton Street, is a good place to buy silk-screened fashions featuring original artwork.

Bicycles are a popular mode of transport in Key West where shady streets are lined with colonial homes, many of them Spanish in style.

LOCAL ATTRACTIONS: The (**2**) **Key West Aquarium**, beside Mallory Square, presents sea life of the Atlantic Ocean and Gulf of Mexico. The (**3**) **Mel Fisher Maritime Heritage Society**, at 200 Greene Street, features artifacts and treasures retrieved from two Spanish galleons that sank off Key West in 1622.

The (**4**) **Audubon House & Tropical Gardens** at 205 Whitehead Street is housed in a restored 19th-century building. The museum commemorates John James Audubon's 1832 visit to Key West and contains a collection of his original engravings.

(**5**) **Harry S. Truman Little White House** has undergone an extensive two-year restoration, and its original furnishings and artifacts recreate the Truman era of the 1940s when the mansion was a presidential retreat.

At 322 Duval Street (near Eaton Street) stands Key West's oldest home, built in 1829 for a wrecker and sea captain. It now houses the (**6**) **Wreckers' Museum** with exhibits including marine artifacts and ship models. Other historic homes of note are the **Curry Mansion** (on Caroline near Duval) and the **Donkey Milk House Museum**, at 613 Eaton Street, a restored 19th-century mansion listed on the National Register of Historic Places. Named for the back alleyway along which donkeys used to pull milk delivery carts, the award-winning mansion features hand-decorated ceilings, Spanish tile floors and verandas off every room.

(**7**) **Ernest Hemingway Home & Museum** at 907 Whitehead Street is a Registered National Historic Landmark. The home was built in 1851 in the Spanish colonial style and contains furnishings and other items that Hemingway and his second wife, Pauline, collected in their travels to Spain, Africa and Cuba. Hemingway wrote some of his greatest works while living here in the 1930s and '40s, and his study in the loft of the pool house remains intact with his desk and typewriter on display. The home exudes Hemingway's forceful presence, and dozens of cats, descendants of those owned by the famous author, still wander the lushly landscaped grounds. **Sloppy Joe's**, Hemingway's favorite watering hole, was moved in 1937 from Greene Street to the corner of Duval and Greene. Its owner, Joe Russell, was Hemingway's boat pilot, fishing companion and a model for the character Freddy in *To Have and Have Not*.

Recently restored and featuring a gift shop, the (**8**) **Lighthouse Museum** at 938 Whitehead Street includes the keeper's clapboard house and the lighthouse itself, built in 1847, with a magnificent view of Key West at the top of its 98 steps.

(**9**) **Fort Zachary Taylor State Historic Site** was part of Florida's coastal defence system. Built from 1845-66, the fort was a base for the Union blockade of Confederate shipping during the Civil War, with captured ships brought to its harbor. Artifacts, models and one of the largest collections of Civil War armaments are on display.

NEW ORLEANS

Louisiana's largest city, New Orleans – the 'Crescent City' – lies within a great bend of the Mississippi. It is one of America's oldest cities and its unique Creole culture, combining French, Spanish and African influences, is a source of fascination to all who visit New Orleans.

Founded in 1718 by the Sieur de Bienville, on subtropical lowlands now protected by levees from flooding, New Orleans soon became the capital of the French colony of Louisiana. Transferred to Spain in 1762, it was a strategic port in the struggle for control of the Mississippi and was briefly returned to France before transferring to the United States with the Louisiana Purchase of 1803. The French-speaking Cajuns of Acadia arrived in 1763, and the westward movement of the 1800s brought growth and prosperity to New Orleans. As the queen city of the Mississippi, this thriving port earned a lasting reputation for elegance and extravagant living.

The Civil War marked the end of the golden era of river steamboats, sumptuous balls and wicked ways, but the city's exotic flavor lives on in its music, cuisine and literature. Jazz was born here among the city's black musicians in the late 19th century, and a park is named for native

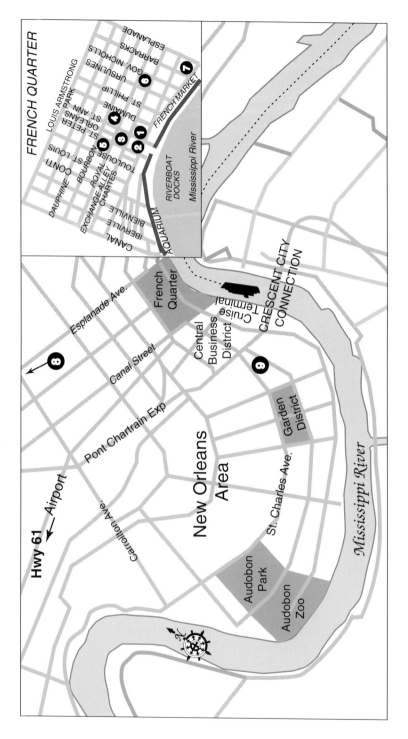

son Louis Armstrong. New Orleans is a city with soul, and its gusto for life reaches a feverish pitch during the annual Mardi Gras festivities.

A city that knows how to throw a party, New Orleans is also a busy commercial port and major U.S. point of entry, lying as it does at the junction of the Intracoastal Waterway with the Mississippi River. Imports here include coffee, sugar and bananas, which are unloaded at wharves that are themselves a local tourist attraction – as are most things in this city of Creole culture where world-famous restaurants serve up shrimp and oysters, and the many parks and museums vie with the historic French Quarter for visitors' attention.

Louisiana Literature

Courtesy U.S. Postal Service

New Orleans, a steamy mix of hedonism and Southern gentility, has stimulated the creativity of many a writer, including William Faulkner and Tennessee Williams. Mark Twain arrived in New Orleans in 1857, on his way to South America to make his fortune, and ended up working as a Mississippi River pilot, a vocation from which he took his pseudonym 'Mark Twain' – the river call for a depth of two fathoms.

Tennessee Williams has been honored by the United States Postal Service with his portrait gracing one of its postage stamps.

William Faulkner worked on his first novel, *Soldiers' Pay*, while living in the city's French Quarter at 624 Pirate's Alley (then called Orleans Alley) which runs parallel with the west side of St. Louis Cathedral. The three-storey building, its narrow facade decorated with wrought iron and ferns, now is a bookstore called Faulkner House.

Tennessee Williams also spent time in the French Quarter, living at 722 Toulouse Street in 1938. His Pulitzer-prize-winning play, *A Streetcar Named Desire*, was set on a tenement street of New Orleans. Streetcars no longer run along Desire Street, which is today the site of a housing project. The playwright Lillian Hellman was born in New Orleans and lived in the stately Garden District, which is where Anne Rice – author of a series of bestselling vampire books – now resides in a Victorian mansion. This district of elegant old homes also contains a cemetery of graves and crypts built above ground, and F. Scott Fitzgerald rented an apartment overlooking this graveyard while reviewing the galleys of his first novel, *This Side of Paradise*.

GETTING AROUND: New Orleans International Airport is approximately 16 miles from the city core and location of the cruise ship pier. The historic **French Quarter** is a short cab ride away from the cruise terminal, and in between are a number of waterfront attractions. In the other direction lies the **Garden District**, one of New Orleans oldest residential areas of stately homes and shady oaks. Local tour operators offer an eclectic choice of tours of these historic districts, including walking tours, cemetery tours and carriage rides.

Gray Line, its ticket office located beside the Jackson (Jax) Brewery, offers a variety of tours. For general sightseeing and shopping, its purple, green and gold trolley picks up passengers at 10 locations throughout the city and makes hourly stops at various attractions, allowing pass holders to hop on and off at their convenience.

The Regional Transit Authority (RTA) operates two streetcars – the red Riverfront Streetcar and the century-old St. Charles Streetcar. A one-day pass allows passengers to ride both cars as often as they like. The St. Charles streetcar, with its reversible wooden seats, rides the oldest working trolley line in the world through the business district. It can be boarded at the corner of St. Charles and Canal Streets. The Riverfront streetcar runs between the Convention Center and the French Market, past the Riverwalk Marketplace, World Trade Center and Aquarium of the Americas.

Mule-drawn buggies can be hired at Jackson Square or throughout the French Quarter for a half-hour tour. Horse-drawn buggy rides are available for both the French Quarter and Garden District. Paddle wheel steamboats, which dock on the waterfront between the cruise pier and Jackson Square, offer local river tours. A ferry runs between the foot of Canal Street and Algiers, on the other side of the river.

SHOPPING: Canal Street has long been famous as a shopping street, as has the French Quarter with its fashion boutiques, museum shops and antique dealers selling everything from rare furniture to objets d'art. **Canal Place** features designer fashions, and the **Jackson Brewery**, which opened in 1984, is a shopping/dining/entertainment complex located beside Jackson Square in a renovated turn-of-the-century brewery. The **French Market** is an open-air produce and handicraft fair overlooking the river, and the **Riverwalk Marketplace** is a retail center located adjacent to the riverboat piers just downstream of the cruise terminal.

DINING: Dining in New Orleans is done in the Continental style, its Creole and Cajun cuisine served with leisurely elegance in world-famous restaurants. The sophisticated sauces of Creole cooking are what distinguish it from the more robust Cajun dishes, but the two traditions – citified Creole and country Cajun – are often blended together and referred to as Louisiana cooking. Well-known and popular dining establishments in the French Quarter include **Galatoire's**, a French bistro on Bourbon Street which serves classic French and Creole cuisine, and internationally-renowned **Antoine's** on St. Louis Street. For Cajun cooking, **K-Paul's Louisiana Kitchen** on Chartres Street serves up blackened redfish and crawfish etoufee in a casual setting.

Local Attractions: The **French Quarter** (*Vieux Carre*) is the heart of New Orleans. It is a vibrant neighborhood of restaurants, hotels, jazz clubs, shops, museums and art galleries housed in 19th-century townhouses. The French Quarter burned twice in the late 1700s, and was last rebuilt by the Spanish, their Mediterranean influence reflected in ornamental cast-iron balconies and fountain courtyards. Most famous of the French Quarter's narrow streets and cobblestone alleyways is Bourbon Street, an entertainment strip packed with revelers during Mardi Gras. A **(1) Visitor Center** is located at 529 St. Ann Street, opposite Jackson Square, a popular starting point for a tour of the French Quarter.

(2) Jackson Square (formerly the *Place d'Armes*) is the centerpiece of the French Quarter. Public meetings, celebrations and the welcoming of heroes have long been held in this square, its focal point a bronze equestrian statue of Andrew Jackson. In 1856 the Baroness de Pontalba transformed this dusty square into a garden park flanked by a pair of red brick apartment buildings which she had built. Fronting the square is the magnificent **(3) St. Louis Cathedral**, completed in 1794, its Spanish style modified in 1851. On one side is the Cabildo, built by the Spanish in 1795, which now houses part of the **Louisiana State Museum**. Its French mansard roof was added in the mid-1800s. The Presbytere, on the other side of the Cathedral, is also part of the Louisiana State Museum, as is the **1850 House** which is an authentic re-creation of an antebellum town house.

Numerous other attractions are found in the vicinity of Jackson Square. These include the **(4) Voodoo Museum** at 724 Dumaine Street, the **(5) Preservation Hall** at 726 St. Peter Street where traditional jazz bands perform each evening, and the **(6) Beauregard-Keyes House** at 1113 Chartres Street which was built in 1826, resided in by Confederate General P.G.T. Beauregard in the 1860s, and later restored by author Frances Parkinson Keyes.

Museum exhibits on jazz and Mardi Gras are housed in the **(7) Old U.S. Mint** at the foot of Esplanade. This restored 19th-century building, an architectural blend of Classical Revival and Victorian, is backed by a courtyard in which stands the 'Streetcar Named Desire'. Beyond the French Quarter, major attractions include the **(8) New Orleans Museum of Art** at #1 Lelong Avenue in City Park, and the **(9) Confederate Museum**, at 929 Camp Street, which is the oldest museum in Louisiana and contains Civil War memorabilia.

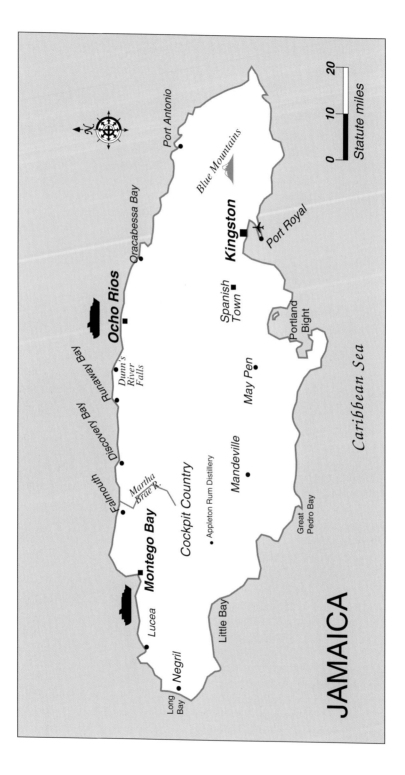

JAMAICA

Port Antonio

Blue Mountains

Kingston

Port Royal

Oracabessa Bay

Ocho Rios

Spanish Town

Runaway Bay

Dunn's River Falls

Discovery Bay

May Pen

Portland Bight

Caribbean Sea

Falmouth

Martha Brae R.

Cockpit Country

Appleton Rum Distillery

Mandeville

Great Pedro Bay

Montego Bay

Lucea

Little Bay

Negril

Long Bay

Statute miles

0   10   20

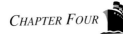

CHAPTER FOUR

JAMAICA

Heart of Caribbean Culture

J amaica, third largest island of the West Indies after Cuba and Hispaniola, is one of the most beautiful in the Caribbean. A lush and mountainous island where rivers rush to the sea and white beaches line sparkling bays, Jamaica has long attracted a diversity of peoples to its shores, from famous buccaneers to famous artists. The country's official motto is 'Out of Many, One People' – acknowledging the range of races and nationalities that have colonized this beautiful island. Its history is turbulent and social problems still exist, but a 'No problem mon' attitude sums up the buoyant spirit of Jamaicans.

A limestone plateau more than 3,000 feet above sea level, Jamaica has a mountainous backbone that rises at its eastern end to the Blue Mountains and the island's tallest peak of Blue Mountain at 7,402 feet. Narrow coastal plains lie on either side of the mountain chain where fertile slopes and broad river valleys support the country's export crops of sugarcane, bananas, ginger, citrus fruits, cocoa, pimento, tobacco and its famous Blue Mountain Coffee. Most of these crops are grown on large plantations while small farms grow subsistence crops such as yams, breadfruit and cassava.

Rainfall, abundant in the mountainous regions, diminishes westward across the rugged plateau of streams and subterranean rivers. The heart of the plateau, called the Cockpits, is used for livestock grazing. During Jamaica's colonial days, escaped or freed slaves – called maroons – fled to Cockpit country where they lived in villages and organized frequent uprisings against the European landowners.

Ocho Rios, Jamaica's busiest cruise port, is set among beautiful beaches, tiered waterfalls and tropical gardens.

Arawaks, an agricultural people, first inhabited the island about a thousand years ago and they called it *Xaymaca* – 'land of woods and streams'. The Spanish began colonizing Jamaica in 1509 under licence from Christopher Columbus's son, and the Arawaks soon died out under Spanish occupation. Captured by the British in 1655 and formally ceded to England in 1670, the island was a haven for buccaneers before becoming a major sugar producer in the 18th century.

Half of Jamaica's population is still rural with much of the work force employed in agriculture. However, the continuing trend is one of migration to the cities. Of the country's 2-1/2 million residents, about 600,000 live in the capital of Kingston. Situated on a deep, landlocked harbor, this port city was established in 1693 after an earthquake destroyed Port Royal at the tip of the peninsula which forms the harbor. Plans are now underway to recreate 17th-century Port Royal and its buccaneering past.

The most famous name associated with Port Royal is Sir Henry Morgan, a Welsh privateer whose daring exploits included the sacking of Portobelo in 1668 and the capture of Panama in 1671. He was eventually arrested on charges of piracy and sent to England where, with war against Spain threatening once more, he was knighted and returned to Jamaica as deputy-governor.

Anther major Jamaican city on the south coast is Spanish Town, founded in about 1525 and, following the destruction of Port Royal, Jamaica's leading city until the capital was moved in 1872 to Kingston.

The entire north coast, from Negril at its western end to Port Antonio at its eastern end, is dotted with beach-lined bays and palm-shaded resorts, including some of the most exclusive in the Caribbean. It also contains Jamaica's two main cruise ports – Ocho Rios and Montego Bay.

Many a famous person has spent time living or vacationing in Jamaica, beginning with Christopher Columbus who first stepped ashore in 1494 at Rio Bueno. On his fourth voyage to the West Indies in 1503, Columbus beached his damaged ships on the island's north shore and spent a year on Jamaican soil awaiting rescue. In more recent times, the swashbuckling movie star Errol Flynn pulled into Port Antonio in his private yacht to escape a storm and ended up building a home there on Navy Island.

For a relatively small country, Jamaica has had a far-reaching impact on the rest of the world with its music, dance and art. Jamaicans are international in outlook and many of its citizens have migrated to other countries, most notably Britain. Over 90% of Jamaicans are of West African descent with Asians and Europeans adding to the cultural tapestry of this dynamic island nation. Yet, the country's rich social fabric has at times appeared to be unraveling, with political tribalism resulting in election violence.

The People's National Party (PNP) was founded in 1938 by Norman Manley. His cousin, Sir Alexander Bustamante, founded the Jamaica Labour Party (JLP). These two parties, their roots in rival trade unions, have dominated Jamaican politics since 1944 when universal adult suffrage was introduced. Jamaica gained its independence from Britain in 1962 but remains a member of the British Commonwealth. The country's economy is one of the more prosperous in the West Indies, despite a recession that persisted throughout the 1970s and 1980s. After embracing socialism in the '70s, Jamaica now has a free market economy based on tourism, agricultural products and the export of bauxite, from which alumina is extracted. Hurricane Gilbert caused widespread devastation when it swept the length of the island in 1988, and the country's tourism industry was crippled.

The island has regained its prominence as a popular Caribbean destination but many tourists stay at all-inclusive resorts. The government is trying to counter this insular attitude with a Meet the People program in which the tourist board will arrange for a visitor to spend time with a Jamaican host who shares a common interest.

Cruise passengers who are apprehensive about venturing ashore can simply book a shore excursion. Those who prefer to strike out on their own will find that Jamaicans, despite their reputation for aggressively selling their wares (including narcotics), are an outgoing people who will respond to a polite but firm 'No thank you' with a 'No problem mon' wave of the hand. Most Jamaicans have a good sense of humor and this, rather than anger, is usually the best way to fend off persistent advances.

Reggae & Rastafarianism

Rastafarianism is a religious-cultural movement that began in Jamaica in the 1930s when Haile Selassie (also named Ras Tafari) became Emperor of Ethiopia, as predicted by Jamaican hero Marcus Garvey. Selassie was hailed as the movement's messiah, Ethiopia was the promised land, and Garvey was considered a major prophet and early leader in creating black awareness and unity.

Reggae,which originated in the 1960s among the poor blacks of Kingston, is the protest music of the Rastafarian faith. Its sound is characterized by an off-beat rhythm that draws on American soul and traditonal African and Jamaican folk music. Reggae's most famous performer is the late Bob Marley, a Jamaican singer, songwriter and guitarist to whom a museum is dedicated in Kingston.

Born in 1945 and deserted by his white Jamaican father, Marley was raised by his mother in Nine Miles village on Jamaica's north coast. As a youth, he and his mother moved to the poor shanty area of Kingston where he worked in the welding trade while seeking success as a musician. Fame finally came to Marley in the '70s when his new group began playing reggae and their songs soared in the charts. When Marley died of cancer at the age of 36, he had achieved international stardom and received his country's highest public honor, the Order of Merit. The worldwide popularity of reggae is attributed in large part to Marley, whose songs supported his belief in non-violence and the Rastafarian religion.

Rastas, who object to shaving and cutting hair, wear their hair in long braids called dreadlocks – a symbolic connection with the Ethiopian lion. They are vegetarians who prefer natural foods and many of them smoke *ganga*, locally grown marijuana. Not everyone wearing dreadlocks is a Rasta and most 'real' Rastas are congenial, generally preferring the country to urban areas.

Photo Johnnie Black

Bob Marley, the 'King of Reggae Music', is credited with spreading Jamaica's musical culture throughout the world.

OCHO RIOS

The original Spanish name for Ocho Rios was *Las Chorreras* – The Waterfalls – an appropriate name for a port situated at the base of lush mountains where rivers and streams spill into the sea. A former fishing village, Ocho Rios has been developed as a tourist destination with high-rise hotels and condominiums lining the beaches to the east of Ocho Rios Bay. The local population numbers about 11,000 and residents speak an English-based patois. Ocho Rios Bay contains two piers – the Reynolds Pier and the new cruise ship pier which is joined by a jetty to shore where telephones, tourist information and a handful of shops are located.

Getting Around

The cruise lines offer organized excursions to the major attractions, or you can hire a taxi. A visitor information booth is located in the terminal building and the taxi fares to various destinations are posted nearby. A dispatcher is also stationed there and, upon telling him where you want to go, he will hail you a driver whose car will carry the red Public Passenger Vehicle (PPV) license plates. If you want to visit a number of destinations, negotiate the fare with your driver before getting in. The fare is per taxi, so travelling in groups of four is the most economical. Some sample taxi tour rates for one to four persons: Dunn's River Falls - $20; Prospect Plantation - $30.

SHOPPING: Jamaica offers good buys in duty-free goods and great bargains in locally produced clothing, wood carvings, coffee and rum. Beautiful, hand-carved walking sticks can be bought for $15 and tee shirts screened with unique Jamaican designs sell for as little as $5. More expensive are the beautiful batik cottons and silks. The exchange rate is approximately 30 Jamaican dollars for 1 US dollar, but there's no need to exchange money because American currency, travellers cheques and credit cards are widely accepted.

Within walking distance of the cruise ship pier are the **(1) Taj Mahal Centre** and **(2) Soni's Plaza,** or you can take a shopping shuttle which costs $2 per person. In between are the **(3) Old Market Craft Shoppes** and **(4) Craft Park,** where local artisans sell their wares. Excellent arts and crafts can also be bought at the Dunn's River Falls marketplace, and paintings by acclaimed Jamaican artists are on display at the Harmony Hall Gallery, about five miles east of the cruise port.

BEST BEACHES: Beautiful white sand beaches line the shoreline east of Ocho Rios Bay. Most of these are backed by hotels and have controlled access to protect tourists from pedlars. The admission fee is usually $1.00 per person. Closest to the pier is Turtle Beach, and an excellent beach lies on the other side of The Point at Mallards Bay.

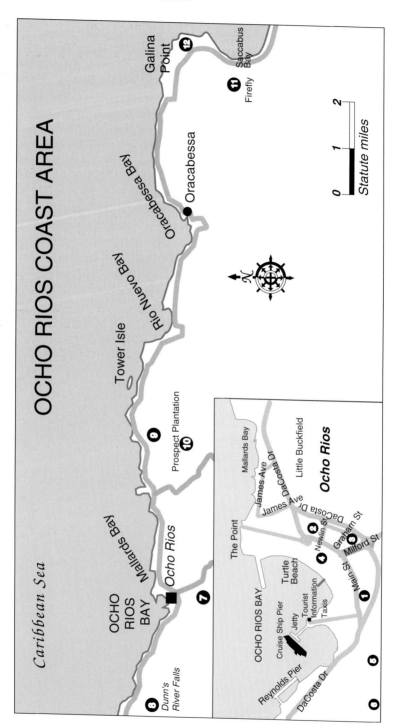

OCHO RIOS COAST AREA

Caribbean Sea

Galina
Point

Saccabus
Bay

Firefly

Oracabessa Bay

Oracabessa

Río Nuevo Bay

Tower Isle

Statute miles

0   1   2

Prospect Plantation

OCHO
RIOS
BAY

Mallards Bay

Ocho Rios

Dunn's
River Falls

Ocho Rios

Mallards Bay

Little Buckfield

James Ave

DaCosta Dr

James Ave

DaCosta Dr

Newlin St

Graham St

Milford St

Main St

The Point

OCHO RIOS BAY

Turtle
Beach

Cruise Ship Pier

Jetty

Tourist
Information

Taxis

Reynolds Pier

DaCosta Dr

DIVE & SNORKEL SITES / GOLF: Snorkeling excursions are available out of Ocho Rios, although some of the nearby shallow reefs have been damaged in recent years by hurricanes. Serious divers recommend going fairly deep to see an abundance of coral and sponge life. Wall diving is popular at Runaway Bay.

Public golf courses are located at Runaway Bay (west of Ocho Rios) and Sandal's Golf & Country Club (east of Ocho Rios on Mallards Bay).

LOCAL ATTRACTIONS: A botanical garden and bird sanctuary, **(5) Shaw Park Gardens** contain a variety of flowers and trees, as well as streams and waterfalls.

The Coyaba River flows through **(6) Coyaba Garden** where riverside paths and boardwalks lead past waterfalls and pools filled with koi carp and turtles. The museum contains pre-Columbian artifacts and the gallery displays creative works by Jamaicans.

Area Highlights: (7) Fern Gully, a former riverbed that went dry following an earthquake, is a three-mile stretch of road that winds into the Blue Mountains and leads, eventually, to Kingston on the other side of the island. The many species of fern that grow in this gully form a lush canopy for vehicles passing beneath it.

One of Jamaica's most popular attractions, **(8) Dunn's River Falls** consist of clear mountain water flowing seaward across a tiered limestone bed. Visitors are charged $5 US to enter the park area, which

The view from Noel Coward's grave site at Firefly, where he enjoyed many an evening aperitif, is one of the most scenic in Jamaica.

includes a guided climb up this stunning set of falls. Guides lead visitors, in single file, along a known route. Operators of the park are fairly insistent you remain part of a guided climb to prevent personal injury. For an additional $5, a guide will hold your camera and other belongings as you scramble up the falls. A pair of running shoes or aqua socks (which can be rented at the Falls) are recommended for the climb over slippery stones and rushing, knee-deep water. Dunn's Falls are about 1.5 miles by road from Ocho Rios and can also be reached by boat, a popular excursion being the party cruise aboard *Sundancer*, a 75-foot yacht that departs the cruise pier for a relaxing boat ride to the mouth of Dunn's River and back, with time allowed for climbing the falls.

Anyone interested in Jamaican folk art will enjoy a visit to **(9) Harmony Hall**, a restored Victorian great house. Set on a small plantation estate four miles east of Ocho Rios, it contains an art gallery, craft and book shops, boutique and restaurant.

Not far from Harmony Hall is **(10) Prospect Plantation** – a working plantation estate where guides take visitors on tractor-drawn jitneys past various flora and agricultural crops including bananas, sugar cane and coffee, as well as the White River Gorge and Sir Harold's Viewpoint from which Cuba can be seen on a clear day. Horseback tours are also available on each of three varied trails that traverse the 900 acres of grounds which also contain a miniature golf course and a gift shop selling local crafts and souvenirs.

About 10 miles east of Prospect Plantation, **(11) Brimmer Hall Plantation** is another working plantation providing tours by tractor-drawn jitney. The beautiful grounds contain an 18th-century great house open for viewing, as well as a swimming pool, bar and shops. Both Brimmer Hall and Prospect Plantation are usually included in the cruise lines' organized shore excursions.

One of the most beautiful views in Jamaica can be enjoyed at Noel Coward's former estate of **(12) Firefly**, 15 miles east of Ocho Rios. Bequeathed to Jamaica in 1975, it has been transformed into a museum administered on behalf of the National Heritage Trust by Island Outpost which charges a small fee to tour the grounds.

The property is set atop a plateau and was originally a lookout for Captain Morgan during his days as a pirate. Coward's house is a modest open-air design which looks east to a dramatic view of the surf pounding into Saccabus Bay. The breeze is dry and warm, the grounds meticulously maintained, and the atmosphere unabashedly nostaglic with strains of "I'll See You Again" floating across the lawn from the recently completed bandshell. When Noel Coward died in 1973 he asked that no fuss be made, and the site of his grave was the spot where he often sat with friends sipping a pre-dinner cocktail while looking out to the sea.

At Oracabessa, the road winds past **Goldeneye**, an estate overlooking a private cove. This was the former winter retreat of the late Ian Fleming, who wrote his James Bond novels at this idyllic location. **OTHER EXCURSIONS:** Helicopter flightseeing trips can be taken from the heli-pad at Reynolds Pier. A 20-minute flight takes in the lush and varied coastal sights of the Ocho Rios area, including aerial views of Dunn's River Falls, sumptuous seaside villas and beaches lapped by an azure sea.

River rafting on the **Martha Brae**, which lies between Montego Bay and Ocho Rios, is a popular attraction. On bamboo rafts carrying two people, the raft man uses a pole to guide the raft gently downstream past bamboo groves and chirping birds. The drive from Ocho Rios to Martha Brae takes 1-1/2 hours along the winding coastal highway, and the river ride is just over an hour in length. An organized shore excursion lasts about five hours, often with a stop at **Columbus Park**, near Discovery Bay, where Columbus first landed at Jamaica. Other notable places along this stretch of coastline include Nine Miles village, the birthplace and grave site of Bob Marley, and the 18th-century Georgian town of **Falmouth** near the mouth of the Martha Brae, about 20 miles east of Montego Bay.

MONTEGO BAY

Jamaica's second-largest city, Montego Bay is one of the Caribbean's most popular resorts, beautifully situated on a beach-lined bay surrounded by green hills. A commercial center and shipping port, it's a growing city of over 70,000 residents, many of whom live in shanty towns on the outskirts. On the lower slopes of the Miranda Hills are luxury hotels set in manicured grounds.

Getting Around

The cruise ships dock at Freeport, about three miles west of downtown. An information booth and telephones are situated on the dock. Nearby is the Montego Freeport duty-free shopping area. The taxi fare into town is about $12 for up to four people, and only JUTA (Jamaica Union of Travellers Association) taxis and mini-vans should be rented.

BEST BEACHES: Doctor's Cave Beach, located just north of the town center, is Montego Bay's most celebrated beach. At the turn of the century it was a fashionable health resort and many distinguished visitors came to bathe here. Today it's Montego Bay's most popular beach, with an entry charge which includes change facilities. Other good stretches of sand are found at Walter Fletcher Beach, south of Doctor's Cave, and at Cornwall Beach which lies directly north of Doctor's Cave with a Jamaican Tourist Board office situated at its south end.

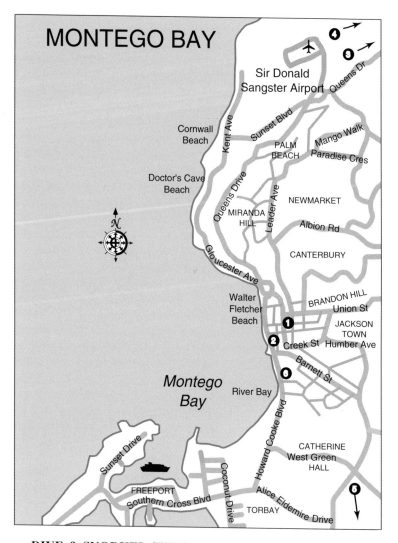

DIVE & SNORKEL SITES / GOLF: Coral sea gardens can be viewed by glass-bottom boat in the clear, sheltered waters of Doctor's Cave, and dives can be arranged through local operators.

A championship golf course is located at the Half Moon Club, east of Montego Bay.

LOCAL SIGHTS & SHOPPING: The city's business district includes a few historic landmarks, most of them situated on or near **(1) Sam Sharpe Square** – named for a Jamaican hero who was hanged in 1831 for leading a slave revolt. On the southwest side of the square stands the Court House, an early-19th century colonial building. The Cage, a small building of the same period on the square's northeast corner, was used for detaining runaway slaves. Nearby, on Church Street, are a number of restored Georgian buildings including St. James's Parish Church which was rebuilt after suffering major damage in a 1957 earthquake. South of Church Street, near the water, is the colorful **(2) Crafts Market**. A few blocks to the north, along the waterfront, stand the remains of Fort Montego which was built by the British in 1752. From here Goucester Avenue, the main shopping thoroughfare, wends north past the hotel strip.

AREA ATTRACTIONS: A British mansion built in 1770 to the east of Montego Bay, **(3) Rose Hall** is Jamaica's most famous great house thanks to a legendary mistress by the name of Annie Palmer. She lived here around 1820 and is said to have murdered three husbands and numerous slave lovers whom she controlled through witchcraft. According to one version of the legend, she was finally murdered by a lover who felt he was destined to be next on Annie's hit list.

(4) Greenwood Great House, located 16 miles east of Montego Bay, was built in the same period as Rose Hall but the domestic scene here was much more sedate. Built by relatives of poet Elizabeth Barrett Browning, the stately mansion is furnished with antiques and contains a rare-book library. A tour of Greenwood gives visitors an inside look at the privileged lives once enjoyed by plantation owners.

(5) Rockland Bird Sanctuary, nine miles south of Montego Bay, is popular with visitors, as is the **(6) Appleton Estate Express**, a train that departs daily from Montego Bay and heads into Cockpit Country, location of the famous **Appleton Rum Distillery** and the **Ipswich Caves** with their limestone stalagmites and stalactites.

Photo Princess Cruises

A number of cruise ships call at Montego Bay where famous beaches and British mansions are among the attractions.

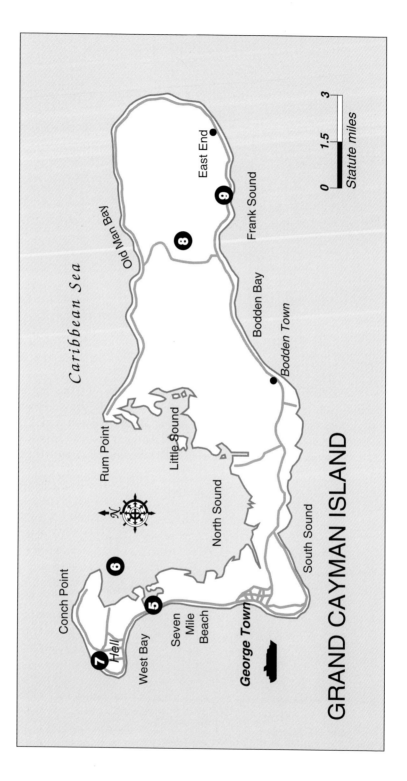

GRAND CAYMAN ISLAND

CHAPTER FIVE

GRAND CAYMAN

Water Sports Mecca

Grand Cayman, an international center for offshore banking, is one of the best-rated dive locations in the world. A person needn't even get wet to enjoy some of the island's remarkable aquatic sights, for a variety of vessels and observatories allow visitors to see the reefs, wrecks and marine life for which the Cayman Islands are famous.

Grand Cayman is the largest of a three-island group which includes Little Cayman and Cayman Brac – a Gaelic word for cliff. The name Cayman is derived from a Carib word for crocodile, although the Caymans were first called *Las Tortugas* by Columbus when he observed, in 1503, the hundreds of turtles living on these uninhabited islands. The Spanish paid these flat coral outcrops little attention as the soil was poor and there were no precious metals to mine, but English, Dutch and French ships pulled in regularly to take on fresh water and salted turtle meat. Today, the green sea turtle is an endangered species and in 1978 the United States banned the import of all turtle products, even those raised at the Cayman Turtle Farm, which releases young turtles into local waters.

Sea turtles are not the only species protected in the Cayman Islands. In 1978 a marine conversation law was passed, and four preservation zones were established in 1986. The Replenishment Zones provide year-round protection of conch and lobster breeding grounds, as well as every other kind of marine life. Line fishing from shore or beyond the drop-off are the only forms of harvesting allowed. Permanent moorings have been installed to protect the reefs which were becoming damaged by the anchors of dive boats. These progressive conservation measures have extended onto land with the establishment of animal sanctuaries and the opening of a botanical park by Queen Elizabeth. Grand Cayman's indigenous animal species include iguanas and parrots. Bird watching is popular here, with more than a hundred species of birds observed, including those on spring and fall migrations. The governor, His Excellency Mr. Michael Gore, is an accomplished ornithologist and wildlife photographer who has written four books on the subject.

The Cayman Islands, a British Crown Colony since 1670, were a dependency of Jamaica when transferred from Spain to Great Britain under the terms of the Treaty of Madrid. Shortly afterwards, the Cayman Islands were settled by a motley collection of British army deserters, shipwrecked sailors, retired pirates and African slaves who gained freedom when ships carrying them foundered on Cayman reefs.

Slavery was abolished by Britain in 1833, a year after a representative government was established on the Cayman Islands. When Jamaica opted for independence from Britain in 1962, a debate ensued among Cayman residents who eventually voted to remain a British Crown Colony. About 30,000 people live on the three islands, the majority on Grand Cayman. Of mixed origin and free of racial tensions, they descend from the English, Irish, Scottish and Africans who first settled

Grand Cayman's tender pier is within easy walking distance of George Town's attractions and harbor-based sightseeing boats.

the islands. With few natural resources on these mangrove-covered islands, the Cayman men traditionally made their living from the sea – turtle fishing, ship building and serving in the merchant marine. As recently as the 1950s, those working on foreign-owned ships were sustaining the local economy with the money they sent back home.

Grand Cayman remained an isolated backwater until 1954 when an airfield was built. But it wasn't until the island's troublesome mosquitoes were brought under control in the '70s that tourists began arriving in droves. The climate is ideal, the beaches are beautiful and the marine life prolific due to the varied underwater terrain which ranges from shallow coral reefs to submarine canyons. Meanwhile, Cayman's political stability and attractive tax laws made it an ideal environment for offshore banking interests. Some 70 financial institutions, six of which are clearing banks, operate on Grand Cayman where local services include offshore incorporation, company management and private banking. Caymanians are said to own the highest number of fax machines per capita in the world and, thanks to telecommunications, Wall Street is as accessible to offshore investors as the Cayman Wall is to offshore divers.

Financial Hub of the Caribbean

Cayman's thriving financial industry, which includes major accounting firms, is subject to strict government controls – which apply to both its banks and its customers. But professionalism and integrity do not provide good material for a Hollywood script, so Caymanians were more than happy to cooperate with Paramount Pictures when its film crew arrived at Grand Cayman to shoot scenes for *The Firm*, a movie of intrigue and corruption based on John Grisham's book and starring Gene Hackman, Tom Cruise and Jeanne Tripplehorn.

The movie's underwater scenes were shot at Soto's Reef and Rhapsody – two dive sites close to George Town. A sheltered cove on North Sound is where the fictitious 'Abanks Dive Lodge' was built, an attraction that will be left intact. The pool bar at the Grand Hyatt Hotel and the Holiday Inn's beachside bar were other film locations, as was Seven Mile Beach and a bank in George Town. A number of locals appeared as extras in the movie, including singer and songwriter George Nowak, who calls himself Barefoot Man.

Getting Around

The cruise ships anchor off George Town and tender their passengers ashore. A visitor information booth and telephones are located at the north tender pier. The town's sights and stores are all within easy walking distance of the waterfront, and a shuttle bus takes visitors to Seven Mile Beach for a fee of $3 per person.

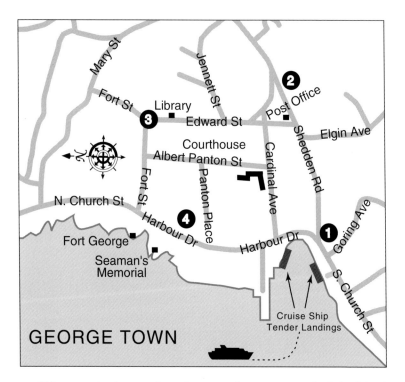

GEORGE TOWN

Ship-organized excursions focus on the western end of the island where most of the major attractions are located. Passengers interested in touring the island can hire a taxi (about $40 US to East End) or rent a car (approximately $40 a day plus $4 for a temporary driving permit) as well as mopeds, motorbikes and bicycles. Driving is on the left.

Shopping: A free port, Grand Cayman carries an assortment of duty-free goods. George Town, where the majority of shops are located (many of which are closed on Sundays), is very clean and orderly with no roadside pedlars. Local items to look for include numismatic jewelry, crafted from old coins retrieved from sunken vessels and featured in exquisite gold-and-diamond settings. Unique to the Cayman Islands are sculptures and jewelry made of an earth-toned, hard dolomite stone called caymanite that was discovered at East End.

The Cayman Island dollar equals $1.25 US, but American currency is accepted throughout the islands. American and Canadian visitors should be aware it is against customs regulations to import turtle products into their countries.

Local Sights: Overlooking the pier area is the **(1) Cayman Islands National Museum**, housed in the former courthouse and containing displays on the islands' natural and cultural history, including artifacts of pirate lore.

Cardinal, one of the main shopping streets, leads to the post office and the adjacent **(2) Elizabethan Square**. A few blocks west on Edward is the **Public Library**. Across the street is a small park containing a massive fig tree. At the intersection of Edward and Fort Streets is **(3) Clock Tower**, a monument to Britain's King George V. Fort Street leads down to the waterfront where the remains of Fort George can be seen, built in the 17th century to protect the island from pirate attacks. Nearby, on Harbour Drive, is the restored 19th-century **(4) Elmslie Memorial Church**.

Best Beaches: The natural choice for cruise passengers is Seven Mile Beach, one of the finest in the Caribbean, which starts just north of George Town and stretches for about five miles along the island's western shore. Lined with hotels, this beautiful white-sand beach is free of pedlars and ideal for swimming, snorkeling and other water sports. Taxi vans run between George Town and Seven Mile Beach at a cost of $3 per person. The cruise lines often arrange with one of the hotels for their passengers to utilize its beach-front facilities for a small fee. Sailboards and other equipment can be rented at the Holiday Inn sports center, located beside the public beach which is usually uncrowded. **(5) Government House**, the Governor's official residence, is on the far side of the public beach area. A regular taxi ride between Georgetown and Seven Mile Beach is $12, and a taxi stand is located at the Holiday Inn. Another way to visit Seven Mile Beach is by glass-bottom party

Much of Grand Cayman's shoreline lies within conservation zones, including Seven Mile Beach which is part of a marine park.

boat, departing from George Town. The cost is about $30, which includes rum and fruit punches.

Dive & Snorkel Sites: Grand Cayman is the top of a submerged mountain and its offshore coral reefs form the famous 'Cayman Wall'. An estimated 60 miles of drop-offs encircle Grand Cayman where the underwater visibility extends to depths of 150 feet. There are more than a hundred dive sites surrounding the island, and they include numerous shipwrecks as well as coral gardens, grottos, caves and canyons which are habitat for rays, turtles, tropical fish and huge, colorful sponges. Whether snorkeling, shore diving or deep diving, Cayman Island offers crystal clear water, an abundance of marine life and a variety of underwater terrain.

This fascinating marine world can also be viewed from vessels that operate out of George Town, including a glass-bottom boat, a semi-submersible and a submarine. There are reefs and wrecks to explore right in Hog Sty Bay, such as Cheeseburger Reef and the wreck of the *Cali*. Other easily accessible dive sites include Eden Rock and Devil's Grotto, just south of George Town, as well as those along Seven Mile Beach. Dive boats take certified divers to the island's incredible drop-offs, such as the West Wall which lies about nine miles offshore. Atlantis Submarine operates out of George Town and offers non-divers the opportunity to view the famous Cayman Wall. Several dive and snorkel shops are located within walking distance of the tender pier, and the cruise lines also offer snorkel and dive excursions.

Golf: There are two golf courses on Grand Cayman, both a few miles north of George Town along West Bay Road. Closest to town is the Hyatt Britannia Golf Course, designed by Jack Nicklaus and offering three courses in one: a nine-hole championship course, an 18-hole executive course and one played with a special Cayman ball. The new Links at SafeHaven is an 18-hole championship course and is reminiscent of those in Scotland.

Island Attractions: (6) Stingray City, located in the protected waters of North Sound, has been described in National Geographic as "one of the most rewarding experiences in the undersea world." From an observatory, visitors can watch the remarkable sight of dozens of stingrays congregating in a shallow area where they nuzzle and brush against the divers feeding them. Visitors can also snorkel with the stingrays, touch their satin-like wings and feed them squid. If you are booking a ship excursion to Stingray City, be sure to take the one that includes your preferred activity, either snorkeling at the Stingray City Sandbar or strictly watching the stingrays from the observatory.

(7) Cayman Turtle Farm, a land-based attraction, is situated in a tidal creek of North Sound. Originally established in 1968 to raise and market turtle products, the farm now concentrates on research and

The Cayman Islands National Museum, housed in Grand Cayman's oldest surviving building, contains a courtyard cafe and gift shop in addition to exhibits.

breeding. Green sea turtles and hawksbill turtles are bred, hatched, raised and tagged before being released into Cayman waters. Tours of the facility are self-guided.

While many visitors like to stop at **Hell** so they can send a postcard, the real attraction is the weathered outcrop of iron shore which, although said to look like the charred remains of a hell fire, is actually made of black limestone about 1-1/2 million years old.

East of George Town, the attractions include Bodden Town with its legendary **Pirate Cave** where pirates are said to have hidden their loot in a series of tunnels. Nearby is the Meagre Bay Bird Sanctuary and further east are the **(8) Botanic Gardens**, officially opened by Queen Elizabeth in 1994. Still being developed, the park's 60 acres of grounds currently include an interpretive trail that winds through woodlands, wetlands, swamps and thickets. The island's eastern shores also contain **(9) The Blow Holes**, saltwater geysers spouting from the coral rock as waves crash onto shore. East End is the oldest town on the island, founded in the late 17th century.

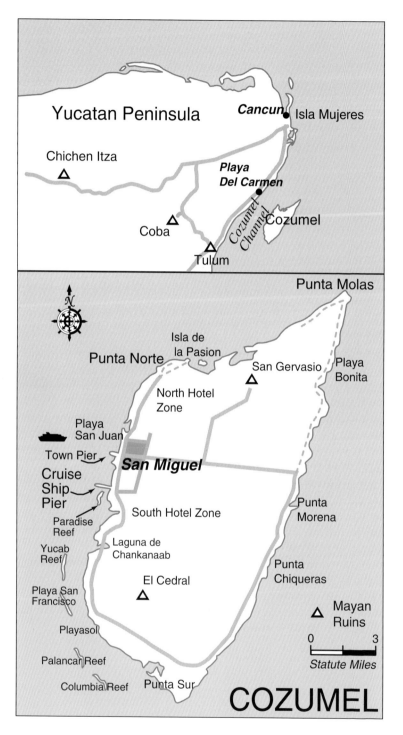

Yucatan Peninsula

Cancun Isla Mujeres

Chichen Itza

Playa
Del Carmen

Coba

Cozumel
Channel

Cozumel

Tulum

Punta Molas

Isla de
la Pasion

Punta Norte

San Gervasio

Playa
Bonita

North Hotel
Zone

Playa
San Juan

Town Pier

San Miguel

Cruise
Ship
Pier

South Hotel Zone

Punta
Morena

Paradise
Reef

Yucab
Reef

Laguna de
Chankanaab

Playa San
Francisco

El Cedral

Punta
Chiqueras

Playasol

△ Mayan
Ruins

Palancar Reef

0   3

Columbia Reef   Punta Sur

Statute Miles

COZUMEL

CHAPTER SIX

COZUMEL

Coral Reefs & Mayan Culture

The coral-fringed island of Cozumel was a sleepy hideaway when Jacques Cousteau paid it a visit in the early '60s and introduced the world to one of the Caribbean's top dive sites. The documentary Cousteau filmed here captured the brilliance of Cozumel's extensive coral reefs which thrive in crystal clear waters teeming with tropical fish and other marine life. The clarity of the water is unsurpassed anywhere in the Caribbean, and the underwater caves and spectacular sponges are considered some of the best in the world. Understandably, about one third of Cozumel's visitors are divers, but the island is also popular for its beautiful beaches and fascinating Mayan ruins which have attracted such notable visitors as Jacqueline Kennedy who came to Cozumel in 1968 while touring the area's archaeological sites.

The ancient Maya, from which Cozumel's inhabitants descend, named the island 'Land of Swallows' and dedicated it to *Ixchel*, the moon goddess of fertility. Remnants of temples and religious artifacts have been found throughout the island which lies 12 miles off the Yucatan Peninsula, separating the Caribbean Sea from the Gulf of Mexico. The Yucatan, low and flat like Cozumel, is a limestone table-land covered with thin topsoil which supports subsistence crops as well as tobacco and corn. It is also one of the world's most important henequen-growing regions, the leaves of these tropical plants containing a strong fiber used for making binder twine. The uncultivated areas are covered with a dense growth of scrub, cactus, sapete wood and mangrove thickets. No rivers run through this area and the light rainfall is absorbed by the porous limestone where it collects in underground rivers and wells (cenotes), and in surface pools called *aguadas*. Scattered throughout the low hills are thousands of pre-Columbian archaeological sites, for the Yucatan was the seat of the great Mayan civilization which flourished for more than two millennium, beginning in about 1500 B.C.

The Maya were an advanced society with an understanding of astronomy and engineering. They built their pyramidal structures oriented to the spring and fall equinoxes, and one of the world's earliest suspension bridges was built by the Maya in the seventh century in Yaxchilan, near Mexico's border with Guatemala. The Mayans also developed a hieroglyphic script, a numerical system and several calendars, some of which were accurate to within 20 seconds over a year.

They practised agriculture and formed a hierarchical society based on patrilineal descent, in which kinship played a major role. There was no widespread political organization of the Mayans; each city state had its own internal structure of dynastic status and power. Their civic centers followed a pattern in which pyramidal structures and temples were built around a central plaza. Built of stone, these buildings were often decorated with elaborate carvings and ceramic paintings.

A common feature of their civic centers was a ball court with stone hoops. Opposing teams played with a heavy rubber ball which players kept in the air by bouncing it off any part of the body except the hands and feet. It's believed that these games were sometimes used as a peaceful means to settle disputes between leaders, with the loser giving up his land and followers to be assimilated with the winning team's people. Another theory is that the losing team offered a human sacrifice – often the team captain.

Mayan civilization reached its height during the Classic period (A.D. 300 to 900), followed by a rapid decline in which much of the population plummeted. In the Yucatan, however, settlement persisted due to the arrival of the Toltec ('master builders') from Central Mexico. Also an advanced civilization, Toltec society was based on a warrior aristocracy. These masters of architecture and arts dominated the Yucatan's Maya from the 11th to the 13th century, at which time the nomadic Chichimec brought about the fall of the Toltec empire, soon to be followed by the rise of the Aztec.

The first Europeans to arrive at the Yucatan were most likely a pair of survivors from a 1511 Spanish shipwreck. One man joined the Maya, the other was rescued by Hernan Cortes in 1519 and became his interpreter. Spanish battles with the Maya began in 1527, with Cozumel used as a staging base, and continued until 1546 when a Mayan revolt

Mexico's Yucatan, the seat of Mayan civilization, is dotted with ancient ruins including the walled city of Tulum.

was crushed. However, resistance to Spanish (and later Mexican) rule continued into the early 20th century.

During the Spanish colonial period, administrative centers were established by Spaniards who imposed their own religious and political organization on the Mayan population. Assimilation, however, was far from complete. The indigenous elite were incorporated into the new colonial system but the rural peasants were left alone. The Spanish were disinterested in the Yucatan, due to its lack of mineral wealth and export crops. Its offshore islands of Cozumel and Isla Mujeres also were of little value to the Spaniards, but they did attract pirates such as Henry Morgan and Jean Lafitte who hid in coves to lie in wait for passing ships laden with gold and other treasures.

In the late 18th century, a growing world demand for cordage and fibers prompted the establishment of huge henequen plantations throughout the northern Yucatan. The local Maya's village lands were expropriated and, as the plantations grew in size, former land owners were pressed into labor. Tensions reached a boiling point in the mid-1800s and sparked a rebellion in which the Maya tried to drive all Europeans off the Yucatan peninsula. They were unsuccessful, but the Spanish were never able to completely suppress the indigenous population, and isolated pockets located outside the plantation zone remained autonomous throughout the 19th century.

Mexico gained independence from Spain in 1821, but widespread political turmoil continued. The social order inherited from Spanish

Cruise ships anchor off Cozumel's port of San Miguel, once a sleepy fishing village until discovered by Jacques Cousteau and other dive enthusiasts.

colonialists consisted of two groups: Spanish-speaking whites and ladinos who resided in the major towns and maintained control of the region's commercial interests, and the much larger group of Mayan-speaking farmers who lived in rural villages. Following the Mexican Revolution of 1910-17, a land redistribution program guaranteed the rural Maya would no longer have their village lands expropriated.

In the early '70s, flush with oil revenue, the Mexican government decided to build a world-class resort and once again the Yucatan Peninsula became the focus of outside interests. The location for a master-plan resort – carefully chosen for its white sand beaches, Caribbean climate, clear waters and access to Mayan ruins – was Isla Cancun, lying off the northeast coast of the Yucutan Peninsula. Modern civilization is very much in evidence at Cancun where hotel towers line the powdery beaches, their design elements including pyramidal forms, stucco walls and other architectural features first used by those accomplished master builders – the Maya.

COZUMEL

Cozumel is a flat island, its highest point only 35 feet above sea level, and is covered with scrub jungle. The majority of islanders live in the town of **San Miguel**, located on the island's sheltered west coast overlooking Cozumel Channel. While no longer the quiet seaside town that greeted visitors back in the '50s, San Miguel has retained much of its early charm. Safe and compact, the port is laid out in a grid pattern with streets running parallel and perpendicular to the waterfront. The locals, of Mayan descent, are generally shorter than the average Mexican and most speak Spanish as well as some English.

The cruise ship pier is situated four miles south of San Miguel, close to good beaches but a short cab ride into town. Ships that anchor off San Miguel transport their passengers by tender to the town pier, right in the heart of downtown opposite the main square. Shops line the streets in either direction, with the upscale boutiques and restaurants located on the waterfront's Avenue Rafael E. Melgar.

Getting Around

A cab ride from San Miguel to Chankanaab Lagoon is about $8 US, to San Francisco Beach - $12, and to Playasol - $15. A passenger ferry runs between Cozumel and Playa del Carmen on the mainland, which is a popular disembarkation port for cruise passengers taking organized shore excursions to Coba, Tulum and Chichen Itza – the Yucatan's three main archaeological sites.

Shopping: Cozumel offers excellent shopping, due in part to the devaluation of the Mexican peso, and many cruise ship passengers spend their day in port searching for gifts and keepsakes. Mexican handicrafts include ceramics, wood carvings, colorful blankets and hammocks, as well as reproductions of Mayan artifacts. All Mexican-made products are duty-exempt and good buys are available in products made of silver, onyx and leather. Small discounts are often given for

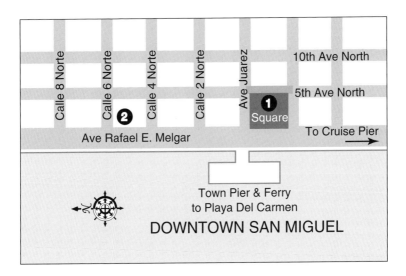

cash purchases and most stores accept U.S. dollars. Passengers taking organized excursions to the Mayan ruins on the mainland will have an opportunity to buy local crafts at outdoor markets.

Local Sights: Located opposite San Miguel's town pier, **(1) Main Square** is pleasant to stroll through with its shady areas, large gazebo, clock tower and a monument to motherhood.

(2) Museum de le Isla de Cozumel, located on the waterfront between Calle 4 Norte and Calle 6 Norte, is a welcome retreat from the busy street and bustling boutiques. For a small admission charge, you can enjoy exhibits ranging from Cozumel's natural habitat to its Mayan and colonial history. A highlight is the replica Mayan house, set in a courtyard, with a garden outside and authentic tools and furnishings inside. A Mayan host demonstrates the various stone tools, identifies foodstuffs on display and generally brings to life the workings of a typical village home. An open-air restaurant on the museum's second floor provides a lovely view to sea and the cruise ships at anchor.

Cozumel Archaeological Park is located on 65th Avenue, a few blocks from the Cruise Ship Terminal and a five-minute cab ride from the town pier. It contains full-size replicas of Mayan and Toltec stone carvings set in a jungle setting. A guided walking tour is included in the admission fee.

Although there are numerous archaeological sites on Cozumel, none reach the scale and architectural significance of those found on the Yucatan peninsula. The most important island site is the Mayan temple of Ixchel located at **San Gervasio**, about 10 miles by road from San Miguel.

Best Beaches: An excellent beach – Playa San Juan – lies a few miles north of San Miguel where the North Hotel Zone is situated, and many more are located south of town, in the vicinity of the cruise ship pier and South Hotel Zone. South of Chankanaab Lagoon lies San Francisco Beach and Playasol Beach, two of the island's most beautiful.

Dive & Snorkel Sites: Chankanaab Lagoon Park (*chankanaab* meaning 'small lake' or 'little sea' in Maya) is connected to the sea by underground channels. This natural underwater preserve contains dozens of species of tropical fish, and its clear water and corals make it ideal for snorkeling, with basic diving instruction available. The admission fee includes entry to a botanical garden and museum dedicated to the local flora, fauna and marine life.

A strong current flows through Cozumel Channel, so drift diving is how the offshore reefs are explored. The continual current carries food to the reefs, which is why the sponge growth is so spectacular.

One of the Caribbean's most famous dive sites is three-mile Palancar Reef at the southern tip of the island with seven different dive sites, ranging from 35 to over 80 feet. Other good dive sites include:

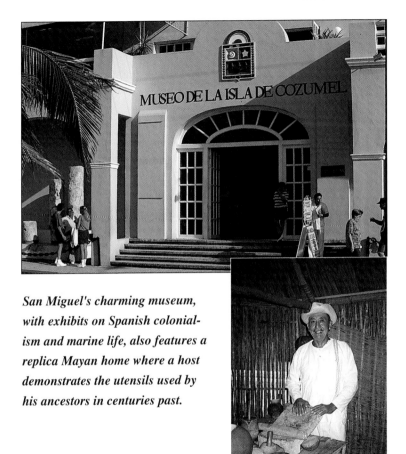

San Miguel's charming museum, with exhibits on Spanish colonialism and marine life, also features a replica Mayan home where a host demonstrates the utensils used by his ancestors in centuries past.

Columbia Reef; Punta Sur with caverns and steep drop-offs; Santa Rosa Reef with its huge coral mounds; San Francisco Reef's valleys and vertical wall; and Yucab Reef, an extensive and shallow dive site encompassing a wide variety of coral formations and fish species.

Cozumel's reefs were protected by presidential decree in 1980 but the current administration has sparked a controversy by approving plans to build a new cruise ship pier at Paradise Reef, a popular beach dive on the island. Several environmental groups, as well as local residents and dive operators, have protested this development and their case will likely be heard by the North American Commission for Environmental Cooperation, established by Canada, the United States and Mexico under the auspices of their trilateral free trade agreement.

Not far from Paradise Beach is Paradise Wall which begins at a depth of 50 feet and contains an abundance of marine life including giant sponges.

The pyramid-shaped temples of Coba are part of the largest Mayan settlement found to date on the Yucatan peninsula.

The Yucatan's Mayan Sites

Chichen Itza: This well-restored and popular Mayan site was founded around two large *cenotes* (deep, natural wells) in circa 514 by the Itza – the last strong, independent Mayan tribe. The site was occupied at various times until 1194 when it was abandoned for the last time. The buildings span two periods of Mayan civilization. The Classic style is reflected in massive structures and heavy, decorative sculpture; the Post-Classic period, with a strong Toltec influence, produced plainer buildings, columns and sculpture based on the Mexican feathered-serpent motif. The site's highlights include the Castillo temple, a ball court and, unusual among Mayan buildings, a round tower called the Caracol (snail shell) which was built in the Post-Classic period, probably as an astronomical observatory. Offerings, including human sacrifices, were thrown into Chichen Itza's sacred well which was a mecca for pilgrimages by other Mayan tribes of Central America and Mexico.

Coba: Dozens of stone roads and causeways once led to Coba – a commercial hub of the Maya which flourished from 400 to 1100. The largest settlement found to date, much of this site is still overgrown but those structures that have been excavated include the 80-foot-high 'Iglesia' temple-pyramid, the 'Crossword' pyramid, and the 'Nohochmul' pyramid which is the tallest on the Yucutan peninsula with 120 steps climbing to the top of its 138-foot-high face.

Tulum: The only known walled city of the Maya, this ancient trading center is a stunning sight perched on the edge of a bluff that overlooks a white sand beach and the blue Caribbean sea. Its stone buildings are surrounded on three sides by a stone wall that dates from 1200 AD and is said to be 16 feet thick in places. Tulum, 'City of the New Dawn', was the only Mayan city still occupied when the Spanish arrived in the early 1500s. The protected cove at the base of this site is ideal for swimming and snorkeling off its white sand beach.

Cancun

Originally a Mayan settlement, its name meaning 'vessel at the end of the rainbow', Cancun consisted of a few hundred inhabitants before an international holiday resort was built on its offshore island in the early '70s. Long and narrow, the island is lined with powdery white beaches and connected to the mainland by a bridge at each end. Its hotel zone contains first-class hotels and recreation facilities which draw over two million visitors annually, mostly from the U.S. The L-shaped island forms a lagoon where water sports can be enjoyed, and the outer beaches are sheltered by coral reefs. Isla Mujeres is a short ferry or water taxi ride from Cancun, and this tiny island is a snorkeling and diving paradise of reefs, lagoons and fine beaches.

Tulum, still occupied when the Spanish arrived in the 16th century, was an important port and religious center of the Maya.
Right: Mayan family sells crafts at market by the walls of Tulum.

*(Top) A cruise ship glides past the Spanish fortress of El Morro, at the entrance to San Juan Harbor.
(Middle, bottom) Danish colonial buildings, Charlotte Amalie, St. Thomas.*

Photo Princess Cruises

*(Top) The U.S. Virgin Islands'
Legislative Building, in Charlotte
Amalie, was built in the late 1800s as
a barracks for the Danish police.
(Middle) Frederiksted, St. Croix.
(Bottom) The ruins of Annaberg
Sugar Mill, St. John.*

(Top) The unspoiled British Virgin Islands. (Right) The beaches on the half-Dutch/half-French island of St. Maarten/St. Martin are beautiful in any language.

Photo Windstar Cruises   Gerald Brimacombe

(Left) Gustavia, on the tiny French island of St. Barts.

Photo Fred Jensen

(Top) Tyrells Catholic Church, Antigua (Left) Nelson's Dockyard, at English Harbour on Antigua, is an 18th-century naval dockyard containing beautiful examples of Georgian architecture.

(Right) From Brimstone Hill Fortress on St. Kitts, the British had a sweeping view across fields of sugar cane to the distant island of St. Eustatius.

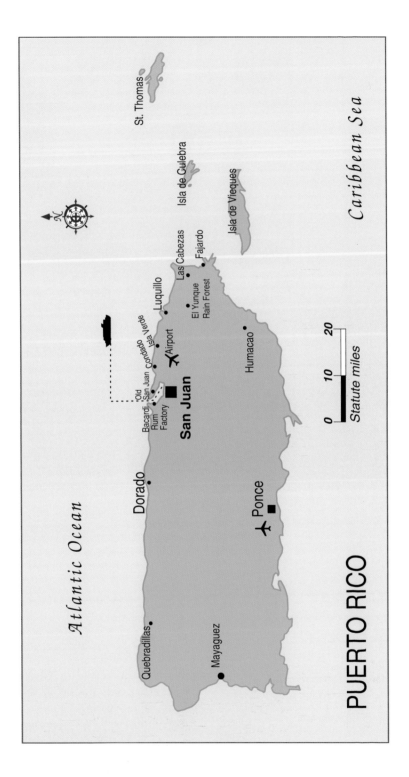

CHAPTER SEVEN

SAN JUAN

Puerto Rico

San Juan, a busy base port for Caribbean cruises, is also one of the best-preserved ports of colonial Spain. The walled city of Old San Juan, the oldest Spanish settlement under American sovereignty, is a World Heritage Site. Its cobblestone streets are paved with ballast from Spanish galleons and the impenetrable citadel of El Morro was once a symbol of Spanish domination in the Caribbean. In contrast to the historic feel of Old San Juan is the nearby Condado area, where modern high-rise hotels line the beaches and a sizzling night life can be enjoyed in the night clubs and casinos.

Puerto Ricans number 3.6 million and they refer to their Connecticut-sized island as the 'continent' of Puerto Rico due to its geographical diversity. Mountains here soar to over 4,000 feet and island vegetation ranges from lush rainforests to low-lying mangrove swamps. Beautiful beaches line much of the coastline and, in the north-west, an extensive system of caves has been carved by one of the world's largest underground rivers.

Puerto Rico is a self-governing Commonwealth of the United States and its infrastructure includes a major airport, well-maintained roads, luxury resorts and championship golf courses. Industrialization came to Puerto Rico in the 1940s when Operation Bootstrap was introduced and its tax exemptions promoted American investment. Manufacturing, pharmaceuticals and the production of high-tech equipment are now major industries, along with agriculture and tourism.

The Condado section of San Juan contains modern resort hotels overlooking the Atlantic Ocean. This area is just two miles from the old part of the city.

Puerto Ricans enjoy the highest annual income in Latin America and are a well-educated work force. Few deny that the island's ties to America are beneficial and worth preserving, but an ongoing debate revolves around the 'statehood versus status quo' issue. The electorate is fairly evenly divided, with those supporting the status quo concerned about preserving their Spanish culture. Those supporting statehood accuse their opponents of 'wanting to have their cake and eat it too'. A small minority support independence, a movement that began in the last century when Puerto Rican statesman and journalist Luis Munoz Rivera led a growing demand for self government, which resulted in Spain granting its Caribbean colony some autonomy in February 1898. However, the Spanish-American war began a few months later and American troops soon occupied the island. By December, Spain had ceded Puerto Rico to the United States.

Puerto Rico remained under direct military rule until 1900 when Congress passed the Foraker Act, setting up a local administration with a U.S. Governor, an elected house of delegates and an upper chamber appointed by the U.S. President. Munoz Rivera, who had moved to New York where he published the *Puerto Rico Herald* before becoming the resident commissioner of Puerto Rico in Washington, was again a driving force for greater autonomy. In 1917 the Jones Act pronounced Puerto Rico a U.S. territory, granting its occupants U.S. citizenship and increased internal self-government.

While Puerto Ricans were making political gains, economic and social conditions were worsening. Much of their subsistence land was encroached upon by the establishment of large sugar plantations. The situation, aggravated by overpopulation, went from bad to worse when the sugar market fell in the 1930s. Recovery measures were taken under Franklin Roosevelt's presidency and the governorship of Rexford Tugwell. In 1948 Puerto Ricans elected their governor for the first time, and in 1952 the Commonwealth of Puerto Rico was proclaimed.

The smallest and easternmost of the Greater Antilles, Puerto Rico is bounded on its north side by the Atlantic Ocean and on its south coast by the Caribbean Sea. The 3,425-square-mile island was originally inhabited by Taino Indians who called the island *Borinquen.* Christopher Columbus visited in 1493 and named the island San Juan Bautista (St. John the Baptist) but sailed on to Hispaniola to establish a settlement. Juan Ponce de Leon began the Spanish conquest of *Borinquen,* after finding gold there in 1508. He established a settlement on the shores of San Juan harbor, calling it Puerto Rico – *rich port.* The names were eventually switched, and rich is what Ponce de Leon became as governor of the island, with the lure of new conquests drawing him away from Puerto Rico from time to time.

In 1521, the Spanish colonists moved their settlement from a low-lying location across the bay to the present-day site of San Juan. Ponce de Leon was in Florida at the time, trying to establish a new colony, where he was felled by the poisoned arrow of a Native American. His party sailed immediately for Cuba where their leader died, his body returned to Puerto Rico for burial.

Meanwhile, hardship, disease and Spanish massacres had eliminated the Tainos and they were replaced with African slaves, first introduced in 1513. Once the island's placer gold deposits were depleted in the 1530s, the

A statue of Ponce de Leon stands outside San Jose Church.

Spanish turned their attention to sugar plantations. Distractions came in the form of raids by Carib Indians and by British, French and Dutch pirates and roving corsairs, all of whom were attracted to this important outpost of the Spanish empire.

Fifty years of empire building had followed Columbus's discovery of Puerto Rico, including the conquest of Mexico and Peru, and twice a year two armed convoys were sent from Spain to collect precious gems, gold and silver. The Spanish ships entered the Caribbean Sea near Puerto Rico, one fleet heading to Veracruz to pick up Mexican gold and silver, the other heading to Cartagena to await treasures arriving from the Isthmus of Panama. The two fleets would then rendezvous at Havana for the return voyage to Spain. To protect her shipping interests, Spain established several military fortifications, the most strategic being San Juan harbor which Spain's King Philip II called 'the key to the West Indies'.

The famous fortress of El Morro stood at the east side of the harbor entrance. It began as a round masonry tower which, over time and following various enemy assaults, was strengthened and expanded until it was a massive citadel. The main purpose of this fortification was to prevent Spain's European enemies from gaining possession of the port and using it as a base for attacks on Spanish settlements and trading ships.

Britain's Sir Francis Drake, justly feared by the Spanish and emboldened by his successful sackings of Santo Domingo, Cartagena and St. Augustine in Florida, was the first to test El Morro. In 1595 he forced

The massive Spanish fortress of El Morro looms at the entrance to San Juan Harbor. Its outer walls are 20 feet thick.

Sentry boxes, called garitas, were positioned along the massive stone walls of Old San Juan, from which guards could keep watch for approaching enemies.

the entrance to the harbor but was repulsed, with heavy losses suffered by the Spanish defenders. Three years later Britain's Earl of Cumberland successfully besieged El Morro, his brief occupation cut short by an outbreak of dysentery. The Dutch were next, in 1625, sacking and burning the town before being driven off by the Spanish.

In response to these attacks, Spain built several fortresses, making San Juan virtually impregnable. Massive walls of sandstone, some 50 feet high and 20 feet thick at the base, were raised around the town. A redoubt named San Cristobal was built about a mile east of El Morro to protect the town from a land-based attack. But it wasn't until the end of the Seven Years War (1756-1763), which left Spain and Britain the two powers in the Caribbean, that San Juan was transformed into the stronghold we see today. Thomas O'Daly, an Irish-born military engineer, was hired by Spain's King Charles III to oversee the completion of the wall, expand San Cristobal into the largest fortress built by Spain in the Americas, and turn El Morro into an impenetrable citadel. Hundreds of workmen were employed in this massive undertaking which took 20 years to complete.

San Juan remained impregnable for more than a century and was one of Spain's last remaining holdings in the Americas when a revolution in Cuba sparked the Spanish-American War. A United States naval flotilla, in search of the Spanish war fleet, bombarded San Juan in May of 1898, and two months later American troops landed on the south coast of Puerto Rico. As soldiers advanced to the outskirts of San Juan, an armistice was signed. Spain's four-century rule of Puerto Rico had come to an end.

Getting Around

San Juan's airport is a $16 (U.S.) taxi ride from the cruise pier. In between lie the hotel-lined beaches of **Isla Verde** and **Condado**, where most passengers stay if spending extra time in San Juan before or after their cruise. The fare from the airport to Isla Verde is $8 and to Condado is $12. The fare from Isla Verde to the cruise piers is $16 and from Condado is $10. Two heritage hotels are located right in Old San Juan – Casa San Jose (a four-storey mansion) and El Convento (a former convent). The brand new Wyndham Old San Juan Hotel & Casino is located on the harbor front.

Parking is limited in Old San Juan and its streets are best explored on foot or by using the free trolley service which originates at the Covadonga parking lot, a block up from the cruise ship piers. Five trolley buses, equipped with wheelchair ramps, operate daily and cover two routes: a central one to **Plaza de Armas** and a northern route to the grounds of **El Morro**. Passengers can hop off and on at any stop.

The El Yunque National Forest, with its varied vegetation and scenic lookouts, is a popular day trip for visitors to San Juan.

*Handmade guitars,
called cuatros, are
among the traditional
items shoppers can
look for in San Juan.*

To see some of the city's outlying districts and area attractions, such as the **El Yunque National Forest**, tours can be booked through the cruise lines' shore excursion office or at the tour desks of the major hotels. Another option is to rent a car. Rental agencies are numerous in the San Juan metropolitan area, including Avis, Budget and Hertz. Road signs indicate distances in kilometers (1 km = .6 mile) but speed limits are posted in miles per hour.

Spanish and English are the official languages. Spanish is predominant, but English is taught in school and is widely spoken. Long-distance phone calls can be made at 'Phones & More' located inside Pier 6. A post office is located opposite Pier 1 where San Justo intersects with Comercio.

SHOPPING TIPS: San Juan has duty-free shopping at its airport and at several factory outlets in Old San Juan. The main shopping streets are Cristo, Fortaleza and San Francisco. Numerous art galleries are located in the shopping area and on San Jose Street.

Traditional items include *cuatros* (handmade guitars), bobbin lace (*mundillo*) and small wood carvings of religious figures called *santos*. Other local crafts include straw work, ceramics, hammocks and carnival masks. The Institute of Puerto Rican Culture operates the Popular Arts and Crafts Center, located at the bottom of Cristo Street near the

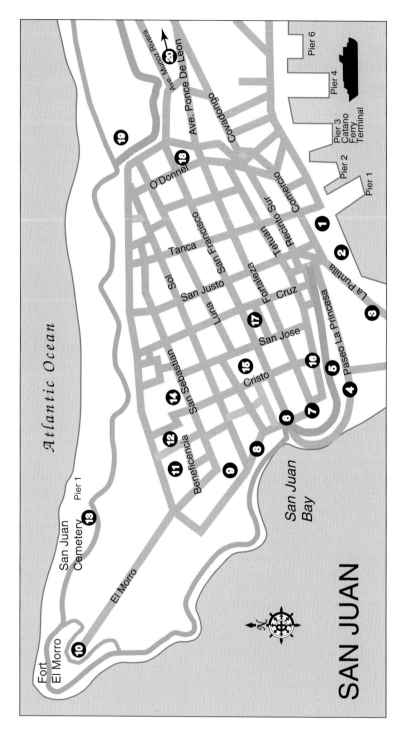

SAN JUAN

Capilla de Cristo, where a variety of island crafts are displayed and offered for sale Monday through Saturday. On weekends, local crafts can be purchased at an outdoor market beside La Casita information center near the cruise piers and along La Princesa promenade. This market is also a popular venue for local musicians.

Rum is another Puerto Rican specialty, with free tours and samples provided at the Bacardi Rum Factory – reached by harbor ferry from the cruise ship pier. Gourmet coffee drinkers may want to purchase a pound or two of flavorful Puerto Rican coffee. If you're looking for fine cigars, there's a boutique catering to connoisseurs at El San Juan Hotel on Isla Verde. Shoppers looking for interesting books and souvenirs should check out the museum gift shops, such as the one at El Morro, where visitors can purchase replica gold and silver coins of the 16th century.

BEACHES: Good beaches in the metropolitan area include El Escambron Beach (near the Condado hotel strip) and Isla Verde Beach, both of which are *balnearios* (government-run beaches with facilities, lifeguards and security personnel). About 20 miles east of San Juan is highly popular and beautiful **Luquillo Beach** – rated one of the world's top ten by National Geographic. A favorite with children is Seven Seas in **Fajardo** at the northeast end of the island. More beautiful beaches lie west of San Juan at **Dorado** where a public beach is located near the hotel and golf resorts.

GOLF: Puerto Rico boasts a dozen public golf courses, including four at the Hyatt Resorts west of San Juan. These courses were designed by Robert Trent Jones Sr. and the par-72 East course at Dorado Beach contains a par-5 thirteenth hole, rated by Jack Nicklaus as one of the top ten in the world. Other courses include Palmas de Mar in Humacao on the island's southeast coast, and three courses at Rio Grande, 16 miles east of San Juan.

Local Attractions:

The cruise ships dock right at the doorstep of Old San Juan, a seven-block area packed with historical and cultural sights which include Gothic churches, restored colonial buildings, townhouses with inner courtyards and wrought-iron balconies, museums, art galleries, boutiques, plazas, fountains and gardens. An information center is conveniently located beside Pier 1 inside **(1) La Casita** (the little house) and is an ideal starting point for a self-guided walking tour of these historic streets and fortifications.

Refreshments can be enjoyed along the way at various restaurants and sidewalk cafes, or from street vendors who sell bottled water and soft drinks. *Piraguas* (fruit-flavored snow cones) and *helados* (coconut and pineapple ices) are popular with the locals.

During colonial times, the heavy wooden doors of San Juan Gate were bolted shut at sundown to secure the fortified city from enemy attack.

(2) **Aduana**, the beautiful pink building overlooking the harbor, is a U.S. Customs House. Nearby (3) **El Arsenal** was built in 1800 as a base for patrol boats and it currently houses Divisions of the Institute of Puerto Rican Culture. Three art galleries are located within the grounds.

An elegant promenade, (4) **Paseo La Princesa**, runs parallel with the city wall and is where Spanish gentry of the 19th century once strolled. Restored for the Columbus Quincentennial, the esplanade is lined with palms and ornate street lamps, and features a large bronze fountain titled *Raices* (Roots), its human figures representing Puerto Rico's Indian, African and Spanish founders.

Paseo La Princesa leads past (5) **La Princesa**, a former jail, which has also been restored to its former colonial grandeur and is now the headquarters for the Puerto Rico Tourism Company, the island's official tourism body.

The promenade curves along the waterfront at the base of the city wall, called *La Muralla*, and leads to (6) **La Puerta de San Juan** (San Juan Gate). This is one of six heavy wooden doors once positioned along the wall and which, for centuries, were bolted shut at sundown to secure the fortified city from enemy attack.

Pass through this gate and make an immediate right on Recinto Oeste Street for a look at (7) **La Fortaleza** (The Fortress) which overlooks San Juan Bay. Built as a fort in 1540, its location proved poor for military defence and its role reverted to that of governor's mansion – the oldest one in use in the Western Hemisphere. The grounds are open weekdays to organized tours that start every hour in a small plaza beside the building.

A turn to the left upon passing through the San Juan Gate will take you to the top of a hill where **(8) Plazuela de la Rogativa** (Small Plaza of the Religious Procession) is a popular gathering place for local residents and the staging of children's puppet shows. A bronze sculpture here depicts an event of 1797 when Old San Juan was under attack by British ships. In desperation, the residents of San Juan, led by their bishop, marched through the streets one night carrying lit torches and praying for their safety. The British apparently mistook this parade of lights for Spanish reinforcements and retreated from the harbor. Opposite the Plazuela de la Rogativa is the **Museo Felisa Rincon de Gautier** (the former home of a popular mayor) and behind it the **Museo del Nino** (Children's Museum).

North of Plazuela de la Rogativa you will come to a fork in the road. On the left is **Casa Rosada** (Pink House) which was built in 1812 for the Spanish army. To the right an upper road leads past a plant-decked wall to a doorway from which steps lead into the lovely gardens of **(9) Casa Blanca** (White House). Built in 1521 as the city's original fortress, this is the oldest Spanish colonial building in Old San Juan and has been modified over the years. It was a gift from Spain's monarch to

Ponce de Leon never lived in the home built for him by the King of Spain, but it remained the family's residence for two and a half centuries.

Ponce de Leon for his settling of Puerto Rico. However, Ponce de Leon died the year the original wooden house was built, but his family resided there until 1779, when it was sold to the Spanish government. Following the Spanish-American war in 1898, the Commander of the U.S. Army lived at Casa Blanca until 1967. It was declared a National Historic Monument in 1968. Recently restored and furnished with authentic 16th- and 17th-century pieces, the mansion now contains two museums – the **Juan Ponce de Leon Museum** and the **Taino Indian Ethno-Historic Museum**. They are open Tuesday through Sunday, 9:00 a.m. to noon and 1:00 p.m. to 4:30 p.m.

Between Casa Blanca and the grounds of El Morro stand two impressive colonial buildings. **Asilo de Beneficenica**, its facade consisting of wrought-iron fencing and green shutters, contains the headquarters of the Institute of Puerto Rican Culture and several galleries which are open Wednesday through Sunday. The red-domed building beside it was built in the 1800s and now houses a school of fine arts.

El Morro

One of the most popular attractions in Old San Juan is the dramatic fort of **El Morro (10)**, part of the San Juan National Historic Site which encompasses the city walls and its massive forts. El Morro and San Cristobal, are both open daily from 9:00 a.m. to 5:00 p.m. Admission is free and a brochure map is available at the entrance.

Administered by the National Park Service, El Morro's full name is *Castillo de San Felipe del Morro* or 'Castle St. Philip of the Headland'. The fort is reached by a long, straight path which leads across a broad grassy area called a *glacis*. This cleared land was smoothed and sloped by the Spanish so that attacking troops had no shelter from the fort's cannon fire. Beneath the ground are tunnels in which kegs of gunpowder were planted should enemy troops try to lay siege to the fort.

From this landward approach, the fort strikes a surprisingly low profile, so engineered to make it a small target for enemy troops approaching by land. This was achieved by a dry moat which was dug along its length so the main wall could be sunk into the ground, yet still present a formidable height for scaling.

The ocean side of the fort, in contrast to the landward side, consists of six tiers of batteries that loom above the water and which protected the fort from sea attacks. Located at the corners of bastions and along the city walls are *garitas* (sentry boxes) from which the posted sentry could watch both sea and land approaches to the fort. The lowest gun platform, the Water Battery, is washed by ocean swells while the uppermost ramparts – the Ochoa and Austria Bastions – stand 145 feet high.

Inside the fort, its entrance guarded by a drawbridge, are storerooms, gun rooms, troop quarters, a chapel and prison. These all open onto a central courtyard beneath which are cisterns. Tunnels and stairways connect different parts of the fort, and a museum is located in one of the bombproof vaults.

The El Morro lighthouse, which took a direct hit during the Spanish-American War, stands on the fort's fifth level. First constructed in 1846, it has been replaced three times since then. A working lighthouse, it helps guide ships entering one of the Caribbean's busiest ports.

Returning to the city streets, the next historic site is **Ballaja Barracks (11)** where Spanish troops and their families once lived. The Museum of the Americas is on its second floor. On the eastern side of the barracks is **(12) Plaza del Quinto Centenario** (Quincentennial Square), constructed for the 1992-93 celebration of the 500th Anniversary of the discovery of the New World. This multi-level square affords a sweeping vista of El Morro and, from its upper western level, a view of the **San Juan Cemetery (13)**.

The steps of the square lead to **Plaza de San Jose (14)** where a statue of Ponce de Leon stands outside **San Jose Church** – the second oldest church in the Western Hemisphere, built in 1532, and the family church of Ponce de Leon's descendants. A beautiful example of Gothic architecture, the church was originally built as a chapel. Next to the church is the **Convento de los Dominicos**, containing the Institute of Puerto Rican Culture book and music store. Tucked in a corner townhouse of the plaza is the **Museo de Pablo Casals**, a small museum containing memorabilia of the famous cellist who spent his final years in

Expansive views can be enjoyed from the upper levels of Quincentennial Square.

Diners enjoy an outdoor cafe near the foot of Cristo Street where Christ Chapel marks the spot at which a horse and rider were miraculously saved, according to an 18th-century legend.

San Juan. On the plaza's eastern side is **Casa de las Contrafuertes** (House of Buttresses), which contains the Museum of Latin American Prints and a Pharmacy Museum.

Cristo Street leads from Plaza de San Jose down the hill to **San Juan Cathedral (15)**. Built in 1540 with early 19th-century modifications, the cathedral contains the marble tomb of Juan Ponce de Leon.

Two blocks south of the Cathedral, at the foot of Cristo Street, you will see **(16) Capilla de Cristo** (Christ Chapel) dedicated to the Christ of Miracles. It was built following a 1753 incident in which a youth was racing his horse down the hill at such a speed that rider and horse could not possibly stop before hurtling over the city wall. One legend is that both miraculously came to a halt just in time, another says the horse stopped but the boy flew over the wall, and a third version claims they both met their maker at this spot. Beside Capilla de Cristo is the small **Parque de las Palomas** (Pigeon Park) with a fine view of the harbor. Lying opposite is **Casa del Libro** (House of Books), a small museum and library with a collection of rare, pre-16th century books.

(17) Plaza de Armas (Army Plaza) lies a block east of Cristo Street on San Francisco. Several government buildings surround the square, which was originally used for military drills, when built in the 16th century, and is now a social gathering place. **City Hall**, completed in 1789, stands on the plaza's north side and was designed to resemble its counterpart in Madrid; it contains a visitor information center. An administration building, at the west end of the plaza, and the provincial delegation building at its northwest corner, are fine examples of 19th-century neoclassical architecture. The century-old statues gracing the plaza represent the four seasons.

At the eastern end of Fortaleza Street, where it intersects with O'Donnel, you'll find **(18) Plaza de Colon** (Columbus Plaza) and Teatro Tapia, a 19th-century theatre. A few blocks north is the entrance to **(19) San Cristobal Fort**. East of the historic quarter is the dome-roofed **(20) Capitol Building**.

Area Highlights

El Yunque National Forest: A 45-minute drive from San Juan, this 28,000-acre tropical forest is one of Puerto Rico's natural wonders. Set in the Luquillo Mountains and named for anvil-shaped El Yunque peak, the park contains 240 species of tropical trees, flowers and wildlife, including ferns, orchids, parrots and tiny tree frogs called *coqui*. Cool and often rainy, the park's verdant forest contains a dozen hiking trails and a lookout tower. Its highest peak is 3,532-foot-high El Toro. A popular restaurant at the entrance to the park is Las Vegas where both Puerto Rican and American cuisine is served.

Las Cabezas de San Juan Nature Reserve: This peninsula at the northeastern tip of the island is often referred to as El Faro, which is the name of the 1882 lighthouse located here. Beautifully restored, El Faro now houses a scientific research center with an observation deck added to the building's exterior. The reserve, situated on land acquired by the island's Conservation Trust, encompasses a dry forest, mangroves, lagoons, beaches, reefs and offshore cays. Guided tours, by reservation only, are conducted in safari buses and include informative walks along trails and boardwalks to observe the various species supported by this diverse habitat.

El Faro Lighthouse

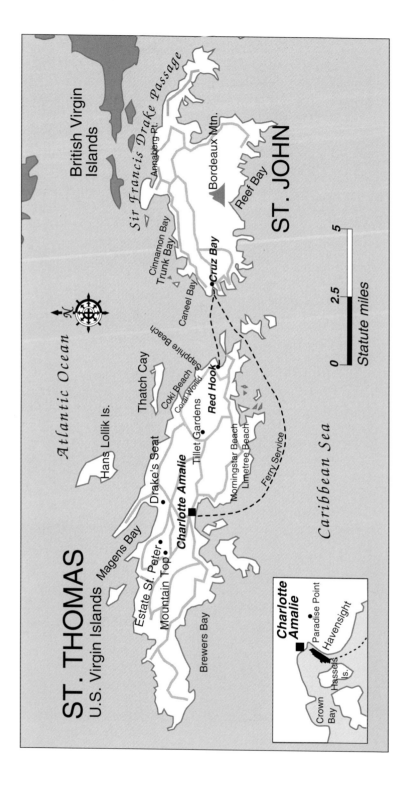

CHAPTER EIGHT

U.S. VIRGIN ISLANDS

The natural allure of the Virgin Islands prompted Christopher Columbus to name them, in 1493, for the legend of Saint Ursula and her 11,000 virgin martyrs. But not even Columbus could have predicted their potential as a tourist mecca. As recently as 1917, when the United States bought these tropical treasures from Denmark for $25 million, it was not for possession of their beautiful beaches and fragrant flowers but to protect America's shipping interests. At the time, after decades of economic decline, the Danish West Indies were valued mainly for their strategic proximity to the recently opened Panama Canal.

A 100-island chain, the Virgin Islands are divided into the U.S. Virgin Islands and the British Virgin Islands. The U.S. Virgin Islands consist of three principal islands – St. Thomas, St. John and St. Croix – and dozens of smaller islands. They contain many sheltered harbors and lie directly in the path of easterly trade winds, which made them an ideal stop-over point for trading vessels in the days of sail.

The capital of the U.S. Virgin Islands, Charlotte Amalie (pronounced Ah-*mahl*-ya), is located on the south coast of St. Thomas and overlooks one of the finest harbors in the Caribbean. The downtown's narrow streets and colonial buildings look much as they did in the mid-1800s when Charlotte Amalie was one of the most important trading centers of the West Indies, bustling with the comings and goings of naval ships, whalers, merchant traders and fishing boats. Import firms

The Danes built steps into the steep hillsides of Charlotte Amalie. This one, beside Government House, leads up Government Hill.

flourished here, their warehouses lining the waterfront, and wealthy merchants lived on the surrounding hillsides where they enjoyed the sea breezes and magnificent harbor views.

Their gleaming white houses, set among terraced gardens and coconut palms, were rectangular in shape with hipped roofs designed to collect rainwater along the gutters. Inside these homes were polished mahogany floors and comfortable furnishings which included rocking chairs and a large sideboard for holding carafes of chilled drinks. Block ice was imported from Boston and stored in wooden ice houses, the spaces of their triple-layered walls filled with sawdust as insulation from the hot sun. The bedrooms contained huge four-poster beds from which hung mosquito netting. As a fire-safety precaution, the kitchen was contained in a separate building, as were the servants' quarters. Mode of travel around the island, up steep winding roads, was by horseback. Life on St. Thomas, however, centered around the town. As the 19th-century Danish naturalist A. S. Orsted wrote, "If you know the town, you know the whole island."

The town began in 1672 when the Danish West India Company established the first permanent settlement here. Fort Christian was completed by the Danes in 1680 and the port quickly became a leading slave-trading center of the West Indies. Denmark allowed the

Brandenburg American Company to operate here for a while and the town's four busy taverns soon earned it the name 'Tap Hus' (Beer Hall). In 1691 the settlement was officially declared a town and named Charlotte Amalie, in honor of the Danish Queen who was consort to King Christian V.

In 1717 the neighboring island of St. John was claimed by Denmark and a fort built at Coral Harbor. Neither St. Thomas nor St. John were ideally suited for agriculture, however, so in 1733 Denmark purchased St. Croix from France. That same year a slave rebellion took place on St. John and the rebels held the island for six months before French soldiers from Martinique helped the Danes recapture it. St. Thomas, meanwhile, was declared a free port and it became a thriving trade center and exporter of contraband trade from the strictly regulated Spanish colonies. It also became a refuge for pirates who sold their cargo here and often hid in the hills overlooking the harbor. The legendary Blackbeard is said to have holed up in a watch tower with a spyglass and supply of rum.

The islands became a Danish royal colony in 1754 and remained thus, apart from two British occupations – the first in 1801, when Denmark allied itself with Russia, and again from 1807 to 1815 when Denmark was allied with Napoleon. St. Croix was devoted to the cultivation and production of sugar, molasses and rum, its countryside covered with sugarcane fields and dotted with windmills. The island pros-

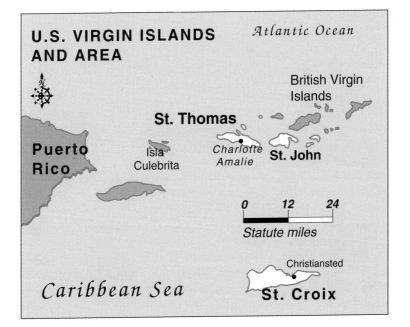

U.S. VIRGIN ISLANDS AND AREA

Atlantic Ocean

British Virgin Islands

St. Thomas

Charlotte Amalie **St. John**

Puerto Rico

Isla Culebrita

0   12   24

Statute miles

Christiansted

Caribbean Sea   **St. Croix**

The Danish fort that once protected Christiansted on St. Croix is now part of a National Historic Site, administered by the U.S. National Park Service.

pered as a producer of sugar cane and the port of Christiansted became Denmark's colonial capital. A town of well-planned streets and handsome buildings, it was protected by Fort Christiansvaern, built of yellow brick and dominating the harbor entrance. A distinct class of Free Blacks, who bought their freedom or earned it through faithful service, emerged on St. Croix and they became local merchants and tradesmen.

In contrast to the orderly development of Christiansted was the haphazard growth of Charlotte Amalie. Between 1804 and 1832, six fires swept through the town's narrow streets. Building codes were eventually enforced that banned frame construction in the commercial area along the waterfront. These masonry warehouses were all fitted with fire-proof roofs of tile or brick which were eventually replaced with corrugated metal due to hurricanes. Following emancipation in 1848, many of the freed slaves moved into town where existing residential lots were re-subdivided into smaller ones.

By the mid-1800s, the Danish West Indies had reached their zenith as colonial holdings. The price of sugar cane had dropped and, with steamships replacing sailing ships, St. Thomas was losing its importance as a stop-over point. Then a labor insurrection on St. Croix in 1878 prompted the remaining shipping companies in Charlotte Amalie to shut down. However, the protected harbors of St. Thomas and St.

John were still of military value and they prompted the purchase of the Danish West Indies by the United States in 1917 to prevent their being used as a German submarine base. The U.S. Navy handled initial administration of the islands and residents were granted U.S. citizenship in 1927. Local government was established in 1954, with a governor and senate locally elected.

During World War II, the military constructed a submarine base, airfield, roads and housing on St. Thomas. Tourism began to flourish following the war, especially after the closing of Cuba to American tourists. A total of 26,650 visitors arrived at St. Thomas by ship or by airplane in 1950. Today that annual number is approaching two million. The U.S. Virgin Islands, despite being hard hit by Hurricane Hugo in 1989 and Marilyn in 1995, have established themselves as America's vacation paradise and Charlotte Amalie is once again the busiest free port in the Caribbean.

ST. THOMAS

Charlotte Amalie is serviced by two cruise ship terminals, the main one being the West Indian Company Dock which is located on the east side of the harbor, about a mile and a half by road from downtown. The other cruise terminal at Crown Bay is about two miles west of downtown. When ships anchor in the harbor, their passengers are tendered ashore to Kings Wharf on the downtown waterfront. The passenger ferry dock, with regular departures to St. John, is at the west end of the harbor, across from Hassel Island which is a national park. St. Thomas is fully geared for visitors with many of the island's 50,000 residents employed in tourism-related industries. English is the official language and the U.S. dollar is the legal tender. Long-distance calls can be direct dialed to the U.S. mainland, and overseas service to Europe is excellent. A U.S. post office is located on Main Street, west of the Grand Hotel.

Getting Around

St. Thomas is only 13 miles long and four miles wide, so the island's beautiful beaches are easily reached by taxi. A number of car rental firms operate on the island. Keep in mind that the roads are narrow and winding, and traffic keeps to the left. The port itself is usually busy with car traffic, and is best explored on foot.

Officially licensed taxis carry a dome light and the letters TP on their license plates. Their rates have been set by the Taxi Commission and approved by the Virgin Islands' Legislature. In the sample fares listed, the one-passenger fare is quoted first followed by the rate paid per passenger if more than one is travelling to the same destination:

West Indian Company Dock to downtown – $2.50 ($2.50)
Crown Bay Dock to downtown – $3.00 ($2.50)
Charlotte Amalie to:
Magens Bay – $6.50 ($4.00)
Morningstar Beach – $6.00 ($4.00)
Sapphire Beach – $8.50 ($5.50)
Coki Beach – $7.50 ($5.00)
Red Hook ferry terminal – $9.00 ($5.00)
Mahogany Run Golf Course – $7.00 ($4.50)

SHOPPING: The Caribbean is famous for its duty-free shopping, and most famous of all is St. Thomas where American visitors to the U.S. Virgin Islands can take advantage of a $1,200-per-person duty-free allowance. The prices in St. Thomas are generally 20% to 50% less than stateside and there's no sales tax. Imported liquor, jewelry, china, crystal, designer leather goods, watches and other items are all offered at substantial savings.

Open-air shuttle buses run regularly between the West Indian Company Dock and downtown Charlotte Amalie, where dozens of duty-free stores are housed in restored warehouses of the town's historic section. The shopping area is concentrated along Main Street, the waterfront and the narrow, palm-shaded alleyways and pedestrian malls that connect these two busy streets. Additional duty-free shops, including branches of downtown retailers, are located at Havensight Mall. The gift shop at Fort Christian sells locally made crafts including hand-carved mahogany rocking chairs, made to order.

DINING: Many fine restaurants are located on St. Thomas. For a taste of authentic Caribbean fare in a casual setting, try **The Jamaican Ackee Tree & Bar**, popular with local business people at lunch time and conveniently located across the street from Havensight Mall. In the downtown shopping core, the Back Street (one block up from Main Street) is a good place to momentarily escape the crowds with a lunch stop at a number of good restaurants, including **Cuzzin's** at the corner of Back Street and Raadets Gade. For fine cuisine, the **Hotel 1829** on Kongens Gade is highly touted.

BEACHES: **Magens Bay**, on the north coast, has been rated by National Geographic as one of the ten most beautiful beaches in the world. The admission charge is $1.00 for adults and 25¢ for children, and changing facilities are available.

Other recommended beaches include **Morningstar Beach** and **Limetree Beach** southeast of Charlotte Amalie. On the northeast side of the island are **Sapphire Beach** and **Coki Beach** – good for snorkeling and adjacent to Coral World where change facilities are available.

SNORKELING & DIVING: Off the island's south coast lie Cow and Calf Rocks, named for two humpback whales once seen at this dive site, which contains dramatic caves, archways and cliff overhangs from 25 feet. The Pinnacle (French Cap), about a mile offshore, consists of two stone pillars atop a seamount at 45 feet. Two miles out, at Buck Island, a World War I freighter is resting in 40 feet.

On the north coast, the calm waters off Coki Beach are excellent for snorkeling and beach dives, with a dive shop right on beach. Lying opposite is Thatch Cay, another popular diving area.

GOLF: Mahogany Run on the north coast is an 18-hole Fazio-designed championship course. Its famous 'Devil's Triangle' consists of three dramatic holes overlooking the Atlantic.

LOCAL SIGHTS: Atlantis Submarine: This two-hour tour departs Havensight Mall for a short boat ride to the dive site located at Buck Island. Here you board the submarine which submerges to depths of 90 feet, providing underwater views of the reef. Divers sometimes swim with the fish and an on-board guide identifies the marine life.

Paradise Point Gondola: Located across the street from Havensight Mall, this tram-way whisks visitors up the mountainside for a sweeping view of the harbor. The complex contains a spacious sun deck, a restaurant/bar with umbrella tables, and a handful of gift shops.

Bluebeard's Tower: Perched on a hill at the east end of town and now part of Bluebeard's Castle Hotel, this stone watch tower is said to have been used by pirates.

Hibiscus Alley is one of many shop-lined pedestrian malls waiting to be explored in downtown Charlotte Amalie.

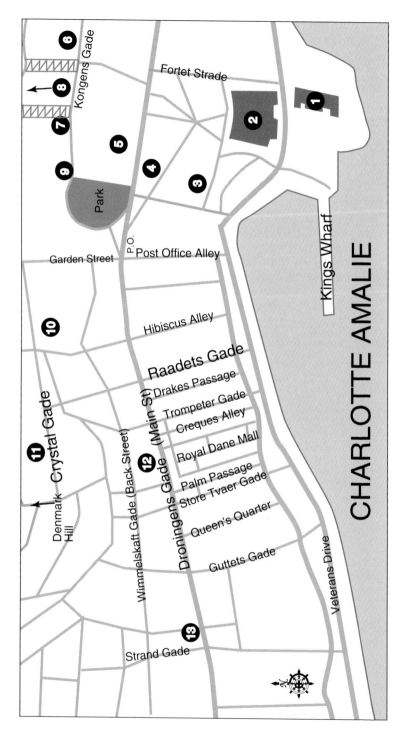

Downtown Charlotte Amalie

The **(1) Legislative Building**, a two-storey green building of Italian Renaissance design, is the seat of the U.S. Virgin Islands Senate. Built in 1874 as barracks for the Danish police, it was later used as housing for U.S. Marines Corps. It's open to visitors Monday through Friday.

Built of red brick and rubble, **(2) Fort Christian** is the oldest standing structure on St. Thomas and a good starting point for a walking tour of Charlotte Amalie. It was begun about 1666, completed in 1680 and altered in 1874 when the watch tower was removed and its north facade, with a crenelated clock tower, was added. The fort was later used as a jail, and is now a museum and National Historic Landmark.

(3) Emancipation Garden, the site of many official ceremonies, commemorates the freeing of slaves in 1848 and contains a bust of Danish King Christian and a small replica Liberty Bell. A tourist information office is located nearby at the corner of Tolbod Gade and Veterans Drive, opposite which is the open-air Vendors Market.

The **(4) Grand Hotel**, originally called the Commercial Hotel & Coffee House, is a Greek Revival structure which occupied an entire block when built in 1840. Formerly three storeys tall, the top floor was presumably damaged by a hurricane sometime after 1896. The former hotel now houses a jewelry studio featuring designs by local artisans.

The official church of the Danish West Indies, the **(5) Frederick Lutheran Church** was established in 1666 with worship services held in the homes of planters and soldiers, and then at Christensfort. The present building was built in 1793, gutted by fire in 1826 and damaged by a hurricane in 1870, after which the tower was added. Completed in 1865, **(6) Government House** is a three-storey masonry building built in the neo-classical design. Its brick walls are painted white, as are the cast-iron verandahs that run the length of the first two storeys. Government offices are located here, including the Governor's Executive Offices. The Governor's official residence is the former Danish Consulate, an imposing two-storey mansion atop Denmark Hill.

Two sets of stairs, the westerly one called **(7) The 99 Steps**, lead up the hillside behind Government House. Standing atop Government Hill is **(8) Skytsborg (Blackbeard's Castle)**, a five-storey conical tower constructed of rubble masonry by the Danish in 1678, with later changes. Now part of a hotel, the stone watch tower is said to have been used by the infamous pirate Blackbeard.

(9) Hotel 1829 (formerly Lavalette House) was built as a residence for a French sea captain and now houses one of Charlotte Amalie's best-known restaurants.

(10) St. Thomas Reformed Church, constructed in 1846, is a good example of Greek Revival building. **(11) Beracha Veshalom U'gemi-

Government House, on Kongens Gade, overlooks the bustling streets and busy harbor of Charlotte Amalie.

lut Hasidim, built of cut stone and brick in 1833, is the second-oldest synagogue in the Western Hemisphere.

The **(12) Camille Pissaro Building** is where the famous impressionist painter lived above the family store in the 1840s. Born in a small Jewish community of Charlotte Amalie in 1830, Pissaro left St. Thomas in 1855 to study art in Paris. He later became a teacher and friend of Gauguin and Cezanne, and died near Paris at the age of 73. The Pissaro building now houses the Tropicana Perfume shop and upstairs, above an inner courtyard entered off Main Street, is an art gallery.

(13) Market Square was, in 1946, officially named Rothschild Francis Square to honor the public service of this champion of civil rights and liberties. The square has long been a central meeting place where fresh produce, fish and spices are sold, with French farmers from the north side of the island bringing their fruits and vegetables to town by donkey. In the early 1900s, an open-air iron shed called the Bungalow was erected and the regular female vendors, called 'Market Women', each had their own spot under the shade of the bungalow – to the exclusion of any male vendors. The annual Carnival Food Fair is held here each April.

Area Attractions:

West of Downtown: **Frenchtown**, founded as a fishing village by French Huguenots from St. Barts, lies west of Charlotte Amalie on the way to the Crown Bay cruise pier. Its restaurants and bars now create a lively night scene. The **University of the Virgin Islands** was founded in 1963 and the campus contains the Reichhold Center for the Arts where concerts and other events are held in its open-air amphitheatre.

East End: **Coral World** at Coki Point is a popular attraction with its underwater observatory, natural reef exhibit, aquarium and semi-submarine rides along a coral reef. Sharks, moray eels, stingrays and pink flamingos are some of the exotic creatures that can be seen here. **Tillet Gardens,** on the way to Coral World, is the site of an historic Danish cattle farm and a gallery featuring local arts and crafts.

North of Town: **Drake's Seat**, said to be used by Francis Drake as a lookout for Spanish ships while his fleet lay concealed in Magens Bay, offers breathtaking views of Magens Bay and the British Virgin Islands.

Estate St. Peter Great House & Botanical Gardens, a former plantation estate, has been developed into a beautiful botanical garden with breathtaking ocean views from its mountainside location. The elegant, open-plan house is wrapped with white latticework and broad decks from which visitors can gaze at more than twenty offshore islands. Local art is displayed in some of the rooms and outside, on the lushly landscaped grounds, are more than 500 varieties of plants and trees.

A drive to **Mountain Top**, highest viewing point on the island, provides stunning vistas of St. John, the British Virgin Islands and Charlotte Amalie Harbor. Refreshments served here include the original banana daiquiri. The attractive complex includes Caribbean shops, an aviary and aquarium.

ST. JOHN

In contrast to bustling Charlotte Amalie, a shopper's paradise, is the peaceful island of St. John, a nature lover's paradise. Lush and mountainous, St. John is indented by numerous bays at the head of which lie some of the world's most beautiful beaches. The island is also a botanist's delight with its proliferation of tropical plants and flowers.

When A. S. Orsted, discoverer of plankton, travelled by barkentine to the Danish West Indies in 1845, he was so captivated by the plant life he found that he changed his field of study from zoology to botany. Born of an illustrious Danish family, Orsted was especially besotted with St. John where uncultivated slopes presented him with an array of indigenous plant species, including bamboo, guava trees, wild pineapple, dodder vines, guava berry, century plant, coconut palms, soursop and tamarind. A century later, in the early '50s, Laurance Rockefeller paid St. John a visit. A member of the wealthy American family famous

The resort at Caneel Bay, located on the west side of St. John, is owned by Laurance Rockefeller.

for its philanthropy, he too arrived by sailboat and he too was so impressed with the serene and natural beauty of the island that he purchased about two thirds of it, which he donated to the United States federal government for the establishment of the Virgin Islands National Park in 1956. The park has expanded since its inception and now covers about three-quarters of the island.

Residents of St. John, who number about 3,000, call their island 'Love City' and most visitors do fall in love with this protected paradise. Its highest point is Bordeaux Mountain at 1,277 feet, and the island's steep slopes provide dramatic vistas of distant islands and nearby cays where a deep blue sea fades to pale aquamarine at the head of beach-lined bays.

Getting Around

Cruise ships stopping at St. Thomas usually offer shore excursions to nearby St. John. Independent travellers can take one of the passenger ferries that connect St. John with St. Thomas, and these depart regularly from both Charlotte Amalie and Red Hook on St. Thomas for Cruz Bay on St. John. The Red Hook/Cruz Bay ferry leaves every hour on the hour both ways, is a 20-minute ride and costs $3.00 one way. The Charlotte Amalie/Cruz Bay ferry ride takes 45 minutes, costs $7.00 one way, and leaves Charlotte Amalie at one- to two-hour intervals throughout the day.

Cruz Bay is the main town on the island and open-air safari buses await here to transport visitors around the island. A Visitors Center at Cruz Bay provides information on the Park – its beaches, trails and activities including organized hikes and historic bus tours.

BEACHES: Inviting beaches line St. John's bay-indented north coast, including the sugary white sands and clear turquoise waters of **Trunk Bay** – considered one the most beautiful beaches in the world. Excellent for swimming, Trunk Bay also has an underwater snorkel trail. On shore are shaded picnic areas and a snack bar.

Cinnamon Bay has open-air dining and a watersports center that rents snorkel gear and beach chairs. Sailing and windsurfing can also be enjoyed here, as well as National Park interpretive programs.

Other lovely beaches include those at Mayo Bay, Hawksnest Bay and Caneel Bay, where a resort owned by Laurance Rockefeller is located.

DIVE & SNORKEL SITES: Cinnamon Bay has good snorkeling and a watersports center that rents snorkel gear. Trunk Bay has an underwater snorkeling trail with red, white and blue markers to guide snorkelers and identify the coral and marine life. Popular dive sites include Steven's Cay, Carval Rock and Congo Cay.

ISLAND ATTRACTIONS: Points of interest on the island include the **Annaberg Sugar Mill** ruins, beautifully situated on the north side of the island overlooking Sir Francis Drake Passage. Also of note are the prehistoric petroglyphs at Reef Bay.

SHOPPING: Cruz Bay is where most of the island shops are located, offering both duty-free goods and local arts and crafts. Mongoose Junction, across from the National Park Dock, is a pleasant shopping complex built of Caribbean stone. Its multi-level design of shaded terraces and tropical foliage contains fine shops, galleries and open-air restaurants.

ST. CROIX

St. Croix (pronounced Croy) was first settled by people who had migrated along the Lesser Antilles from South America. By the 4th century A.D. they had established a village at Salt River Bay on the island's north coast and eventually constructed the only ceremonial plaza/ball court discovered to date in the Lesser Antilles. When Columbus arrived at Salt River Bay in 1493, on his second voyage to the Caribbean, the boat party he sent ashore was met by a canoe filled with Carib warriors. A skirmish took place that resulted in the death of two Caribs and one Spaniard – the first fatal confrontation between Europeans and New World natives. Columbus called the island Santa Cruz (Holy Cross) but it was the English and Dutch who first colonized

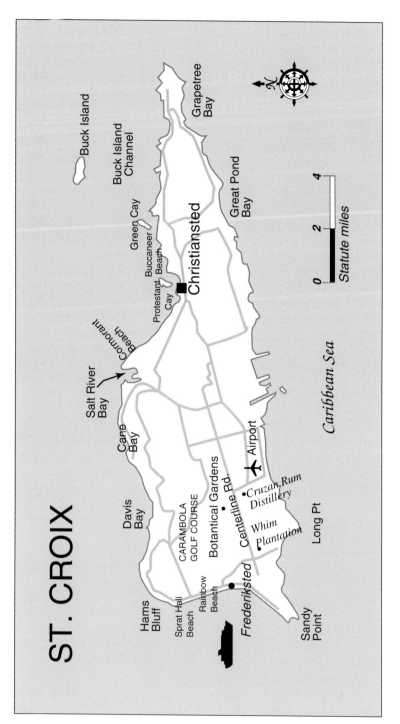

ST. CROIX

Buck Island

Buck Island Channel

Green Cay

Buccaneer Beach

Protestant Cay

Christiansted

Cormorant Beach

Salt River Bay

Cane Bay

Davis Bay

Hams Bluff

Sprat Hall Beach

Rainbow Beach

Frederiksted

CARAMBOLA GOLF COURSE

Botantical Gardens

Centerline Rd.

Airport

Cruzan Rum Distillery

Whim Plantation

Sandy Point

Long Pt

Great Pond Bay

Grapetree Bay

Caribbean Sea

N

0   2   4
Statute miles

the island, followed by the French who sold it to Denmark in 1733. In the late 1700s and early 1800s, St. Croix was one of the wealthiest sugar islands in the West Indies and Christiansted's waterfront was busy with ox-drawn carts driven by slaves and laden with barrels of sugar and molasses to be loaded onto waiting ships.

In 1803, Peter von Scholten arrived as a young officer and rose through the ranks to become Governor-General of the Danish West Indies in 1827. Born of an aristocratic family (his father served as Commandant of St. Thomas in the early 1800s), von Scholten issued a decree in 1848 abolishing slavery. His companion Anna Heegaard, a woman of color, no doubt influenced his views on slavery. Denmark's king confirmed von Scholten's emancipation decree but von Scholten paid dearly for his benevolence, for he was dismissed from office and stripped of his pension. The man who had governed his country's Caribbean colony with military efficiency, graciousness and compassion, was crushed. Returning to Denmark, he died a few years later.

Before Peter von Scholten's arrival in the West Indies, a distinct class of Free Blacks had already begun to escape slavery on St. Croix. With money saved selling produce at the local market, they would buy their freedom; others earned it with faithful service. In a designated section of town, established in 1747 and called Neger Gotted (Free Gut), they built their own houses and worked as merchants, tradesmen and fishermen. In 1834 the Free Blacks gained full equality. As for Peter von Scholten, he is today honored throughout the U.S. Virgin Islands.

Getting Around

St. Croix, about 20 miles long and up to seven miles wide, is the largest of the U.S. Virgin Islands and its topography is fairly flat. Most ships dock at Frederiksted at the west end of the island. A small cruise ship dock is located at Chistiansted for shallow draft vessels. Centerline Road, a four-lane highway that runs the length of the island, connects the two ports with taxi vans running regular shuttles ($5 each way). Per-person fares to various destinations are set by law and posted in each taxi. A three-hour island tour by taxi costs $20 per person.

BEACHES: Lovely beaches abound on St. Croix and those closest to Frederiksted are **Rainbow Beach** ($5 round trip taxi fare from Frederiksted), **Sprat Hall Beach** ($6 round trip) and Sandy Point where the beach closes each spring when sea turtles come ashore to lay their eggs. Popular beaches near Christiansted include Buccaneer, Cormorant Beach, and Protestant Cay which is a $3 ferry ride from the Christiansted waterfront.

SNORKEL & DIVE SITES: St. Croix is a superb snorkel and dive destination, with its clear waters and extensive coral gardens. **Buck Island Reef National Monument**, two miles off St. Croix's north

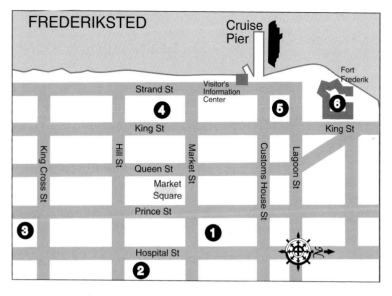

coast, is one of the most popular underwater sites in the Virgin Islands. First protected in 1948 and proclaimed a national monument in 1961, it encompasses 176 acres of land, 704 acres of water and a magnificent coral reef system. Numerous endangered species nest at Buck Island, including the brown pelican and the hawksbill, leatherback and green sea turtles. Much of this dry-forest island is surrounded by an elkhorn coral barrier reef that reaches 30 feet in height. The lagoon, formed by the barrier reef, contains clear calm water and large brain corals that nearly reach the surface. A snorkel trail with underwater interpretive signs lies off the east end of island.

Good snorkeling can also be found at Cane Bay and Green Cay. One of the island's most beautiful dive sites is the Old Frederiksted Pier where the marine life includes orange sea horses.

GOLF: There are three golf courses on St. Croix. Closest to Frederiksted is the 18-hole course at Carambola Golf Club, designed by Robert Trent Jones. At the eastern end of the island is The Buccaneer Hotel's 18-hole course and a 9-hole course called The Reef.

SHOPPING: The stores on St. Croix offer both duty-free goods and local crafts, but on a much smaller scale than St. Thomas. The largest selection of stores (and restaurants) is at Christiansted, where Queen Cross and Strand are the main shopping streets. In Frederiksted, most of the shops are located on Strand Street facing the harbor.

FREDERIKSTED HIGHLIGHTS: Frederiksted's shady streets and arcaded sidewalks contain a number of historic buildings, many of them rebuilt in the Victorian ginger-bread style following the 1878 labor riots during which much of the town was burned.

(1) **St. Patrick's Catholic Church**, (2) **Holy Trinity Lutheran Church** and (3) **St. Paul's Anglican Church** were all begun in the 1840s. (4) **Victoria House** and the (5) **Customs House** were built in 1803. (6) **Fort Frederick**, overlooking the local beach, was begun in 1752. Now a museum, it has been restored to its 1820s appearance.

CHRISTIANSTED HIGHLIGHTS: Christiansted is one of the Caribbean's best-preserved colonial ports and is ideally suited to a self-guided walking tour. The town's historic buildings are located on or near the waterfront and are administered by the National Park Service. Their architectural designs reflect the West Indian neo-classical style that dominated the Danish islands during their golden age of colonial wealth. Features include rows of arches that run the length of arcaded sidewalks and upper-floor galleries designed to catch the breezes and provide shade from the tropical sun.

The gift shop at the entrance to (1) **Fort Christiansvaern** contains an official map and guide to the historic area. There is a small admission fee to enter the fort, which was completed in 1749, with later additions in 1835-41. Built of yellow brick brought to the island as ship's ballast, this carefully preserved fort once protected the town from pirates and slave uprisings. Under the governorship of Peter von Scholten from 1827 to 1848, Christiansvaern was well manned with a garrison of 215 officers and men, with Free Blacks serving in the fire corps.

The (2) **Steeple Building**, built from 1753 to 1796, was St. Croix's first Lutheran Church. After 1831, when the congregation moved to the Lutheran Church on King Street, the Steeple Building was used for various functions, including that of bakery, hospital and school.

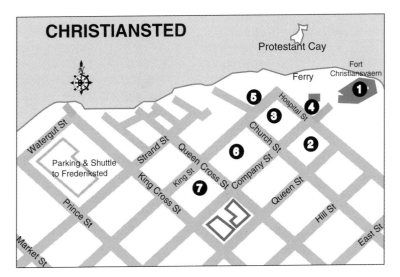

The Visitors Bureau in Christiansted is housed in the town's former Scale House.

The **(3) Danish West India & Guinea Company Warehouse** was built in 1749 to house offices and storerooms. The courtyard was used for auctioning slaves.

In 1840 the **(4) Customs House** was constructed and the town's post office was located upstairs.

Imports were inspected and sugar was weighed prior to export at the **(5) Scale House**, built in 1856 to replace a wooden structure. It is now the location of a **Visitors Bureau**.

Also in this area is the dock used by a passenger ferry that runs between Christiansted and **Protestant Cay**, the location of a hotel and beach. The small island was formerly a burial ground for Protestants barred from the Catholic cemetery. The ferry ride costs $3 for adults and $1 for children.

A short walk from the waterfront is **(6) Government House**, comprising two palatial townhouses that were built in the mid-1700s and connected in the 1830s. Usually open to the public, the second-floor reception hall has been restored to its 1840s appearance.

Built as the Dutch Reformed church in 1744, the **(7) Lutheran Church** was sold in 1831 to local Lutherans who vacated the Steeple Building, bringing its furnishings with them. The Church's steeple was added by the Lutherans.

Island Attractions

Whim Plantation Museum, featured in most island tours, is located two miles east of Frederiksted on Centerline Road. This sugar plantation estate consists of an elegant, 18th-century great house built of stone and elegantly furnished with colonial antiques. Other buildings on the grounds include a cookhouse, sugar mill and gift shop that sells West Indian crafts and prints. Tours run every half hour, Monday through Saturday.

Other island attractions include the **Cruzan Rum Distillery** with tours and a tasting bar; **St. George Botanical Gardens** with self-guided tours of this 17-acre park; and the restored ruins of **Estate Mount Washington Plantation**.

Oil refining has replaced sugar production on St. Croix, and just outside of Christiansted is the sprawling Hess Oil Refinery – one of the largest in the world.

St. Patrick's Catholic Church in Frederiksted was built with limestone blocks in the Gothic Revival style.

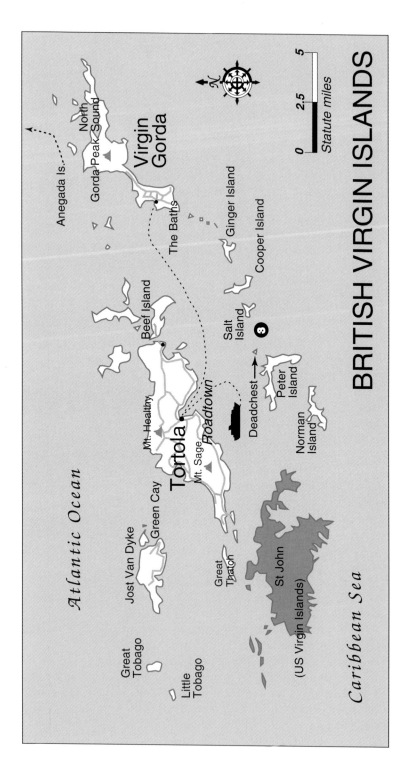

Atlantic Ocean

Great
Tobago

Little
Tobago

Jost Van Dyke

Green Cay

Great
Thatch

St John

(US Virgin Islands)

Caribbean Sea

Mt. Healthy

Mt. Sage

Tortola

Roadtown

Deadchest

Norman
Island

Peter
Island

Salt
Island

Beef Island

The Baths

Cooper Island

Ginger Island

Gorda Peak Sound

North

Virgin
Gorda

Anegada Is...

N

0   2.5   5

Statute miles

BRITISH VIRGIN ISLANDS

CHAPTER NINE

BRITISH VIRGIN ISLANDS

Pirates, Rum and Road Town

Christopher Columbus named the Virgin Islands in 1493, but Francis Drake set the tone a century later when he sailed along the channel now bearing his name. Sir Francis Drake Channel runs through the middle of the British Virgin Islands, commonly called the B.V.I., which are a labyrinth of islands and channels rich in pirate lore and legend. The island of **Jost Van Dyke**, popular with yachtsmen who frequent famous Foxy's Tamarind Bar, was named for a Dutch pirate. **Norman Island** was the inspired setting for Robert Louis Stevenson's *Treasure Island*, an adventure story published in 1883 about a search for Captain Kidd's buried treasure. And **Peter Island** is associated with the pirate Blackbeard who is said to have anchored in Deadman's Bay after a successful raid. While splitting the booty, an argument ensued and Blackbeard marooned 15 of his men on the nearby island of **Dead Chest** with a bottle of rum and their sea chests. The following lyric is attributed to this incident: *Fifteen men on dead men's chest, Yo ho ho and a bottle of rum!*

The B.V.I., with their steady breezes and pristine anchorages, have long been a mariner's mecca. They were ideal for buccaneers who hid in secluded coves when fleeing enemy ships, and today they attract island-hopping yachtsmen from around the world. Large charter fleets are moored at marinas on the main islands of **Tortola** and **Virgin Gorda**, and boat bunks account for nearly half the total tourist beds in the B.V.I. There are no high-rise hotels in this chain of 30-plus islands, just plenty of white beaches and blue bays dotted with sailboats.

The British Virgin Islands are renowned as a yachting destination, with numerous islands and protected bays. Sail boats lie at anchor in beautiful Cane Garden Bay on Tortola.

Inhabited by Taino Indians when discovered by Columbus, the B.V.I. were first settled by the Dutch in 1648, then annexed by Britain in 1672. Plantations were established during the 18th century's sugar boom and fortifications were erected at strategic points to protect the islands from seaborne attacks. In the hills surrounding **Road Town** are the ruins of forts built by the Royal Engineers in 1794 – Fort George on Fort Hill and Fort Charlotte on Harrigan's Hill. Another fort west of Road Town at Pockwood Pond, called the Dungeon, contains a set of stairs leading to an underground cell.

Other vestiges from colonial times include the remains of a stone windmill in Mount Healthy National Park, and a round tower at Fort Recovery on Tortola's West End – believed to be built by Tortola's earliest Dutch settlers. Salt Island contains evaporation ponds that are still panned for salt just as they were two centuries ago, and at the south end of Virgin Gorda is an abandoned copper mine worked by Cornish miners between 1838 and 1867 – the year in which the HMS *Rhone* sank off Salt Island during a hurricane. This wreck is now one of the Caribbean's most popular dive sites and the centerpiece of Rhone National Marine Park.

The first national parks were established in the 1960s, when the Rockefellers gave three sites to the B.V.I. government: Devil's Bay and Spring Bay on Virgin Gorda, and Sage Mountain on Tortola. Reforestation and the re-introduction of original vegetation in Sage Mountain National Park have returned this 92-acre parcel of land to its

Goats graze at the roadside on the pastoral island of Tortola. Car traffic throughout the BVI's is usually very light.

original habitat. At 1,780 feet, Sage Mountain is the highest point in all of the Virgin Islands. Views from its hiking trails are dramatic and, although the mountaintop receives only 100 inches of rain a year, its vegetation is similar to a rainforest with tree ferns and bromeliads thriving in the ocean mist that's carried upwards by the wind.

Other natural attractions include The Baths – beached granite boulders forming a series of pools and grottoes on Virgin Gorda, which are equally popular with snorkelers and swimmers. **Green Cay**, ringed with white sand beaches, is your classic 'desert isle' and has been featured in various commercials. The islands' marine life includes tropical fish, eagle rays and nurse sharks. In winter, humpback whales arrive in local waters to breed.

The B.V.I. are volcanic in origin, except for the low-lying coral and limestone atoll of **Anegada** which lies about 15 miles to the northwest. Its highest point is 28 feet above sea level, and the island is ringed with extensive beaches and reefs that have claimed more than 300 ships. Animals outnumber people on this island of about 200 residents. Wild goats, donkeys and the Anegada iguanas all live here, as does a colony of flamingos for which a bird sanctuary has been established at one of the island's salt ponds. This protected nesting ground is also used by herons, ospreys and terns.

Piracy and plantations have been replaced with tourism and offshore banking as the major industries in the B.V.I. A politically stable British crown colony, the territory is ruled by a governor who is appointed by

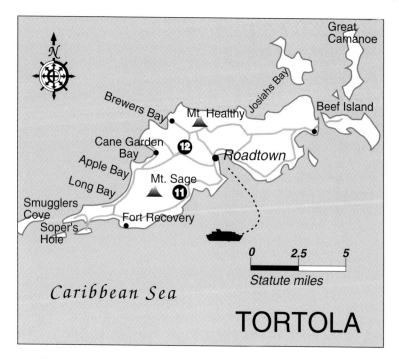

the Crown and by an elected chief minister and government. Tourism was introduced to the islands in the mid-1960s when Laurance Rockefeller built a resort at Little Dix Bay on Virgin Gorda. This was followed by the opening of The Moorings in 1969 which marked the beginning of the local charter yacht business. The future development of tourism is being planned carefully to preserve the islands' natural beauty – the most precious treasure to be found here.

ROAD TOWN, TORTOLA

Tortola, named for the turtle dove, is the largest island of the B.V.I. chain. Most of the island's 17,000 inhabitants live in Road Town, the colony's capital, administrative center and main harbor. The recently completed cruise pier is located at the north end of town on Wickhams Cay. Nearby is the **(1) Tourist Information Office** and the Cable & Wireless Public Office, on Waterfront Drive near Nibbs Road, which sells Caribbean phone cards and other long-distance services. Road Town is a charming port of shuttered wooden houses, brightly painted and trimmed with fretwork.

Getting Around

The B.V.I. Taxi Association is located at Wickhams Cay and its fleet includes open-air safari buses and air-conditioned vans. Rates are unmetered and some sample fares are: Road Town to Cane Garden Bay, $15 for 1-3 passengers, $20 for 4 passengers; Two-Hour Island Tour, $45 for 1-3 passengers, $60 for 4 passengers. A Budget Rent-A-Car office is located in the **(2) Mill Mall** near the pier.

Passenger ferries connect Tortola with Virgin Gorda, Peter Island and Jost Van Dyke. The ferry dock is opposite the town center and ferries depart two or three times daily from Road Town, Beef Island and West End. The 1/2 hour ride from Road Town to Virgin Gorda is about $10 one way. For an up-to-date schedule, visit the Tourist Information Office.

BEST BEACHES: Tortola's best beaches are concentrated on the northwest coastline. **Cane Garden Bay** is a beautiful, crescent-shaped beach with watersports, restaurants and bars. To the south is **Long Bay**, a mile-long stretch of white sand. **Apple Bay** is the 'surfing beach' and location of Bomba's Shack, a popular beach bar. **Brewers Bay** has two beach bars and good snorkeling, as does **Smugglers Cove**, a small sandy beach at the northwest end of the island. **Josiahs Bay** is a dra-

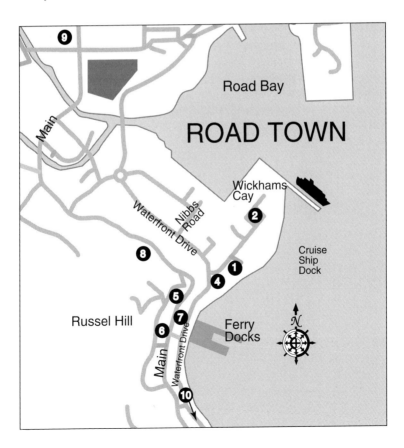

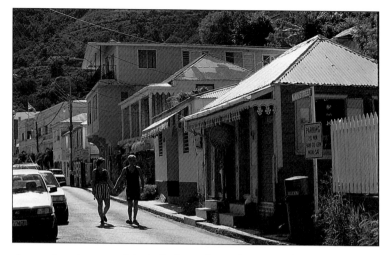

A couple enjoys a quiet stroll along the main street of Road Town. Quaint shops selling a variety of local and imported crafts add to the charm of this port.

matic beach on the north shore, and **Long Bay** on Beef Island offers seclusion and sheltered waters.

DIVE & SNORKEL SITES: There are two dozen established dive sites in the B.V.I.'s sheltered waters, a number of which can be enjoyed by snorkelers.

(3) Rhone National Marine Park was established to preserve the wreck of the *Rhone*, a 310-foot mail ship that went down in a hurricane off Salt Island in 1867. (See map on page 228.) Its broken hull, encrusted in coral, lies 20 to 80 feet beneath the water's surface and is frequented by schools of tropical fish such as the queen angelfish and the parrotfish. Underwater footage in the movie *The Deep* was filmed at this famous wreck which can be viewed by snorkelers. Blonde Rock – a pinnacle between Salt Island and Dead Chest – has ledges that descend from 15 to 60 feet, the top one crowned with fire coral. Dead Chest Island is also part of the park and Painted Walls, off the island's southern point, consists of four long gullies covered with corals and sponges in depths of 20 to 30 feet.

On Tortola, Smugglers Cove at its western tip and Brewers Bay on its north coast both offer good snorkeling. On Virgin Gorda, The Baths and Spring Bay are excellent snorkeling sites. The Caves on Norman Island are ideal for snorkeling, as is nearby Angelfish Reef where divers will find excellent visibility at 90 feet. Santa Monica Rock, a pinnacle about a mile south of the island, is a good spot to see eagle rays and other open-ocean fish in depths of 10 to 100 feet.

SHOPPING & DINING: The **(4) open-air market** on Wickhams Cay includes the B.V.I. House of Crafts where locally made tropical clothing and souvenirs can be bought. Main and Waterfront are the primary shopping streets. Main used to run along the waterfront before a land fill expanded the town site. Its quaint shops sell Caribbean arts and crafts, spices and preserves, wines and spirits, and cotton clothing.

Pusser's Co. Store is located on Waterfront Drive and its famous Royal Navy Rum is sold here along with unique nautical gifts and sports clothing. Adjoining the store is Pusser's Pub where an English-style pub lunch can be enjoyed. Next door is Tavern in the Town, another British-style pub that's open for lunch.

The North Shore Shell Museum at Carrot Bay is a good place to buy shell art and other local crafts.

LOCAL SIGHTS: Most of the town's historic sites are on Main Street. The **(5) Virgin Islands Folk Museum**, housed in a traditional West Indian building, contains artifacts from the islands' Taino and plantation eras, as well as pieces from the wreck of the RMS *Rhone*. A few doors down from the museum is the **(6) post office**, built in 1866 with stone walls and Gothic arches. Across the street is **(7) Sir Olva George's Plaza**, a shady spot that once served as a busy market place.

Farther north on Main is **(8) Britannic Hall**, an interesting structure perched atop a massive boulder, which houses a private business. Also on Main are St. George's Anglican Church, rebuilt following the hurricane of 1819, and the Methodist Church, built after the hurricane of

Local business people head to Road Town's British-style pubs for lunch.

Ruins of sugar mills and forts can be viewed in the British Virgin Islands. Shown above is a 17th-century round tower at Fort Recovery, built by Tortola's early Dutch settlers.

1924. In between the two churches is HM Prison where the infamous William Arthur Hodge was executed for murdering a slave. The **Sunday Morning Well** on Upper Main Street is marked with a plaque commemorating it as the site where the Proclamation of Emancipation was read in 1834.

The **(9) J.R. O'Neal Botanic Gardens**, created by the B.V.I. National Parks Trust, are located northwest of the town center and contain nearly three acres of indigenous and exotic tropical plants. Landscaped paths lead past flowering hibiscus and bougainvillea, a lily pond and a waterfall.

(10) Government House, overlooking Road Harbor, is south of the ferry docks on Waterfront Drive. A bit further along is **Queen Elizabeth Park**. Part of the B.V.I. national park system, this small waterfront park contains shrubs, flowers and rows of White Cedars.

Island Attractions

The architect William Thornton, who designed the Capitol in Washington, was born on Tortola in 1759. He trained as a physician in London and practised medicine on Tortola before emigrating to the United States in 1787. The ruins of his family plantation estate can be seen at **(11) Pleasant Valley**.

The **(12) Briercliffe-Davis Observatory**, established in 1984 atop Tortola's mountain ridge, provides panoramic views of the B.V.I. and

U.S. Virgin Islands. Located along Ridge Road, a half-mile north of the Cane Garden Bay turn-off, it is part of a complex containing the Skyworld restaurant and bar, and a gift shop selling local artwork.

Callwood Rum Distillery at Cane Garden Bay is housed in a stone building from the plantation era. Copper boiling vats, an old still and a cane crusher remain in use, and bottles of Arundel Rum line the shelves.

Sopers Hole at the West End is where Dutch settlers first landed in 1648. A sheltered harbor with several restaurants and shops, it is today a major anchorage and location of Tortola's main ferry terminal. A bridge here connects Tortola to **Frenchman's Cay**.

Beef Island, at the eastern end of Tortola, used to be a buccaneer hang-out and is now the location of the B.V.I.'s international airport. Beef Island is connected to Tortola by the Territory's only toll bridge – a one-lane structure dedicated by Queen Elizabeth in 1966.

Virgin Gorda

Virgin Gorda (the fat virgin), was named by Columbus who may have anchored off the island in 1493. Today about 2,500 people live on the island, which consists of three distinct sections.

The northern third rings **North Sound**, a beautiful blue lagoon of protected coral reefs and white beaches. Yachts anchor here and the shore facilities include a number of resorts, dive operators and the famous Bitter End Yacht Club. The island's middle section is mountainous and crowned by **Gorda Peak** which, at 1,370 feet, rises in the middle of Gorda Peak National Park.

The southern third is flat, its west side lined with lovely beaches. The ferry from Road Town pulls into **St. Thomas Bay**, just north of the Yacht Harbor which is home to luxury yachts and charter fleets, as well as a shopping center which includes a dive shop, bar and restaurant. South of here is Little Fort National Park where a wildlife sanctuary and ruins of a Spanish fortress are located.

The beaches of Trunk Bay and Spring Bay lie to the south, as does Virgin Gorda's famous landmark – **The Baths**. The beach here is dominated by unique rock formations containing sea caves and shallow pools of seawater connected by passageways. Geologists remain puzzled by the origin of these enormous granite boulders which could be the result of glacial action.

Virgin Gorda's most popular beaches for both swimming and snorkeling are The Baths and neighboring Spring Bay. Trunk Bay, a wide sandy beach, can be reached by a rough path from Spring Bay.

Chapter Ten

ST. MAARTEN / ST. MARTIN

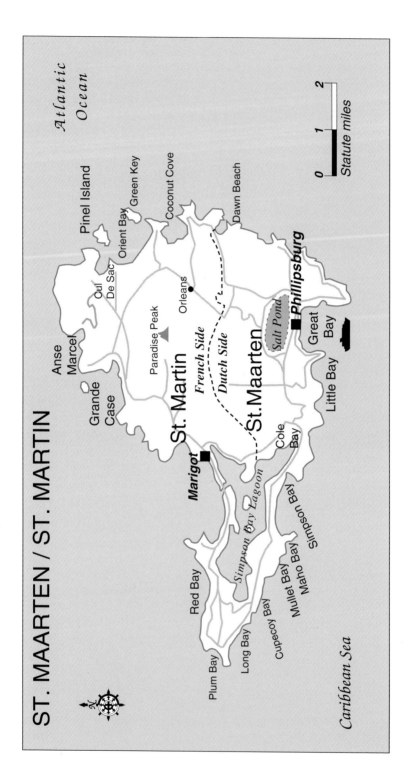

Atlantic Ocean

Pinel Island
Green Key
Orient Bay
Coconut Cove
Dawn Beach
Cul De Sac
Orleans
Paradise Peak
Anse Marcel
St. Martin
French Side
Dutch Side
St. Maarten
Phillipsburg
Salt Pond
Great Bay
Little Bay
Grande Case
Marigot
Cole Bay
Simpson Bay Lagoon
Simpson Bay
Maho Bay
Mullet Bay
Cupecoy Bay
Long Bay
Plum Bay
Red Bay
Caribbean Sea

N

Statute miles
0   1   2

ST. MAARTEN / ST. MARTIN

Beaches and Bistros

I t's been called the island with a split personality, but both sides are friendly. The Netherlands and France have peacefully shared this arid island since 1648 when a border was established dividing it in two. Variations of a popular legend explain why the French ended up with 20 square miles versus the Dutch share of 17 square miles. A foot race, so the story goes, was held between a Frenchman and a Dutchman, who walked in opposite directions around the shoreline until they met again and a line was drawn across the island between these two points. The Frenchman was drinking either wine or brandy, while the Dutchman was indulging in gin or perhaps beer. One version of the legend has the Frenchman abstaining, but this seems unlikely. Whatever their respective choices of beverage, the Frenchman walked faster than the Dutchman. Some say the critical factor was not the drink but the fetching French maiden deployed to delay the Dutchman.

Foot races aside, the Dutch were no doubt happy with their share of the island for the Great Salt Pond, with its high-quality salt, was what they wanted and what they got. *Sualouiga* (Salt Land) is what the island's original inhabitants, the Arawaks, called it. A seafaring people from South America, their ancient artifacts are still being discovered by local archaeologists. Columbus was the first European to sight and name the island in 1493, although some historians believe it was another island he saw.

The Spanish were seeking gold and they paid St. Maarten little attention. The Dutch and French, however, saw great worth in the island's salt flats. The Dutch West India Company needed a secure source of salt for preserving fish and in the mid-1620s some Dutch traders landed on St. Maarten's south shore. About the same time, a handful of French families settled on the island's north side and a peaceful co-existence prevailed until a Spanish fleet landed 1,300 soldiers on the island in 1633. The Dutch company's 80-man garrison was quickly overcome and a force of Spanish soldiers held the island for the next 15 years, fending off a Dutch attack in 1644 led by Curacao governor Peter Stuyvesant, who lost a leg in the battle and soon afterwards was appointed governor of New Amsterdam (later New York City).

In 1648, Spain withdrew and the remaining Dutch and French inhabitants returned to their peaceful co-existence, dividing the island along a customary boundary (or perhaps one determined by that legendary foot race). A hilly island, St. Maarten was cultivated with sugar plantations during the 18th century, along with cattle ranches. Britain seized it and other Dutch colonies after Napoleon invaded Holland in 1795, then returned the island in 1815.

When France ended slavery on St. Martin in 1848, slaves on the Dutch side simply took their freedom. Official emancipation came in 1863 and the plantation system disappeared, with planters unable to pay wages and still make a profit. The freed slaves and white settlers grew subsistence crops in the arid climate and sought seasonal work on other

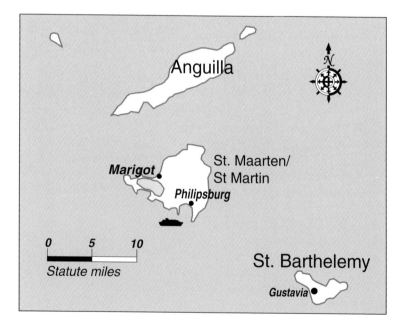

*As morning breaks, a cruise ship pulls into Great Bay on the Dutch
side of St. Maarten.*

islands. The island lacks an adequate water supply and a desalination
plant now provides fresh water for today's influx of tourists and an
exploding population which now exceeds 60,000 residents.

St. Maarten was one of the first Caribbean islands to open up to
tourism, which has boomed since the early 1970s. An extensively
developed island with an infrastructure to accommodate the thousands
of tourists who come here each year, St. Maarten calls itself the
Friendly Island. There are no border checks here, just a monument
commemorating the 300th anniversary (1648-1948) of the two nations'
peaceful sharing of the island. Both sides have retained their colonial
ties – St. Martin is an overseas region of France and a prefecture of
Guadeloupe, while St. Maarten is part of the Netherlands Antilles, an
autonomous part of the Kingdom of the Netherlands. Capitalizing on its
strong links to Europe, the island has forged its own identity in which
French and Dutch influences have combined with West Indian heritage
to create a vibrant Creole culture. It's a high-energy island offering cosmopolitan flair with a calypso beat.

Today it's a toss-up which country got the better half of the island.
Philipsburg, the Dutch capital, is where most of the cruise ships moor
while Marigot, the French capital, is where cruise passengers go to
sample French boutiques and bistros. The Dutch side has gambling
casinos and a golf course; the French side has Fort Louis and topless
sunbathing. Both capitals are free ports and the entire island contains
beach-lined bays which attract tourists in such numbers that the road

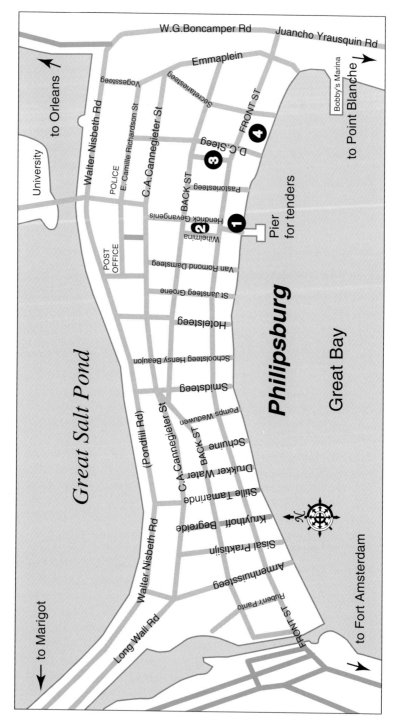

W.G.Boncamper Rd

Juancho Yrausquin Rd

Emmaplein

to Orleans

Vogtesteeg

Secretariesteeg

FRONT ST

Bobby's Marina

to Point Blanche

University

Walter Nisbeth Rd

POLICE

E. Camille Richardson St

C.A.Cannegieter St

D.C.Steeg

❹

❸

Pastoriesteeg

BACK ST

Hendrick Gevangenis

❷

❶

Wilhelmina

Pier for tenders

POST OFFICE

Van Romond Damsteeg

St Jansteeg Groene

Philipsburg

Great Bay

Hotelsteeg

Schoolsteeg Hensy Beaujon

Great Salt Pond

Smidsteeg

Pomps Weduwen

(Pondfill Rd)

C.A.Cannegieter St

BACK ST

Schuine

Drukker Water

Stille Tamarinde

Kruyhoff Begraide

Walter Nisbeth Rd

Sisal Prakisirin

Ammuniussteeg

FRONT ST

Ruben' Panto

to Marigot

Long Wall Rd

to Fort Amsterdam

leading from Philipsburg to Marigot is often clogged with bumper-to-bumper traffic. The Princess Juliana International Airport is one of the busiest in the West Indies and the island is one of the Caribbean's most popular ports of call, offering great shopping, dozens of beaches, and an impressive array of shore excursions. Yet, in spite of the island's high level of development, it's still possible to find a quiet stretch of sand on which to enjoy the island's ever-present sunshine.

Philipsburg

The majority of cruise ships currently anchor in Great Bay and tender their passengers ashore to the Town Pier adjacent to **(1) Cyrus Wathney Square** where a Tourist Information Bureau and taxi stand are located. Philipsburg is easy to explore on foot with its two main streets – Front and Back (*Vorstraat* and *Achterstraat*) – running parallel with the waterfront. Front Street, lined with duty-free shops, features West Indian-style buildings trimmed with gingerbread fretwork. Back Street, the former site of salt warehouses, is connected with Front Street by a series of interesting alleyways called *steegjes*.

Getting Around

There are plenty of taxi drivers awaiting your arrival at the town pier. Their rates are unmetered and a few sample one-way fares in US $ from Philipsburg (1-4 per taxi) are:

to Marigot	$16
to Maho Beach	$14
to Dawn Beach	$12
to Orient Beach	$18

The cheapest way to travel directly between Philipsburg and Marigot is by public bus. These vans pick up passengers on Back Street and drop off in downtown Marigot. The fare is only $1.50 each way and the buses run regularly throughout the day.

Rental cars are available here, with numerous rental agencies in both St. Maarten and St. Martin, including Avis, Budget and Hertz.

Dutch and French are the official languages but English is widely spoken.

SHOPPING: The official currency is the Netherlands Antilles florin and the French franc, but U.S. dollars are accepted throughout the island.

With about 500 duty-free shops and savings of up to 50%, the island is a great place to shop for such goods as French perfume, Irish linen and designer fashions. Good buys are available in cameras, electronics, watches, jewelry, china, crystal, leather shoes and handbags, and Finnish stoneware. Bargains in liquor include fine cognac and St. Maarten's own guavaberry liqueur.

Cruise visitors to St. Maarten are tendered ashore at Philipsburg, where an 18th-century courthouse overlooks the town's central square.

GOLF: An 18-hole course is located at Mullet Bay Resort on the Dutch side.

LOCAL SIGHTS: Overlooking the square, on Front Street, is the **(2) Courthouse**. Built in the 1790s, it has at various times housed a barracks, prison cells, secretariat and post office, in addition to its courtroom. The original wood-and-stone building was repaired following hurricane damage in 1819. Its most recent restoration was completed in 1969, and the building is now occupied by the Court of First Instance.

A few blocks east along Front Street and entered through a wrought-iron gate is the **(3) Old Street Mall**, a colorful shopping alley of potted palms and old-fashioned lamp posts. Nearby, at the east end of Front Street, is **(4) Pasanggrahan Royal Guest House**. The oldest and most authentic colonial style inn on St. Maarten, it used to be the Governor's home and was a royal residence for Dutch Queen Juliana during World War II when, as a princess fleeing the Nazi invasion of her homeland, she stayed there while en route to Canada.

At the west end of Front Street is the **Museum of St. Maarten**, tucked away in a West Indian colonial building that also houses Le Bec Fin, an elegant French restaurant.

Area Attractions

The ruins of Fort Amsterdam stand on Great Bay's western point, and directly north atop Fort Hill are the remains of Fort William. The St.

Maarten Zoological and Botanical Garden, which focuses on education and contains baboons and St. Kitts monkeys, is located just north of Great Salt Pond.

The winding road from Philipsburg to Marigot provides scenic views of yacht-filled Simpson Bay Lagoon as it ascends the hilly terrain. An observation platform on top of **Cole Bay Hill** offers sweeping views of neighboring islands, including Anguilla and St. Barts. The Cole Bay Hill Cemetery contains the grave of Scottish adventurer John Philips, for whom Philipsburg is named.

Paradise Peak is the island's highest point at 1,500 feet above sea level and a number of hiking trails lead in all directions from this point. It can be reached by a secondary road from Rambaud, which is located on the main road leading north of Marigot to **Grande Case** – a fishing village renowned for its gourmet restaurants and restored creole houses. This waterfront village is also the location of the Seaworld Explorer, a semi-submersible glass-bottom boat that provides narrated tours of the coral reefs around Creole Rock. The northern tip of the island, around **Anse Marcel**, consists of secluded coves and scenic hiking trails. The island's oldest French settlement of **Orleans** is located on the island's east side.

Marigot

A pretty port of French colonial buildings and elegant shops, the Marigot harborfront has undergone a recent multi-million dollar

Fort St. Louis stands atop a hill overlooking Marigot Bay on the island's French side.

makeover. It's a pleasant place to stroll along the water's edge and gaze at anchored sailboats or relax at an outdoor cafe beneath the shade of colorful awnings and umbrellas.

Marigot's tourist information center is located near the waterfront, at the north end of Rue De La Republique. Beside it is a taxi stand and opposite is an open-air market where vendors sell their wares beneath multi-colored canopies.

Perched above this festive scene is **Fort St. Louis**, its hilltop ruins reached by stairs leading from the Sous-Prefecture parking lot. With its breathtaking view over Marigot Bay and the lagoon, the site is a wonderful place to indulge in a picnic while wandering about the site. Built in 1767 during the reign of Louis XVI, the fort was armed with 15 cannons.

BEACHES: On St. Maarten/St. Martin, there's a beach – 37 in total- to suit everyone's taste, whether it's resort facilities, coral reefs or sandy solitude that you're seeking. All beaches have public access and those designated 'topless' and 'clothing optional' are on the French side.

Fine beaches on the Dutch side include Great Bay, just a few steps from Front Street. Nearby is **Little Bay**, a small but lovely beach backed by a number of resorts.

Maho Bay has sparkling white sand and a surf that is sometimes rough. Facilities are available at the Maho Beach Hotel.

The mile-long beach at **Mullet Bay** also has resort facilities. The island's only golf course is located beside this beach.

Cupecoy Bay's beach of powdery white sand is backed by sandstone cliffs and caves. A dramatic setting, there are no change facilities or watersports here, and there is topless bathing at the far end.

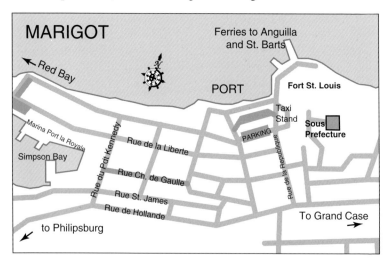

Two 12-meter yachts tack their back to Philipsburg, their deckhands enjoying one of the Caribbean's most popular shore excursions.

More beautiful beaches await on the French side. Those near Marigot include **Red Bay**, with snack facilities and good snorkeling at its eastern end.

Long Bay is one of the island's largest beaches and is fairly quiet with little resort development here. Topless bathers frequent this beach, and the neighboring beach at **Plum Bay** can be reached by walking west around Canonnier Point. Plum Point is a good snorkeling spot.

At the north end of the island is **Orient Bay** – one of St. Martin's busiest beaches, offering restaurants, snack bars, watersports and a non-stop water taxi to **Green Key Island**. Beach chairs, umbrellas, catamarans and windsurfers can all be rented here and those who like sunbathing in the buff can do so in front of the Club Orient Hotel.

For visitors with children, the beaches at **Anse Marcel** (north end) and **Coconut Grove** (east side) are quiet and shady. The one at Coconut Grove has change facilities, refreshments, chairs and sailboard rentals.

SNORKEL & DIVE SITES: At the island's north end, **Flat Island**, **Pinel Island** (reached by boat from Cul de Sac) and **Orient Bay/Green Key** are part of a Regional Underwater Reserve and offer excellent snorkeling. Also within the reserve is Grand Cayes, a unique diving site on the coral reef barrier.

On the east side, **Dawn Beach** has some of the island's best snorkeling along its offshore reefs, and refreshments are available here.

Dive shops are located at various hotels, including Mullet Bay Resort. Some fascinating wrecks are within easy reach, such as the

British ship HMS *Proselyte* which sank in 1801 about one mile off the eastern entrance to Great Bay. Near the western entrance point, off Fort Amsterdam, a 17th-century warship is resting on Man-O-War Reef, its scattered cannons still visible.

BOAT EXCURSIONS: St. Maarten offers visitors a good selection of boating excursions, including lively sightseeing cruises with unlimited rum punch and private-island beach stops for a chance to swim, snorkel and sunbathe.

A unique and highly popular boating attraction is the 'America's Cup' Sailing Regatta out of Philipsburg. No sailing experience is necessary to sign on as 'deckhand' in this friendly regatta that takes place outside Great Bay onboard original 12-meter yachts that were raced in the 1987 America's Cup in Fremantle, Australia. The boats, about 70 feet in length, are manned with an experienced skipper and crew who assign each deckhand a task and explain its execution. A few practice tacks and jibes are made on the way to the race course, and then it's time to leap into action and experience the exhilaration of world-class yacht racing.

St. Barts

Named St-Barthelemy by Christopher Columbus and once governed by Sweden, the island everyone calls St. Barts is unabashedly French and very chic. It lies 15 miles southeast of St. Maarten and is part of the French overseas departement of Guadeloupe. The island's capital is Gustavia, its sheltered natural harbor often filled with sailing craft and luxury yachts, its streets of northern-European style homes overlooked by the ruins of forts that once defended this tiny island.

During colonial times, in about 1660, the island was settled by Huguenots from Brittany and Normandy. Then, in 1784, France's Louis XVI ceded the island to King Gustav III of Sweden in return for duty-free trading rights in Gothenburg. Gustavia was soon declared a free port and the island, benefiting from Swedens' neutrality, prospered until struck by hurricanes and a great fire in Gustavia in 1852.

In 1877, France bought the island back for 320,000 francs and to this day the island's French culture remains strong. Residents, about 5,000 in number, speak a French patois sprinkled with English and Swedish words, and women can still be seen wearing starched white caps like those of their Norman ancestors. The population is predominantly white, for the arid island never supported a plantation economy, and in the past local commerce was based on trade and fishing. That all changed when the jet set discovered this island hideaway, and tourism is now its major industry.

The Rockefeller, Ford and Rothschild families all have vacation homes on St. Barts, and this 8-1/2-square mile island is dotted with luxury resorts. Its varied shoreline of pristine coves and idyllic beaches includes Anse du Gouverneur, accessible only on foot and considered one of the finest in the West Indies, and Saint-Jean, the island's most photographed beach with its two crescents of pale sand separated by a rocky promontory. The remote beach at Columbier on the island's north shore is where David Rockefeller built a vacation home, and Grand Cul-de-Sac Bay, a favorite with windsurfers, has two beaches – one embracing the tranquil waters of a sheltered bay, the other facing the ocean.

Beach hopping can be done by rented mini-moke and beach buggy, or by taxi. A taxi stand is located in Gustavia where local attractions include duty-free shops and the town's two historic churches – the Roman Catholic French church and the Anglican Swedish church. Seventeenth-century Fort Oscar stands at the tip of a peninsula and is occupied by the Ministry of Armed Forces. The ruins of Fort Carl stand in the heights of Gustavia and provide a spectacular view of the harbor. Fort Gustave also provides panoramic views of Gustavia and neighboring islands.

Other island attractions include the Wall House Museum & Library, housed in a Swedish colonial building, and the Inter Oceans shell museum which is located in Corossol, one of the island's oldest villages.

French is the official language on St. Barts and the franc its official currency, but English is widely spoken and prices are often quoted in U.S. dollars.

Anguilla

Anguilla is a short ferry ride from St. Martin but it's a world apart in terms of atmosphere. Northernmost of the Leeward Islands, Anguilla is a true island hideaway with pristine beaches and luxury resort accommodations. The likes of Denzel Washington, Janet Jackson and Phil Collins have vacationed on Anguilla, a British territory of 10,000 residents where visitors come to find peace and relaxation.

A unique feature on Anguilla, in the process of being developed as a public attraction, is the Fountain – a cavern containing several freshwater pools, a fountain and a dozen or so petroglyphs as well as a 16-foot stalagmite which was carved by Taino Indians. Archaeologists believe this dome-shaped cavern was a major Amerindian center for worship.

Anguilla's main attraction is its miles of white powdery beaches and coral reefs. For visitors with an urge to shop, the duty-free boutiques of Marigot are just a 20-minute ferry ride away.

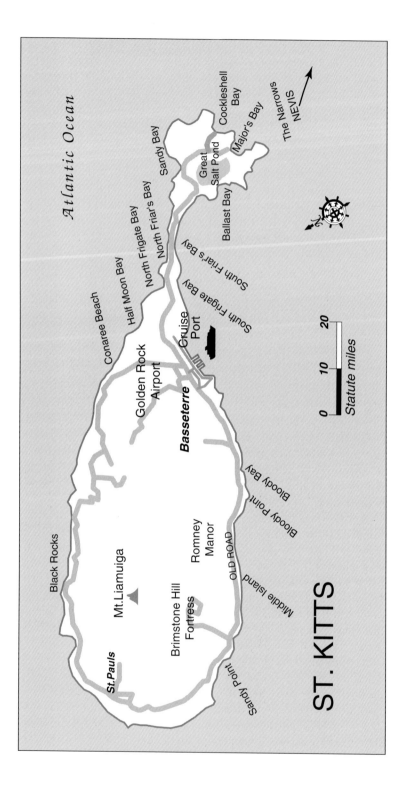

ST. KITTS

Atlantic Ocean

Black Rocks

Conaree Beach

Half Moon Bay

North Frigate Bay

North Friar's Bay

Sandy Bay

Great
Salt Pond

Cockleshell
Bay

Major's Bay

The Narrows
NEVIS

Ballast Bay

South Friar's Bay

South Frigate Bay

Cruise
Port

Golden Rock
Airport

Basseterre

Bloody Bay

Bloody Point

Middle Island

OLD ROAD

Romney Manor

Brimstone Hill
Fortress

Mt. Liamuiga

St. Pauls

Sandy Point

0   10   20
Statute miles

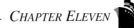

CHAPTER ELEVEN

ST. KITTS

Mother Colony of
British and French West Indies

The verdant mountains of St. Kitts are a beautiful sight for cruise passengers as their ship draws close to this island of patchwork fields and sandy beaches. Its pastoral charm belies the bloody battles that took place on the island called *Liamuiga* – fertile land – by its early Carib inhabitants. So valued was St. Kitts for its sugar cane, the British eventually built a massive fortress on Brimstone Hill which became known as the 'Gibraltar of the West Indies'.

A massive fortification of volcanic rock and limestone mortar, the fortress took more than a century to build using slave labor. When completed in 1794, its walls encompassed a citadel, bastions, barracks, officers quarters, storehouses, cookhouses and a hospital. Both impregnable and impressive, the Brimstone Hill Fortress loomed nearly a thousand feet above the surrounding countryside with sweeping views of the coastline and other islands. Its name refers to the odor of sulphur that seeps from nearby volcanic vents. The fortress itself stands atop an upthrust of solidified lava covered by limestone.

St. Kitts and its neighboring island of Nevis are the upper slopes and cones of volcanoes resting on a submarine rock base. Mount Misery, the highest peak on St. Kitts at 3,793 feet, was last active in 1692. Nevis Peak, a single volcano in the center of Nevis Island, rises to 3,232 feet. The two islands are separated by a two-mile-wide channel called the Narrows, its shallow sea floor covered with coral reefs.

Brimstone Hill Fortress, built of volcanic rock and limestone mortar, took over a century to complete.

The climate of St. Kitts and Nevis is particularly pleasant. Clouds collect around the island's mountains and the breezes that blow along its western coastline are warm and dry. The vegetation on St. Kitts is layered according to altitude, starting with grass at the highest summits, below which grows a mist forest and, below that, an evergreen tropical rain forest. On the lower slopes, the land is cultivated right to the coast. At the south end grows thorny scrub and dry forest, and this relatively undeveloped area is inhabited with Green Vervet monkeys, often seen scampering across the road. They were brought to St. Kitts by the French who, along with the British, drew supplies of salt and building timber from the island in the late 1600s. A hundred years earlier, the island had been named St. Christopher by Columbus, in honor of his patron saint, but it became known as St. Kitts and the name was officially changed in 1988.

In 1605 England took possession of St. Kitts and in 1623 the island's first white settlers arrived, led by Sir Thomas Warner, a Suffolk gentleman who planned to grow tobacco here with the financial support of a syndicate of British merchants. He drove off a small group of hostile Carib natives, cleared the land and established the first permanent British settlement in the West Indies, only to have a hurricane destroy his first crop of tobacco. But Warner and his followers persevered and a new crop was planted the next year. They soon had company in the form of French pirates, their damaged ship putting in to what is now Basseterre for repairs. The French, led by Belain d'Esnambuc, decided to stay and plant tobacco too.

The British and French joined forces to massacre some avenging Caribs and wipe them from the island. They then divided the island, which is 23 miles long and up to seven miles across. The central mountainous region went to the English; the north and south ends went to the French. But the living was far from easy, and frequent quarrels flared between the British and French farmers, many of whom died of diseases such as yellow fever and malaria. In 1628, a wealthy British planter led a group of settlers to Nevis, and by 1632 others had left St. Kitts to settle on Montserrat and Antigua. The French also used St. Kitts as a staging area for the settlement of their other islands, such as Guadeloupe, Martinique and St. Martin.

Mother colony of the West Indies for both the British and the French, St. Kitts was battled over for the next century and a half until the 1783 Treaty of Versailles recognized it as a British possession. In 1871, St. Kitts and Nevis were incorporated in the colony of Leeward Islands, and in 1983 they became, along with a small coral island called Sombrero that lies about 35 miles northwest of Anguilla, an independent state within the British Commonwealth.

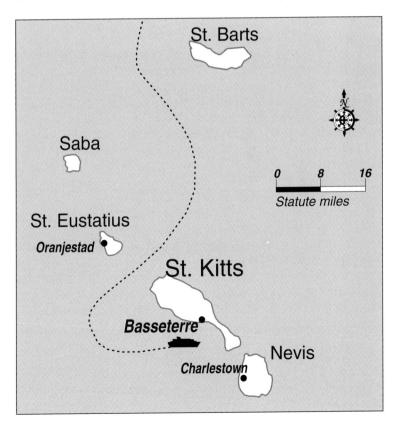

Photo Michael DeFreitas

A narrow-gauge railway encircles St. Kitts. It was built in the early 1900s to transport sugarcane to Basseterre.

The fertile soil on St. Kitts supported three centuries of sugar cane crops and showed no signs of exhaustion until the 20th century, when modern methods of cultivation initially doubled the yield per acre, followed by a marked decrease. Total output has been halved in the last twenty years, but agriculture is still the island's major export with the entire sugarcane crop of St. Kitts and Nevis processed at a refinery in Basseterre. Nearly 40 miles of narrow-gauge railway encircles St. Kitts, built between 1912 and 1925 to transport wagon loads of cane from the plantations to the refinery.

The majority of St. Kitts's 44,000 residents live in Basseterre (pronounced *bass-terr*), originally founded by the French but developed by the English from 1706 onwards. The island's chief town since 1727, it suffered widespread destruction from an earthquake in 1843 and was rebuilt in 1867 following a great fire that destroyed most of the town. The 20th century has also brought a series of natural disasters: a hurricane in 1928, an earthquake in 1974, and more hurricanes in 1979, 1980 and 1988. The town's deep-water harbor, 2-1/2 miles south of the town center, opened in 1981 but tourism has barely touched this scenic island of fields and fortress.

Basseterre

A tourism information booth is located on the cruise pier, right beside some pay telephones. A tourist office is located on the downtown waterfront overlooking the Treasury Pier, at Bay Road and Fort Street.

The Treasury Building stands at the foot of Fort Street in downtown Basseterre.

Next door is the Treasury Building and beside that is a post office (just west of the Pelican Mall).

American money is widely accepted although the official currency is the Eastern Caribbean dollar worth approximately $2.70 EC per $1 US (or approximately $1 EC per 40¢ US).

Getting Around

St. Kitts, has good roads and beautiful scenery, so touring the island by taxi, rental car or organized shore excursion is a pleasurable way to spend your time in port. English is the official language and residents also speak a local patois.

Arranging for a taxi at the cruise pier is a well-organized procedure with drivers lining up outside a cordoned-off area while a dispatcher deals with disembarking passengers seeking a cab. Upon stepping ashore, you simply tell the dispatcher where you would like to go and he will tell you what the fare is and direct you to a driver. The set fare is per car, one to four persons.

Sample fares (in U.S. dollars) from cruise port:
Downtown Basseterre (one-way) $5
Romney Manor (return) $22.50
Romney Manor and Brimstone Hill (return) $41
Frigate Bay (one-way) $7; Friars Beach (one-way) $8
Tour of South East Peninsula $31
Island Tour $45

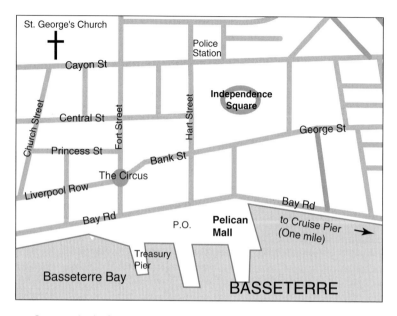

On round-trip fares, a 15-minute wait at each destination is included. After that, a small waiting fee is charged.

There are several car rental agencies in Basseterre, including Avis and Budget. A visitor's driving license ($12 U.S.) is required, available at the Police Station, and driving is on the left-hand side of the road.

BEACHES: St. Kitts has some attractive beaches at its southern end. **South Frigate Bay** has resort facilities and watersports equipment rental, including snorkeling gear. **South Friars Bay** is a quiet, undeveloped beach with good snorkeling.

At the southern tip lie more remote beaches at **Cockleshell Bay** and Banana Bay, with an excellent view across the Narrows of conical-shaped Nevis Island. Some dramatic beaches with surf on the Atlantic side include **North Frigate Bay** and **Conaree Beach**.

DIVING & SNORKELING: The Caribbean side of the island has protected waters and extensive reefs that begin in shallow water and drop off to depths of 100 feet or more. There are a couple of dive operations in Basseterre, one on Bay Road and another at the Bird Rock Beach Hotel. Dive sites on St. Kitts include Bloody Bay Reef, laced with small caves filled with purple anemones and yellow sea fans, and the Grid Iron, an undersea shelf in the Narrows which is covered with shallow-water corals, sea fans and sponges. Snorkeling can be enjoyed at many of the island's beaches, especially those on the Caribbean side, such as South Frigate Bay and South Friars Bay.

GOLF: There are two courses on St. Kitts: the Golden Rock Golf Club near the airport north of Basseterre, and the Royal St. Kitts Golf

Course at Frigate Bay. The latter is an 18-hole championship course bordered by both the Atlantic Ocean and the Caribbean Sea. Designed by the Golf Course Architectural Group, this par-72 course is both challenging and scenic, its fairways and greens adorned with ponds, palm trees and tropical flowers.

SHOPPING: St. Kitts is famous for its locally produced clothing made of beautiful batik and tie-dyed cotton. Other local crafts include hand-embroidered items, straw goods and ceramics. Duty-free items sold here include perfumes, jewelry, crystal and porcelain.

Shopping areas in Basseterre are found along Bay Road, Liverpool Row and Fort Street. The Circus is where Island Hopper sells Caribelle Batik's famous dresses, caftans, wraps and wall murals. The Caribelle Batik studio, where these exquisite fashions are designed and made, is located at Romney Manor (northwest of Basseterre). Duty-free shopping can be found on Liverpool Row and at the Pelican Shopping Mall on the downtown waterfront. A philatelic bureau selling colorful collectors issues of postage stamps is also located in this mall.

Local art, including the renowned Carnival Clown series by Rose Cameron Smith, can be bought in The Spencer Cameron Gallery on North Independence Square. The Plantation Picture House, home to Kate Spencer's studio and gallery, is at the northwest end of the island near Rawlins Plantation.

A colorful public market is located on Bay Road, a few blocks west of the Treasury Pier, and local merchants also set up tables on the cruise pier when a ship is in port.

Eight paths converge on a central fountain of Independence Square, in a pattern that resembles the Union Jack when seen from the air.

LOCAL SIGHTS: The Circus, in the heart of Basseterre, is a traffic circle modeled after London's famous Piccadilly Circus. In the center of this busy hub stands the Berkeley Memorial, a Victorian clock-tower monument commemorating a former president of the General Legislative Council.

Bank Street leads off The Circus to **Independence Square** (originally called Pall Mall Square) which was built in 1790 for slave auctions and council meetings. This open square is graced with a fountain and lined with well-preserved colonial buildings such as the brick-built Georgian House which now contains a gourmet restaurant. Facing the square on its east side is the Roman Catholic Church of the Immaculate Conception, and at its southeast corner is the Court House with a public library upstairs.

St. George's Anglican Church, an impressive brownstone structure surrounded by lawns and flowering shrubs on Cayon Street, was originally called Notre Dame when built by the French in 1670. Burned to the ground by the British in 1706, it was rebuilt four years later and named for England's patron saint. Two fires and an earthquake between 1763 and 1843 resulted in the church being rebuilt three more times, followed by its most recent restoration in 1869.

Area Attractions

Bloody Point at the mouth of Stone Fort River is the former site of a Carib village. Within the walls of the river's narrow canyon, 2,000 Carib Indians were massacred by the British and French in 1626. The Caribs, unhappy with the increasing number of Europeans settling their island, had been planning their own attack when they were trapped here and slaughtered. The river is said to have run red with their blood. Local taxi drivers will stop at Bloody Point if asked and young children with pet monkeys often wait here for camera-toting tourists. Carib carvings (petroglyphs) can be seen on the canyon walls which are about a half hour hike from Bloody Point.

Old Road Bay is where Thomas Warner landed on St. Kitts in 1623 and established the first permanent British settlement in the West Indies. It was the island's capital until 1727. Nearby, at what is now Wingfield Estate, are Carib petroglyphs and pictographs sketched on boulders – reminders of the Caribs who initially befriended Warner and allowed his party of farmers to settle on St. Kitts.

Romney Manor, site of a 17th-century great house and plantation, is now home to **Caribelle Batik** where local artisans practice the Indonesian art of batik to produce high-quality fabrics and fashions of striking designs and colors. The lovely grounds feature an enormous 350-year-old Saman (rain) tree and five acres of flowers, shrubbery and terraced lawns.

The island of Nevis lies across a narrow channel at the southern end of St. Kitts.

Thomas Warner's tomb is located in the churchyard of St. Thomas Church in **Middle Island**.

One of the most famous historic sites on St. Kitts, and the second largest fortress in the Caribbean, **Brimstone Hill** was inaugurated as a national park by Queen Elizabeth in 1985. The impressive fortifications contain a visitor center at the base of the restored citadel, atop which 24-pounder cannons overlook the sea and surrounding countryside. The sweeping view includes the island of St. Eustatius to the northwest.

Beyond Brimstone Hill, at the northwest end of St. Kitts, are scenic sugarcane plantations and estates. At **Black Rocks**, on the northwest coast, you can view black cliffs and boulders formed by lava flowing from Mount Liamuiga and eroded by a pounding sea.

The island's **Southeast Peninsula** is easily accessible by modern highway from Basseterre. The Frigate Bay area contains several luxury resorts, sandy beaches and a golf course. At the far end of the peninsula, nestled among the cone-shaped hills, is the Great Salt Pond. This undeveloped area of breathtaking vistas and pristine beaches is also the place to spot wild monkeys in the low scrub that lines the quiet roads.

Nevis

Dominated by a single central mountain peak, the small island of Nevis (pronounced Nee-vis), is steeped in Old World charm. It was called *Nieves* (Spanish for snow) by Columbus because cloud-covered Nevis Peak reminded him of a snow-capped mountain. The main port of

Photo Michael DeFreitas

St. John's Church, in Fig Tree Village on Nevis, is where Horatio Nelson married a local woman named Francis Nesbitt.

Charlestown is where most of the island's 9,000 residents live and is connected to Basseterre by passenger ferry.

Charlestown was once a fashionable health spa destination for the wealthy who stayed at the grand Bath Hotel and Spring House, built in 1778. The resort's bath houses were positioned on a fault over a hot spring, and a soak in the thermal mineral water brought relief from rheumatism and gout. Today's visitors can still take a mineral bath and tour the reconstructed hotel, much of its original structure destroyed by a 1950 earthquake.

Other historic attractions in Charlestown include a cotton ginnery (still used during the March/April picking season), and the Alexander Hamilton House, birthplace of the American statesman and aide to Washington. The Hamilton Museum, housed in a Georgian-style building, contains papers by Hamilton and other archival documents. Nevis's other famous figure is Horatio Nelson, the British naval hero who, as a young captain stationed in the West Indies, met and married in 1787 a local woman named Francis Nesbitt. A record of their marriage (and Alexander Hamilton's birth) is registered at St. John's Church in Fig Tree Village. There's also a Nelson Museum in Morning Star, and Nelson's Spring is where he took on water for his ships before sailing to North America during the War of American Independence. Other attractions on Nevis include its restored plantation estates, the golden sands of Pinney's Beach, and an 18-hole championship golf course at the Four Seasons Resort Nevis.

St. Eustatius

The small Dutch island of St. Eustatius, commonly called Statia, was known as the 'Golden Rock' during colonial times when, as the headquarters of the Netherlands West Indies Company, its population grew to almost 20,000 and trade in rum, sugar and tobacco was brisk. The island also served as a transhipment port for supplies to the American colonies during the American War of Independence. A salute fired by an American warship on November 16, 1776, was replied to by Fort Oranjestad, thus making the Netherlands the first foreign power to recognize America's new flag, the Stars and Stripes. The fort, perched on a crag above the sea, was built in 1636 and restored in 1976. The town of Oranjestad contains a number of historic sites, including one of the oldest synagogues in the Western Hemisphere and a number of restored 18th-century houses such as the one Admiral Rodney used as his headquarters when he captured the island for Britain in 1781.

Peaceful times now prevail on Statia, its population a mere 2,000. The island's scenic beauty can be enjoyed on nature trails that crisscross the island, including one that leads through tropical rain forest to the crater of an extinct volcanic peak called The Quill. For snorkelers and scuba divers, the island's surrounding waters are dotted with ship wrecks, coral reefs and rare fish.

Saba

The tiny volcanic island of Saba (pronounced Say-ba) is part of the Netherlands Antilles and is a unique piece of Caribbean geography. There are no beaches on Saba, which is the top of a dormant volcano, and its steep coastline consists of cliffs that plunge into the sea. Only five square miles in size, Saba's single road – called The Road – winds across the island and connects a handful of villages of red-roofed houses nestled at the base of green slopes.

The waters surrounding Saba contain a microcosm of sea life due to the continual currents flowing past the island's shores. A marine park completely encircles the island and features groove channels filled with juvenile tropical fish, underwater tunnels, barrel sponges and soft corals. Nearby is a range of underwater sea mounts, their peaks 80 feet beneath the surface. Thirty permanent moorings have been installed in Saba Marine Park to accommodate dive boats while protecting the coral. The island's decompression chamber at the Fort Bay Pier was donated by the royal Dutch Navy, and local dive operators help with many of the park's projects, which include the ongoing collection of data and sharing of marine information.

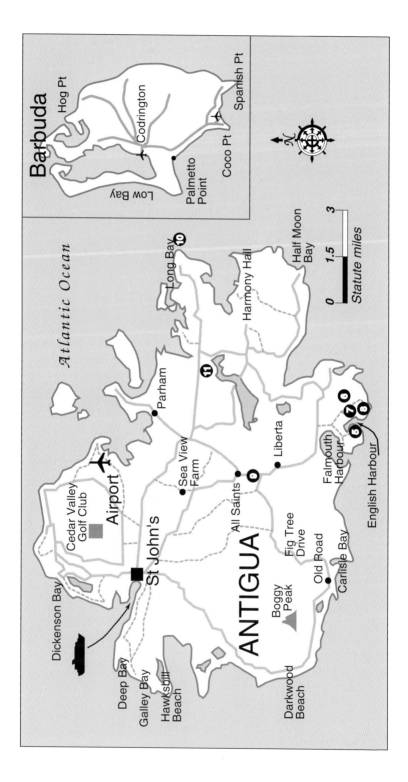

CHAPTER TWELVE

ANTIGUA

A beach for each day of the year

Antigua's beautiful bays and harbors have been providing shelter to seagoing vessels since the days of Columbus. English Harbour was already a popular hurricane haven when the Royal Navy began using it in 1725 as a dockyard. One of the finest natural harbors in the world with its narrow entrance and surrounding hillsides, English Harbour soon became Britain's major naval port in the West Indies. Fortifications were built on hilltops overlooking this and other harbors on the island, and ships would regularly pull in for repairs and provisions, or to ride out a storm during the hurricane season. This busy dockyard reached its zenith in the late 18th century when 26-year-old Horatio Nelson was headquartered here as commander of the Northern Division of the Leeward Island Station.

The sailing tradition continues today with Antigua's annual Sailing Week in April. One of the world's largest ocean racing events, attracting over 200 yachts from nearly 40 countries, this regatta has been called a 'sailor's Woodstock' for the fun-loving spirit of its competitors. The racing is serious but away from the course the rum punch flows and the dockside events are pure frivolity. A certain decorum does prevail, however, when the winning prizes are presented from the Old Officer's Quarters Balcony in Nelson's Dockyard, after which the Royal Antiguan Police Band 'Beats the Retreat'. The festivities conclude with the Lord Nelson Ball, a formal-dress affair complete with fireworks display.

Darkwood Beach on the west coast of Antigua is one of many beautiful beaches lining the island's shores.

Such is Antigua, an island conducive to languid lazing on beautiful beaches, but with a hint of British crispness in the accents of its people whose friendliness is tempered with a touch of reserve. The local school children wear uniforms, and cricket is a popular here with international matches played at the Recreation Ground in St. John's. The bat used by Antigua-born Viv Richards, famous captain of the West Indies cricket team, is on display at the local museum.

Antigua is also a recluse for British royalty and rock stars, with the Queen herself once taking a dip in the sea at one of many secluded beaches. Princess Margaret and Lord Snowden honeymooned on Antigua and, more recently, Princess Diana visited Antigua's sister island of Barbuda for a tropical respite away from the prying lenses of the paparazzi. Eric Clapton has a home near English Harbour, and Michael Jordan, Whitney Houston and Elton John have all vacationed on Antigua, its powdery white beaches stretching past some of the Caribbean's most exclusive resorts.

Antigua (pronounced An-tee-ga) was named in 1493 by Columbus for Santa Maria de la Antigua, a miracle-working saint in the Seville Cathedral in Spain. The island's earliest signs of habitation date back to 1775 B.C. and settlement by the Arawaks, who migrated here from South America, began in about 35 A.D. The island's lack of natural springs discouraged European settlement until, in 1632, some hardy English farmers arrived from St. Kitts, claimed the island for the English crown, and planted crops of tobacco, indigo and ginger. The island remained under British rule for the next three and a half centuries, apart from a brief occupation by the French in 1666.

In 1674, Sir Christopher Codrington arrived from Barbados and, with an army of slaves, established the island's first large sugar plantation, naming it Betty's Hope for his daughter. The plantation's success encouraged others and within 25 years the island's landscape was transformed. Its natural vegetation was cleared to grow sugar cane, and more than 150 sugar mills dotted the countryside. The slave laborers plotted an insurrection in 1736 but the slave trade didn't end until 1808, followed by the abolition of slavery in 1834. The boom market in sugar collapsed but, despite the demise of plantation estates on Antigua, the production of sugar remained the island's major industry well into the 20th century, until surpassed by tourism.

Antigua, the neighboring island of Barbuda and the tiny uninhabited island of Redonda, 20 miles to the west, gained their partial independence from Great Britain in 1967 and have been independent since 1981. The islands' population of 64,000 is mostly of African origin with a small community of Europeans, Americans and Canadians living here. English is the official language.

St. John's is the capital and although this historic trading port has been ravaged by earthquakes, hurricanes and fires over the centuries, its colonial past endures in the British street names and restored harborfront warehouses. Rising above the narrow streets and hip-roofed build-

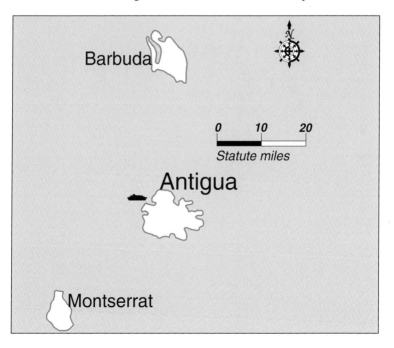

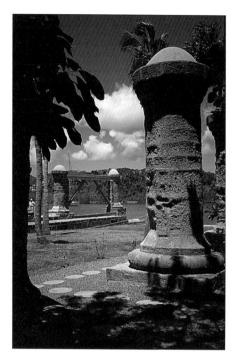

The sail loft pillars remain intact at Nelson's Dockyard.

ings are the twin spires of St. John's Cathedral – easily visible as your ship pulls into port and docks at the town's doorstep.

Lord Nelson

Horatio Nelson, Britain's celebrated naval hero, was a man of great leadership abilities who inspired devotion and exceptional service in his men. Yet, while serving his only peacetime commission in the West Indies from 1784 to 1787, the young captain was anything but popular with the merchants of Antigua. As leader of the Leeward Islands Squadron, Nelson strictly enforced the Navigation Act which prevented trade with American ships. This enraged the local merchants who threatened legal action over lost business. Nelson, to avoid arrest, confined himself to his ship for eight weeks, which was no great sacrifice for he regarded the island as 'barbarous' and the dockyard that today bears his name as 'vile'. In fact, he always slept aboard his ship while in English Harbour – a common practice among naval officers of the day who wished to avoid the mosquito-carried diseases of yellow fever and malaria.

A plantation owner on the nearby island of Nevis posted Nelson's bail, and when he went ashore at Nevis to thank his benefactor, Nelson met his future wife, a young widow named Fanny Nesbit. At their wedding in 1787, the bride was given away by Nelson's friend and fellow naval captain, Prince William Henry, who eventually became England's King William IV. As for Nelson, he returned to England with his wife and stepson, and pursued a brilliant naval career that ended with his historic victory at the Battle of Trafalgar in 1805. His marriage to Fanny came undone when he fell in love with Lady Emma Hamilton in 1798, but the notoriety of this liaison did not tarnish his reputation with the British public and his legendary status endures to this day.

Getting Around

Cruise passengers step ashore at Heritage Quay, a duty-free shopping complex where a tourist information booth and public telephones are located. The post office is beside Heritage Quay on High Street.

Taxi fares are regulated but you should agree on the price in advance. Sample fares (for the whole taxi in US$) from Heritage Quay:

Dickenson Bay $8

Deep Bay/Ramada Renaissance $10

Hawksbill Beach Resort $14

English Harbour $16-$20

Local car rental agencies include Avis and Budget. Driving is on the left side of the road and a temporary licence ($12 US) is required. Many of the roads are unmarked, unpaved and in need of repairs.

The shore excursions organized by the cruise lines usually include an island drive to Shirley Heights and Nelson's Dockyard, a Jolly Roger Pirate Cruise along the northwest coast, and a catamaran cruise featuring a stop at a secluded beach for snorkeling, swimming and sunbathing.

Official currency is the Eastern Caribbean (EC) dollar which is tied to the U.S. dollar at approximately $2.70 EC to $1 US (or $1 EC to 40¢ US), but American currency is accepted everywhere.

SHOPPING: Batik island cotton, hand-painted clothing and tropical jewelry are among the Caribbean keepsakes sold on Antigua. Duty-free shopping is available at **Heritage Quay** with its dozens of international and local stores, and at adjacent **Redcliffe Quay** where the 19th-century warehouses have been carefully restored and transformed into a shopping district with inviting boutiques and courtyard cafes. More shops are located on **St. Mary's Street**, including Caribelle Batik, and on High and Long Streets. A colorful produce market is located at the junction of Valley and All Saints Roads and is a good place to buy some local pineapple – highly touted for its delicious sweetness.

Out-of-town shopping opportunities include The **Art Center** at Nelson's Dockyard which features the island's largest collection of local art. Local handicrafts are also sold at Dow's Hill Interpretation Center and Shirley Heights Lookout. **Harmony Hall**, on the east side of the island, is a complex built around an old sugar mill which houses an art gallery featuring works by local artists. At **Sea View Farm**, a traditional pottery-making village in the middle of the island, residents still make and sell pinched pots from the local clay.

BEACHES: Antiguans claim their island has 365 beaches – one for every day of the year. Watersports equipment and lounge chairs can be rented at most of the beach-front resorts, many of which are located along the island's northwest coast.

Dickenson Bay, at the northwest end, is the island's most popular beach with its resort facilities, dive shop and glass-bottom boat tours. **Deep Bay**, due west of St. John's and the location of a Ramada Renaissance resort, is also popular with cruise visitors. Directly south of Deep Bay the beaches become progressively quieter. **Galley Bay** is good for windsurfing and **Hawksbill Beach Resort** is located adjacent to four beach-lined coves, the southernmost one used by nude sunbathers.

Secluded and beautiful beaches lie south of St. John's, such as **Darkwood Beach,** popular with locals on the weekend but usually quiet during the week, and **Carlisle Bay** where an exclusive resort hotel stands atop Curtain Bluff at one end of this inviting stretch of sand.

On the Atlantic side, **Half Moon Bay** is considered by many Antiguans to be their most beautiful beach with its circular shape and ocean surf that can range from crashing waves to gentle swells. **Long Bay Beach**, also on the Atlantic side, is just around the point from Devil's Bridge, one of the island's most impressive natural attractions where waves shatter onto an eroded arch of limestone.

SNORKEL & DIVE SITES: Barrier reefs surround much of the island and wrecks are plentiful, including three in **Deep Bay**, with the *Andes* lying just off the beach in 20 feet. Most dives are fairly shallow, to about 60 feet, except off **Shirley Heights** where depths surpass 100 feet. **Cades Reef**, off the southwest coast, is a popular dive site and an underwater park. Dive shops are located around the island and include those at Dickenson Bay, Nelson's Dockyard and Club Antigua on Lignumvitae Bay.

GOLF: The 18-hole course at The Cedar Valley Golf Club (462-0161), just a few minutes from St. John's, is a 6100-yard, par-70 course

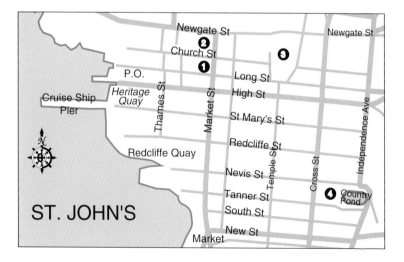

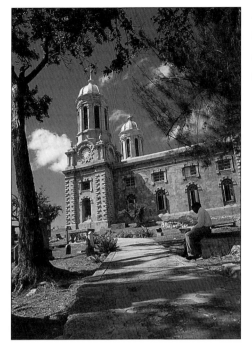

In St. John's, the twin baroque spires of the Anglican Cathedral are a town landmark.

where the Antigua Open is played each March. The 9-hole course at Half Moon Bay (460-4300) has lovely sea views.

LOCAL SIGHTS: The **(1) Museum of Antigua and Barbuda** is housed in the Old Court House, Antigua's oldest building, which was built in 1747 from stone quarried on some of Antigua's satellite islands. The museum is located at the corner of Long and Market Streets, and contains hands-on exhibits designed with children in mind, including a life-sized Arawak house. Nearby is the **(2) Police Station**, built in 1772 with a fence railing made from musket barrels, some with bayonets still attached.

The twin baroque spires of the **(3) Anglican Cathedral of St. John the Divine** stand 70 feet high and are a town landmark. The third church built on this site, it is made of freestone with an interior encased in pitch pine to protect the structure from ruin during an earthquake or hurricane. The first church was built here in 1681 and the second one was destroyed by an earthquake in 1843. Five years later the present structure was completed and locals refer to it as 'big church'. The pillars of the south gate are topped with white-painted figures representing St. John the Divine and St. John the Baptist, and are said to have been taken from a French ship.

The **(4) Country Pond**, at the top of Tanner Street, was constructed in the mid-1700s by early settlers. Its name is likely a corruption of

St. Mary's Street, in the heart of downtown St. John's, runs past Heritage Quay on its way up the hillside from the cruise pier.

'Congo Pond' because this and other ponds on the island were built by contract workers from the Congo. Its purpose was to collect water during heavy rainfalls, with the overflow running into a drainage ditch that divides Tanner Street and runs down to the waterfront. During prolonged droughts, as the Pond's water level dropped, it could be accessed by steps built along its western wall.

Area Attractions

(5) Nelson's Dockyard at English Harbour is the premier attraction on Antigua. The island's first national park, this 18th-century naval dockyard maintained a continuous squadron of British ships in the Caribbean and contains beautiful examples of Georgian architecture which now house a museum, two inns, boutiques, restaurants, several businesses and a major marina. Established at its present site in 1743, the dockyard came under the command of Nelson from 1784 to 1787. Its historic buildings include the Admiral's House, which now houses a museum; The Copper and Lumber Store (now a hotel and restaurant); the Engineer's Office (now the Admiral's Inn Hotel & Restaurant); the Officer's Quarters Building where officers lived during the hurricane season (now housing an art gallery, craft shop and other businesses); and the site of the Capstan House, where the walls no longer remain but the capstans used to careen the ships have been restored. Also intact are the Boat House Pillars that once supported a sail loft and the 200-year-old Sandbox Tree which stands beside the Admiral's House. The dockyard, closed by the Royal Navy in 1889, was reconstructed in the 1950s and officially reopened in 1961. Many of the businesses operating here now serve the local sailing community, a reflection of the dockyard's original function.

Situated on a ridge overlooking English Harbour, **(6) Dow's Hill Interpretation Center** is an educational complex in which visitors can watch a 15-minute light and sound show, imaginatively presented and depicting six different periods of Antigua's history.

(7) Clarence House, the official country residence of the island's Governor General, was built in 1787 as a residence for Prince William Henry while stationed in Antigua as a captain of the Royal Navy. This Georgian country house overlooks Nelson's Dockyard and, following the Prince's departure, was used as a residence for senior naval officers.

(8) Shirley Heights, a fortified ridge of hills above the town of English Harbour, is one of the most famous views in the Caribbean. With its panoramic perspective of the harbour and surrounding bays, it was the principal lookout for enemy ships approaching English Harbour and is today a popular photo opportunity for visitors. Its restaurant facilities and refreshing breezes make it the ideal spot for a regular Sunday barbeque popular with both locals and tourists, and featuring plenty of music and festivities. The heights are named after one of the island's early governors, Sir Thomas Shirley.

The Dow's Hill Interpretation Center includes a viewing platform overlooking English Harbour.

*English Harbour, location of Nelson's Dockyard, is one of the most
sheltered anchorages in the Caribbean.*

Natural attractions on Antigua include **Boggy Peak**, the island's
highest point at 1,360 feet, and **Fig Tree Drive** – four miles of hilly
road that winds from Carlisle Bay to Liberta past groves of fruit trees.
These include the mango, coconut and fig, which is the Antiguan name
for banana. At the east end of Fig Tree Drive is eye-catching **(9)
Tyrells Catholic Church**, made of pink coral, and south of here, on the
way to English Harbour, is the town of **Liberta** which was one of the
first to be settled by freed slaves.

At the northeast end of Antigua at Indian Town Point stands a natural limestone arch called **(10) Devil's Bridge**. Carved by the sea, this
rock formation is a dramatic sight when a surf is running.

(11) Betty's Hope, located southwest of Devil's Bridge, is a recently restored historical site. The original sugar plantation was founded
here in the mid-1600s and its cotton house storeroom has been converted into a small museum. One of its twin windmills has been restored to
a fully operational wind-powered sugar mill.

Barbuda

Barbuda is a flat coral island lying 30 miles north of Antigua.
Dominated by a large lagoon on its western side where watersports are
enjoyed, the island's handful of resorts are located on the south coast
where beautiful pink coral beaches lie between Palmetto Point and
Coco Point. The Martello Tower, not far from Palmetto Point, is 56 feet
tall with a view of almost the entire island.

The Frigate Bird Sanctuary, in the northwest area of the island, is a breeding ground for various indigenous species, including thousands of frigate birds that nest here in the tops of mangrove bushes.

Montserrat

The green and mountainous island of Montserrat, named by Columbus and claimed by the British, is also a wee bit Irish. With a shamrock for its official logo and place names such as Galway and Cork Hill, the island's Irish heritage is very much apparent. Under Cromwell's rule in the18th century, Irish Catholics were forced from their homeland and some of them arrived at Montserrat, the Caribbean's 'emerald isle'. The island, with only 11,000 inhabitants, is peaceful, friendly and uncommercialized. Hidden coves lie at the base of steep mountains, their rivers and streams flowing through dense rainforests to grassy lowlands once covered with sugarcane plantations.

The island's main town of Portsmouth contains Georgian houses, a colonial-style post office and an 18th-century courthouse. Government House, a Victorian mansion set in lovely gardens, is south of the town. The ruins of Fort St. Georges provide a spectacular view of Plymouth and the sea. Montserrat also has a number of stone churches, but it's the natural attractions that make this island special. These include Chances Peak (the island's highest point at 3,000 feet), Great Alps Falls, the bubbling hot springs and steam vents at Galways Soufriere, and the nature trail at Bamboo Forest with views across White River Valley. The island also has a bird sanctuary at Fox's Bay and a 9-hole golf course. Most of its beaches are of dark volcanic sand while the island's most beautiful white sand beach is found at secluded Rendezvous Bay.

Photo Michael DeFrietas

Government House, Montserrat

Photo Michael DeFreitas

(Top) Gosier, Guadeloupe.

(Middle) Pastry shops and
sidewalk cafes line the
streets of Pointe-a-Pitre and
Fort-de-France.

(Bottom) Pointe-a-Pitre's
tourism office is housed in a
colonial building overlooking Victory Square.

(Top) Schoelcher Library, Fort-de-France.

(Middle) A cruise ship docks at Fort-de-France's downtown pier.

(Bottom) St. Pierre on Martinique, with Mount Pelee rising above the town.

Photo Windstar Cruises / Harvey Lloyd

(Top) Tobago Cays, Grenadines.

(Middle) The Sisserou Express travels the roads of Dominica in support of forest conservation.

(Bottom) Marigot Bay, St. Lucia.

*(Top) St. George's,
Grenada*

*(Left) The Penha building
in Willemstad, Curacao.*

*(Right) Harrison's Cave,
Barbados*

(Bottom) Crane Bay, Barbados

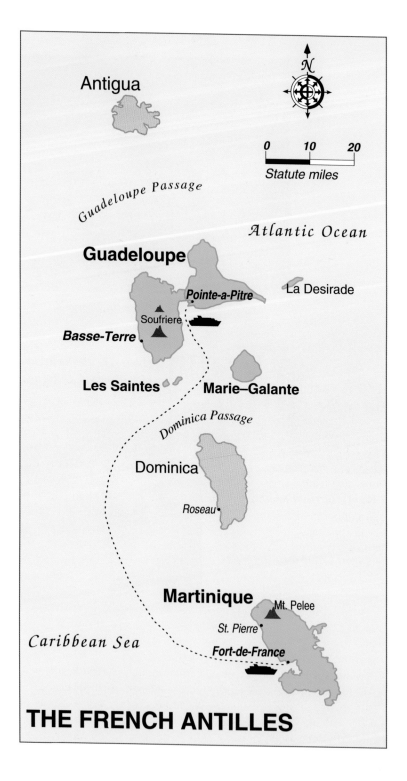

THE FRENCH ANTILLES

CHAPTER THIRTEEN

GUADELOUPE & MARTINIQUE

The French Antilles

Guadeloupe and Martinique, the major islands of the French West Indies, have a great deal in common besides active volcanoes, lush rainforests and beautiful beaches. Former colonies of France, they both became *departements* in 1946 and are now full-fledged *regions* with representation in the French government. These islanders, as citizens of France, can exercise their right to fine wines and fresh pastries while retaining customs of their African and East Indian ancestors. The result is a vibrant Creole culture, and one that visitors can experience firsthand on the crowded streets of Fort-de-France and Pointe-a-Pitre, where Parisian-style shops stand next to public markets selling piles of papayas and breadfruit. Here the aroma of freshly baked baguettes mixes with the pungent spices used in Creole cooking, and boutiques featuring imported porcelain and crystal compete with street vendors selling hand-painted wood carvings.

Roman Catholicism is the dominant religion and a *joie de vivre* prevails. The graceful Creole women combine their taste for bright colors with French sophistication, and even the children are stylishly dressed. Busy as the port towns are with their traffic-clogged streets and narrow sidewalks, the main squares are an oasis from the heat and bustle, with lawns that sweep past historic monuments and palm-shaded benches.

English-speaking visitors are encouraged to try a few words of French with the locals who, when conversing with each other, speak a Creole dialect based on West African grammatical structures and

*(Left) Court of Justice,
Fort-de-France,
Martinique*

*(Below) Centre St. John
Perse, Pointe-a-Pitre,
Guadeloupe*

French vocabulary. A smile and a gesture are often all that's needed to communicate, especially if you're interested in purchasing something, and most shopkeepers can speak at least a smattering of English.

The economies of Guadeloupe and Martinique are based on food exports – bananas, pineapple, sugar and rum – and tourism is steadily increasing, but unemployment is widespread and there is a heavy reliance on subsidies from France. Funds used to flow the other way when these islands were major sugar producers and prized colonies of France.

The French connection began in 1635, when settlers from France landed on the two islands. Those arriving at Guadeloupe spent the next five years repelling attacks by the resident Caribs, while those on Martinique built Fort Saint-Pierre on its west coast. For 20 years they shared the island with the local Caribs before driving them away. Within a century both islands were covered with sugar plantations which employed tens of thousands of African slaves. Meanwhile, the French repelled attacks by the British who eventually conquered Guadeloupe during the Seven Years War and held it for four years. This change of ownership did not, however, slow sugar production, and about 25,000 more slaves were imported and additional windmills were built under British occupation. In 1763, a bargain was struck with the Treaty of Paris in which Britain returned Guadeloupe to the French in exchange for Canada.

This allocation of New World colonies was short lived, for the American War of Independence began in 1776. Continued fighting ensued between the British and the pro-revolutionary French, including a famous naval battle off Les Saintes in 1782 in which a fleet of French warships was defeated by the British under Admiral Rodney. Turmoil continued with the outbreak of the French Revolution and the subsequent abolishment of slavery by the new Convention. A mini-French Revolution was staged on Guadeloupe when Victor Hugues, commissaire of the Convention, arrived from France in 1794 and, after defeating the British, proceeded to guillotine the local plantation owners. This action made their counterparts on Martinique understandably nervous and they welcomed British occupation of their island until 1802, when it was returned to France under the Treaty of Amiens. At this point, slavery was reinstated in the French West Indies by Napoleon Bonaparte whose Creole wife, Josephine, was born on Martinique.

Nelson's annihilation of Napoleon's fleet at the Battle of Trafalgar in 1805 all but eliminated the French West Indian planters' lifeline to France. There was also, in keeping with the romantic spirit of the French, a hero by the name of Victor Schoelcher – son of a Parisian porcelain merchant – who campaigned for 15 years to free the slaves of the French West Indies. When the French Republic was proclaimed in Paris in 1848, Schoelcher drafted a decree that freed the 160,000 slaves of Guadeloupe and Martinique. Following the emancipation of slavery, contract workers from India took up the slack, but the era of plantation prosperity had ended. France's sugar islands, for two centuries a prolific source of 'white gold', were now bastions of black freedom.

GUADELOUPE

Guadeloupe consists of two main islands – Basse-Terre and Grande-Terre (separated by a narrow saltwater channel) – and the smaller islands of Marie-Galante, Les Saintes and La Desirade. As an overseas department of France, the administrative region of Guadeloupe also includes the distant dependencies of St. Barthelemy and St. Martin.

Named by Columbus in 1493 for a monastery in Spain, Guadeloupe is shaped like a butterfly with outstretched wings. Its western island (the left wing of the butterfly), is mountainous and volcanic in origin, while the eastern island (the right wing) is chalky and flat.

Basse-Terre, situated on the island of the same name, is the capital of Guadeloupe, and **Pointe-A-Pitre** on Grande-Terre is the major port

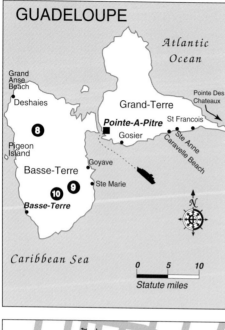

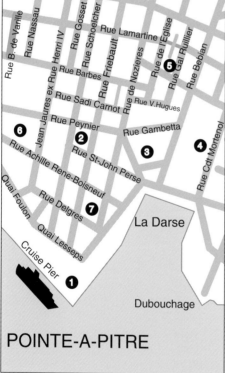

and commercial hub, its modern cruise facility located right downtown.

Adjacent to the cruise pier is the **(1) Centre St. John Perse**, an air-conditioned complex designed in the French West Indies style. Here you will find a number of shops and restaurants as well as a currency exchange, car rental agency and public telephones.

Getting Around

Most taxi drivers can speak English and are eager for business. The one-way fares (in US dollars) from Pointe-a-Pitre to the beaches east of town are, per vehicle (holding one to four persons): $20 to Gossier; $30 to Caravelle Beach; and $50 to St. Francois. A two-hour tour to Ste. Rose or Vernou is $20 per person, and a 3-hour tour to the Carbet Falls, based on four to six persons per vehicle, is $30 each. Guadeloupe has a network of modern highways and its car rental companies include Avis, Budget, Hertz and Thrifty. Ship-organized excursions often include a tour of Basse-Terre to view its lush rainforest and mountain waterfalls.

BEACHES: The most accessible of Guadeloupe's beaches lie east of Pointe-a-Pitre. Closest is **Gosier**, where many of the island's resorts are situated along a white sand beach. Watersports equipment, change facilities and beach chairs are available to non-guests for a small fee.

Caravelle Beach, outside Sainte-Anne, is the island's longest stretch of powdery white sand and, protected by reefs, is ideal for snorkeling. Watersports equipment can be rented at the Club Med. The **Raisins-Clairs Beach** at Saint-Francois is another lovely beach where sail boards and other watersports equipment can be rented at the Meridien Hotel. **Pointe Des Chateaux**, at the island's eastern tip, is a rugged section of coastline with wave-pounded boulders and beaches, including Beach of Tarare which attracts skinny dippers.

On **Basse-Terre**, many of the beaches have dark sand. One of its best beaches is **La Plage de Grande-Anse** – a stretch of golden sand near Deshaies on the northwest coast.

SNORKEL & DIVE SITES: Pigeon Island, off the west coast of Basse-Terre, has been described by Jacques Cousteau as "one of the world's 10 best diving spots." Glass-bottom boats and snorkeling trips can be taken to the underwater reserve at Pigeon Island from Malendure Beach. The snorkeling is also good at **Caravelle Beach** on Grande-Terre's south coast.

GOLF: An 18-hole golf course, designed by Robert Trent-Jones, is located at the Meridien St. Francois. At 6,755 yards with a par-71, the course is fairly challenging.

SHOPPING: 'Made in France' luxury items are good buys, sold at French domestic prices, and these include scarves, perfume, porcelain, crystal and liquor. Foreigners are entitled to a 20% discount on purchases made with traveller's cheques or a major credit card.

In **Pointe-a-Pitre**, the shops are concentrated at **Centre St. John Perse**, and on the main shopping streets of **Rue Frebault**, **Rue Schoelcher** and **Rue de Nozieres**. For local wares, the **(2) public market** on Rue Frebault features hand-painted wood carvings, jewelry and spices. In **Basse-Terre**, the principal shopping streets are rue Maurice Marie-Claire, rue du Cours Nolivos and rue du Docteur Cabre. An outdoor market is located on Boulevard du General de Gaulle opposite the Conseil General.

LOCAL SIGHTS: Pointe-a-Pitre was named for a Dutch fisherman and was first developed by the British in 1759, when they held Guadeloupe during the Seven Years War. The town was damaged by an earthquake in 1843, followed by a fire in 1899. Hurricanes have also wreaked devastation, the most recent being David and Frederick in 1979.

A number of attractions are in the vicinity of the cruise port, and a walk along the waterfront will take you past a bustling produce market to the **(3) Tourism Office** which is housed in a colonnaded colonial building overlooking the old harbor (*La Darse*) and **(4) Place de la Victoire** – an expansive square lined on three sides with French colonial architecture and shaded with flamboyant trees and other tropical vegetation. Commemorating Victor Hugues's 1794 defeat of the British, this square is where he guillotined the island's aristocracy. Today the square is an inviting place to linger and visit one of the sidewalk cafes tucked beneath the brightly colored awnings on Rue Bebian.

A block west of Rue Bebian is the **(5) Cathedral of St. Pierre and St. Paul**, built in 1847. Fresh flowers of the tropical variety are sold at a stand in front of the church.

The **(6) Schoelcher Museum** on rue Peynier is housed in a beautiful colonial building, its rose-colored facade decorated with relief stonework and ornate ironwork. Inside are exhibits dedicated to Victor Schoelcher, a key figure in the movement to abolish slavery.

The **(7) St. John Perse Museum**, a colonial-style house on Rue de Nozieres, is dedicated to the great poet and diplomat who was born Alexis Saint-Leger Leger in Guadeloupe in 1887. He served in France's foreign office and, as an opponent of Nazi appeasement, he became one of Europe's foremost diplomats. His reputation grew as a poet following his self-imposed exile to the U.S. in 1940. Using the pseudonym St. John Perse, he was awarded the Nobel Prize in Literature in 1960.

Isles des Saintes, off Guadeloupe, contain spectacular mountain-bounded anchorages and beach-lined coves.

Photo Windstar Cruises / Harvey Lloyd

ISLAND ATTRACTIONS: Some of Guadeloupe's most scenic attractions are on the island of **Basse-Terre**. These include the **(8) National Park** which covers 74,000 acres of rainforest and includes 186 miles of trails. To the south is **(9) Carbet Waterfalls**, its three separate cascades spilling 400 feet. The **(10) Soufriere** volcano, surrounded by rainforest and banana plantations, is still active, with puffs of steam rising from its summit.

Basse-Terre is Guadeloupe's secondary cruise port, its historic architecture including the Cathedral of our Lady of Guadeloupe, the Conseil General, Palais de Justice and the Prefecture. Nearby is massive Fort Louis Delgres, dating back to 1650 and the site of numerous battles between the French and British.

Iles des Saintes, a cluster of islands off Guadeloupe's south coast, is a port of call for the smaller cruise ships. They often anchor in the spectacular harbor of Terre-de-Haute where a village of the same name is nestled at the base of a mountain, its streets of gingerbread houses easily explored on foot. A bus or taxi ride away is Fort Napoleon with its barracks, drawbridge, art gallery and exotic garden. Nearby are underwater grottoes, coral beds and numerous beach-lined coves.

MARTINIQUE

Martinique – beautiful, sophisticated and slightly snobbish – has long been a flower in the lapel of France. The Caribs originally called her *Madinina* – 'Island of Flowers' – and Columbus, who first laid eyes on Martinique in 1493, was so moved by her beauty when he came ashore in 1502, he described the island as "the most fertile, most delightful and most charming land in the world." But it was the French who eventually conquered Martinique and established the island's first capital of St-Pierre located on the west coast..

Called the 'Paris of the West Indies', the town's 30,000 residents were so enamoured by their surroundings they ignored warning signs that the nearby volcano – Mount Pelee – was about to erupt. The local wildlife evacuated the area before the town was smothered in ash and stones on the morning of May 8, 1902. Only one person survived; he was inside a prison cell at the time, the walls of which protected him from the hail of ash and burning gases. As the sole survivor of this catastrophic explosion, he became a sideshow with Barnum's Circus, complete with a replica of his prison cell.

Following the destruction of St-Pierre, the island's new capital became Fort-de-France, where about a third of Martinique's 360,000 residents now live. Often compared to the French Quarter of New Orleans with its narrow streets and iron grille balconies, Fort-de-France is a fascinating port to explore on foot.

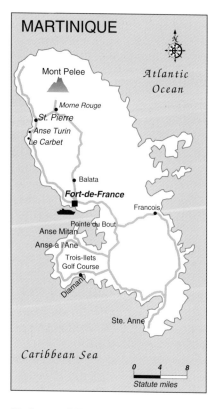

MARTINIQUE

Atlantic Ocean

Mont Pelee

Morne Rouge
St. Pierre
Anse Turin
Le Carbet

Balata

Fort-de-France

Francois

Pointe du Bout
Anse Mitan
Anse à l'Ane
Trois-Ilets
Golf Course
Diamant

Ste. Anne

Caribbean Sea

0   4   8
Statute miles

Getting Around

For passengers disembarking at the pier east of downtown, it's a 15- to 20-minute walk or an $8.00 (US) cab ride into town. Passengers disembarking at the western pier are a 5-minute walk from the main shopping streets and attractions. The round-trip ferry ride from the Fort-de-France waterfront to the beaches at Pointe du Bout is about $6.00.

Unless you're fluent in French, you may want to tour the island with an organized shore excursion. The roads here are good, although steep and winding, and driving is on the right, so renting a car is an option if you're not intimidated by the French road signs and speedy drivers. Local rental agencies include Avis, Budget and Hertz, and the average daily cost is $60. Taxis can be hired beside the cruise piers, along the downtown waterfront and beside Savannah Park. Many of the drivers speak basic English but they tend to strike a hard bargain, so indicate on a map exactly where you want to go, the stops you would like to make along the way, and write down the price agreed upon so there is no misunderstanding and renewed bargaining at the end of the tour. A round trip from Fort-de-France to St. Pierre with a half-dozen stops, including Morne-Rouge and Balata, costs about $100 (based on one to four persons sharing a taxi).

The cruise line shore excursions usually feature tours to St. Pierre, Balata and a butterfly farm, with opportunities to see the abundant flora of a tropical rainforest. Boat excursions include a catamaran cruise to a beach-lined cove and an opportunity to view a coral reef along the way.

Tourist Information is provided at various locations, including the cruise piers. A post office is at Rue de la Liberte and Rue Blenac.

BEACHES: A 20-minute ferry ride from Fort-de-France provides access to some excellent beaches. The blue ferry goes to **Plage Pointe du Bout** where a there's a marina and luxury resorts. The red ferry goes to **Plage Anse Mitan**, a public beach of white sand with superb snorkeling, and to quieter **Plage Anse a l'Ane**, with picnic tables and a hotel/bar nearby. Either ferry costs about $6, return trip. More beautiful beaches lie along the island's south coast at **Diamant** and near **St. Anne** (about 30 miles from Fort-de-France), but reaching these beaches entails an expensive cab ride.

SNORKEL & DIVE SITES: There are good reefs for snorkeling around **Pointe du Bout** and off **Anse Mitan**. Two dive operations are located at Pointe du Bout.

GOLF: The Golf Country Club is located one mile south of Pointe du Bout near the birthplace of Empress Josephine. A par-71 course designed by Robert Trent-Jones, its rolling hills offer scenic sea views.

SHOPPING: Best buys are in French-made luxury items, including perfume, jewelry, designer fashions, cosmetics, leather goods, watches, crystal, china and porcelain, with savings as high as 40% thanks in part to the 20% tax refund available to foreigners who pay by credit card or traveller's cheque. Local items of note include rum, fruit-flavored liqueurs and jams, wickerwork and handicrafts of bamboo, shell and madras cotton. Rue Victor Hugo is a major shopping street, with more shops located in the blocks between it and Rue Victor Severe. A produce market is located at the corner of Rue Isambert and Rue Blenac, and there's a handicraft market at the Park de La Savane.

LOCAL SIGHTS: Originally a parade ground, **(1) Place de La Savane** (Savannah Park) is 12 acres of lawns, stately palms and statues. It contains a children's playground and is a lively place during Carnival. A bronze statue of Pierre Belain D'Esnambuc (who led the first party of settlers to Martinique) faces the ferry pier, and a white

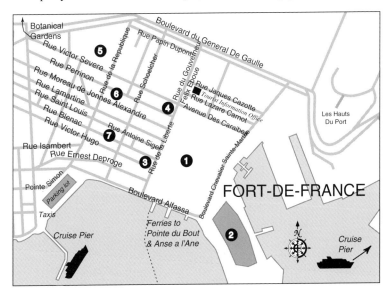

Old City Hall, Fort-de-France. In 1964, General De Gaulle delivered a speech from its balcony.

marble statue of Empress Josephine, a gift from Napoleon III in 1859, stands near the park's northwest corner. The statue was beheaded in 1991 as a rather gruesome reminder that native-born Josephine, of Creole ancestry, was the Emperor's consort when he restored slavery in the French West Indies a decade after the Republic had abolished it.

The construction of **(2) Fort Saint-Louis** took three centuries to complete, starting in the 1600s. Standing on a point of land overlooking the harbor, it is surrounded on three sides by water.

The **(3) Museum of Archaeology** is located beside Savannah Park and its exhibits of pre-Columbian art include pottery and ceramic pieces that date back 1,700 years.

Designed by the 19th-century architect Henri Pick (a contemporary of Gustave Eiffel), the **(4) Schoelcher Library** was shipped in pieces from France and completed in 1893. Restored between 1980 and 1982, this magnificent multi-colored chrome structure with a Byzantine glasswork dome is registered as a historical monument of France. It's named for Victor Schoelcher, humanitarian, writer and book collector, who believed that freedom for slaves would be in vain without their receiving an education, and so donated his own library of 9,000 volumes to Martinique in 1883 to provide free access to knowledge. These books were destroyed in the huge fire of 1890, but Schoelcher's good intentions survive in the library now bearing his name.

The Prefecture (police station) on Rue Victor Severe (facing the library) is the former Government House and beside it is a colonial-style villa now housing an exhibition gallery. A few blocks down the street is the **(5) Old City Hall**, now a theatre, built in 1912. French President Charles De Gaulle gave a speech from its balcony in 1964.

Nearby is the **(6) Court of Justice**, built between 1906 and 1907 when iron and glass were widely used. A statue of Victor Schoelcher stands out front in a garden setting of greenery and benches. Three blocks over is the **(7) Saint-Louis Cathedral**, inaugurated in 1895 and designed by Henri Pick to resist fire, hurricanes and earthquakes.

ISLAND ATTRACTIONS: A few miles north of Fort-de-France, at Balata, is the **Sacred Heart Basilica**, an exact but smaller replica of Montmartre Basilica in Paris. It was built in 1915 to accommodate the influx of worshippers to the Fort-de-France area following the eruption of Mount Pelee in 1902. The **Balata Tropical & Botanical Park** features plants and flowers from around the world and offers breathtaking views of Fort-de-France and the peaks of Carbet.

The inland route between Fort-de-France and St. Pierre winds past volcanic peaks and verdant rainforests. **Le Morne Rouge**, a pleasant resort town at the north end of this scenic drive, provides good views of Mount Pelee, as does **St. Pierre**, where a museum recalls that fateful day in 1902 when the mountain looming to the north brought death and destruction to this coastal community. South of St. Pierre along the coast is **Anse Turin**, where the French painter Paul Gauguin lived in 1887, and **Le Carbet**, where Columbus is believed to have landed.

South of Fort-de-France, near Les Trois Ilets, is the **Pagerie Museum**, a stone house commemorating the birthplace of the Empress Josephine, born in 1763 as Marie Josephe Rose Tascher de La Pageriein. Her first husband was guillotined during the French Revolution, in 1794, but she escaped with a brief imprisonment, and in 1796 she married Napoleon Bonaparte. In 1804, as consort of Napoleon I, she became the Empress of France and her two children by her first marriage became titled heads of Europe. However, her union with Napoleon produced no heir and he had the marriage annulled in 1809 so he could marry the daughter of the Austrian emperor. Josephine, who had played a prominent role in the French court's social life, lived in retirement until her death in 1814.

The church at Balata is a smaller version of Montmartre Basilica in Paris.

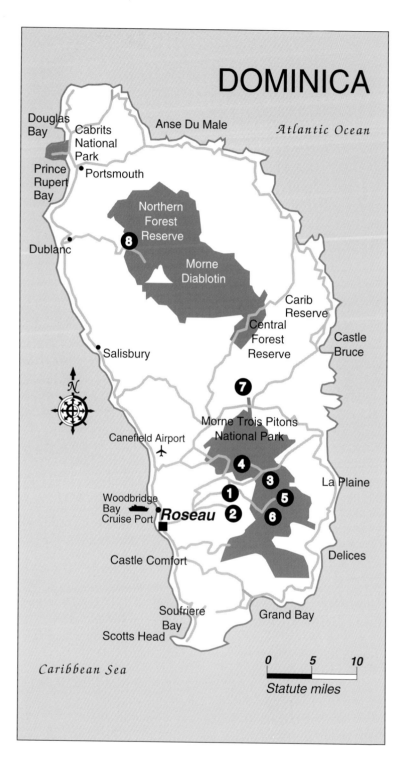

CHAPTER FOURTEEN

DOMINICA & ST. LUCIA

The 'South Seas' Islands

D ominica and St. Lucia are two of the largest Windward Islands, and it's a toss up which is more ruggedly beautiful. Both consist of volcanic peaks, dense tropical forests and fertile valleys filled with banana plantations. Each were coveted by the British and French who battled one another, and the local Caribs, for ownership. Neither nation fully succeeded, for the mountainous interiors of these islands discouraged colonization and provided cover for resisting Caribs and runaway slaves.

About 3,000 descendants of the early Caribs now live on a 3,700-acre territory of Dominica, their final enclave in a region they once dominated. The inhabitants of both islands are today mostly of African descent and, although both islands entered the 20th century as British colonies with English the official language, the unofficial culture is French. The common language is a Creole dialect like that used on Martinique and Guadeloupe, the dominant religion is Roman Catholic and the place names are frequently French. Still, the surname of many an islander reflects a British past, as does their love of cricket.

It's the natural beauty of these two islands, however, that most encourages comparison, their similar vegetation including plants and animals that are South or Central American in origin. Each island is a naturalist's dream with towering mountains, verdant valleys, rushing rivers and cascading waterfalls. The people who live on these lush islands are among the friendliest in the Caribbean and they proudly welcome visitors to their islands of untamed beauty.

DOMINICA

Pronounced Dom-in-*eek*-a, this island of 74,000 inhabitants was named by Columbus when he sailed past on a Sunday in 1493. One of the least spoilt of the West Indies, Dominica rightly calls itself the 'Nature Island of the Caribbean'. Large areas of virgin forest remain more or less intact, and are now protected within parks and reserves. Dominica has 20 major rivers and two freshwater lakes, both located in the National Park, and the government is committed to protecting this precious watershed. Water is currently shipped to St. Maarten, and bulk water could become a chief export. Meanwhile, bananas are a major export, as well as citrus fruits and coconut oil.

The island was badly hit by Hurricanes David and Frederick in 1979, with David causing 37 deaths and leaving 80% of the population homeless. The island's social history has also been stormy. The Caribs refused to give up their island without a fight and, in 1748, the British and French, both thwarted in their attempts at conquest, agreed to leave the island to its warlike inhabitants. But neither power could resist trying to conquer this fertile island, and France finally ceded it to Britain, but not before burning the capital of Roseau. The Commonwealth of Dominica gained independence from Britain in 1978, and its first election was held in 1980.

Dominica's unspoiled forests contain pristine trails and cascading waterfalls, such as those at Trafalgar Falls.

A Dominican man sells flowers at the parking lot near Trafalgar Falls.

Getting Around

Roseau, located at the mouth of the Roseau River on Dominica's southwest coast, is the island's capital and chief port, with a population of approximately 20,000. The Woodbridge Bay Deep Water Harbor is about a mile north of the town center, and a shuttle runs between the two locations and to nearby beaches. A Tourist Information Office at the cruise pier provides general information and prices for visitors looking to hire a taxi/tour operator.

Dominica's other cruise ship pier at Prince Rupert Bay, near Portsmouth, was inaugurated in 1992 and is unique in that passengers disembark directly into a national park. The terminal building has displays and presentations to introduce passengers to the area's attractions.

Local taxi drivers are friendly, informed guides and their hourly sightseeing rate is about $20 US per hour. Some sample fares from the Woodbridge pier: Botanical Gardens – $2; Trafalgar Falls – $15 per person round trip; and Morne Trois Piton National Park – $20 per person round trip.

Several car rental firms operate on Dominica, including Avis and Budget. Driving is on the left side of the road and a local driver's permit is required at a cost of EC $50 (approx $20 US).

Ship-organized shore excursions often feature island drives to the Botanical Gardens, Morne Bruce, Trafalgar Falls and the Emerald Pool.

Longer tours take in the Northern Forest Reserve and the Carib Territory, terminating at Cabrits National Park where passengers are picked up by the ship. Passengers interested in an extensive hike should make arrangements ahead of time for a local guide.

BEACHES: Most of Dominica's beaches consist of dark to silver-grey volcanic sand, although a few are honey-colored. Two of the best, both of which are golden brown in color, are found at Prince Rupert Bay, just north of Portsmouth, and at nearby Douglas Bay.

DIVE & SNORKEL SITES: Coral reefs lie within Cabrits National Park, along its northern shores, and at the south end of Dominica off Scotts Head which is the location of the Scotts Head/Soufriere Bay Marine Reserve. A half-dozen dive operators are located on Dominica, including two in Portsmouth, two in Castle Comfort (just south of Roseau) and one at Soufriere.

SHOPPING: Local handicrafts are sold at both cruise piers. Items to look for include straw crafts, pottery, hand-painted candles, wood carvings, handmade cigars and coconut-oil-based soaps, as well as unique Carib crafts such as tri-color baskets woven of larouma reeds.

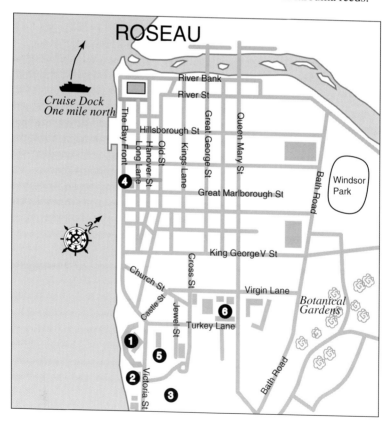

Authentic Carib weave baskets and hats are sold throughout the Carib Reserve and at various shops in Roseau, including Tropicrafts at the corner of Queen Mary Street and Turkey Lane. Cotton House Batiks at 8 Kings Lane sells original hand-painted clothing, as does the Artwear Gallery at 54 King George Street. The NDF Small Business Complex at 9 Great Marlborough Street houses a collection of craft shops selling batiks, jewelry and other handcrafted items. Local currency is the EC Dollar (approximately EC$2.70 per US$1).

LOCAL SIGHTS: The historic buildings in downtown **Roseau** are clustered near the harborfront on Victoria Street, including the 18th-century **(1) Fort Young** (now a hotel) and a number of Georgian-style buildings: the **(2) Public Library, (3) Government House** and the **(4) Court House.** Also in the vicinity is **(5) St. George's Church**, a 19th-century Anglican church, and the **(6) Cathedral of Our Lady of Fair Haven,** the island's principal Roman Catholic church.

The town's main attraction is the **Botanical Gardens**, 40 acres of landscaped gardens nestled at the base of Morne Bruce hill on land once cultivated with sugar cane. The planning and planting of the Gardens began in 1890, and the many exotic and indigenous trees and shrubs that grow here are identified with a tab number or letter to which visitors can refer on a written guide. Also located here is the Aviary – a breeding facility for Dominica's endangered parrots, namely the Jaco and the Sisserou (Dominica's national bird). The Gardens were once a popular cricket ground and have been visited twice by Queen Elizabeth. Sometimes seen parked at the Botanical Gardens is the **Sisserou Express**, a bus painted with tropical flora and fauna that travels the roads of Dominica to raise local awareness of conservation issues. Equipped with video recorder, t.v. monitor and other visual aids, its exhibits are used to further environmental education among the island's pre-school children. A look-out at the top of **Morne Bruce** provides panoramic views of Roseau and the coastline.

Island Attractions (see map – page 290)

(1) Trafalgar Falls, not far from Roseau, can be reached by a steep winding road that terminates within a 15-minute walk to the base of the falls. A path, lined with ferns and mosses, leads from the parking lot to Trafalgar Falls, which consists of two major falls where visitors can bathe in rocky pools. Plants in the area include nutmeg, coffee, cocoa and banana, and the songbirds that can be heard include the Mountain Whistler. The **(2) Wotten Waven Sulphur Springs** are located across the valley from Trafalgar Falls.

Morne Trois Pitons National Park, named for a three-peaked mountain within the park, was established in 1975, its 16,000 acres of steep volcanic landscape filled with natural wonders. Water from **(3)**

Freshwater Lake feeds the Trafalgar Falls which flow into the Roseau River, and a hydro power plant is being developed to provide island-wide electricity. A trail, which takes about three-quarters of an hour to hike, leads from Freshwater Lake to **(4) Boeri Lake** – a crater 3,000 feet above sea level which is filled with fresh water. In the other direction is **(5) Boiling Lake**, the largest of its kind in the world. It's cupped in a volcanic crater, the heat of which keeps the water bubbling.

Nearby, on the flanks of Morne Watt, is the **(6) Valley of Desolation** – a barren landscape where smoking fumaroles and boiling sulphur springs indicate there are heated rocks lying just below the surface. The sights include pools of grey, bubbling mud and multi-colored streams, their water containing minerals from old volcanic activity.

The **(7) Emerald Pool**, at the north end of the park, is a grotto filled with water that is brilliant green in color and fed by a waterfall. This Garden of Eden setting, with its profusion of plants, flowers and ferns, is an easy 10-minute walk through woodlands from the main road.

The 22,000-acre **Northern Forest Reserve** contains Dominica's highest peak – Morne Diablotin – which rises to 4,747 feet. The reserve's vegetation runs the gamut of a mountain ecosystem, with secondary and rain forests at lower levels, a montane (mist) forest at higher altitudes, and an elfin woodland near the summit.

A tract of land bordering the northwest side of the reserve, often referred to as the **(8) 'Parrot Preserve'**, is a habitat for the indigenous and endangered Sisserou and Jaco Parrots. The **Syndicate Nature Trail**, less than a mile long and easy to walk, loops through the Parrot Preserve's stand of mature rain forest, where orchids and bromeliads grow. The bird life here, in addition to parrots, includes blue-headed hummingbirds and broad-winged hawks.

The **Carib Reserve** is situated on the northeast side of the island, where about 3,000 descendants of the Caribbean's original inhabitants engage in farming, fishing and their traditional basket making and canoe building.

Portsmouth's Attractions

Dominica's second town, Portsmouth is situated on a natural harbor backed by mountains. It contains sheltered Prince Rupert Bay, originally home to the Caribs and a port of call for Spanish conquistadors heading to the South American mainland. Beautiful beaches are found at Prince Rupert Bay and at nearby Douglas Bay.

Cabrits National Park is situated on a forested peninsula at the north end of Portsmouth Harbor. The park contains two peaks which can reached by hiking trails, and the restored ruins of historic Fort Shirley stand on the hillsides. The park's extensive marine area offers good snorkeling among corals and tropical fish.

Rowboat rides are available on the **Indian River** which winds past mangroves south of Portsmouth.

ST. LUCIA

Saint Lucia (pronounced Loo-sha) is the Caribbean's poster island. Gracing many a brochure (and the cover of this book) is its famous landmark, the Pitons – twin volcanic peaks rising from the water's edge. Conical in shape and lushly vegetated, they are evocative of the South Pacific. St. Lucia also has a 'drive-in volcano', and its National Rain Forest, home to the jacquot (St. Lucia's parrot), is a tropical paradise of wild orchids and giant ferns.

It's believed Columbus's navigator, Juan de la Cosa, was the first European to discover St. Lucia in 1499. When the British first attempted to colonize the island, it was inhabited by Caribs with whom the British signed a treaty in 1660. This situation was short lived, for the French West India Company took control of the island in 1667. This too was short lived, and from 1674 to 1814 the French and the British fought over possession of St. Lucia, the island changing hands no less than 14 times.

Since 1979 St. Lucia has been an independent country within the British Commomwealth, and its population of about 153,00 enjoys a stable parliamentary democracy. This tiny country is the birthplace of two Nobel Laureates – the late Sir W. Arthur Lewis (Nobel Prize in Economics in 1979) and the poet Derek Walcott who won the 1992 Nobel Prize in Literature.

A cruise ship pulls into Soufriere Bay, where St. Lucia's famous Pitons form a dramatic backdrop.

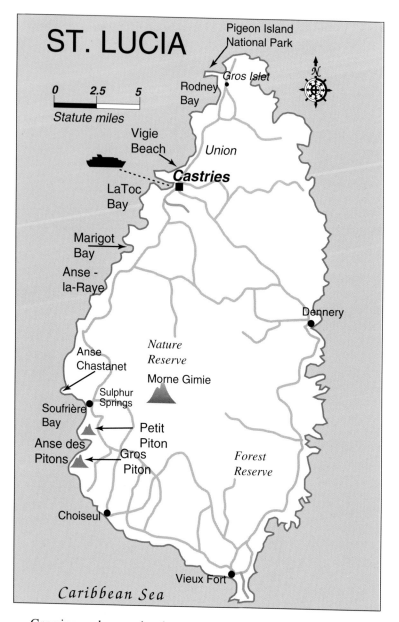

Growing and exporting bananas and other tropical produce is a major industry in St. Lucia. An oil refinery and trans-shipment facilities are also located here, near the capital of Castries on the northwest coast. Castries, named for a French colonial minister, is the island's main cruise port. The Elizabeth II dock is right downtown at the commercial docks, and another pier is located at Pointe Seraphine, which is where the St. Lucia Tourist Board office is located. AT&T telephones are also located here and on Jeremie Street in downtown Castries.

Getting Around

The roads on St. Lucia are steep and winding, with many a hairpin turn, so booking a ship-organized shore excursion or hiring a taxi are the best ways to see the island. The Courtesy Taxi Co-Operative Society operates at the waterfront and its drivers are capable, courteous guides. They charge government-set rates for standard trips, and island tours (1-4 persons) are $20 (US) per hour. Some sample fares are:

From Elizabeth II Dock
Bagshaw Studio – $6; Pigeon Island – $16; Marigot Bay – $16

From Pointe Seraphine
Bagshaw Studio – $10; Caribelle Batik – $12; Pigeon Island (return) – $34; Marigot Bay – $20; Vigie Beach Hotel – $5.

A water taxi ($1 each way) travels between the Castries cruise pier and Pointe Seraphine. The cab fare between these two points is $4.00.

Ship-organized shore excursions often include a scenic drive to Marigot Bay. A longer tour to the Sulpher Springs and Diamond Falls usually terminates at Soufriere where passengers are returned to their ship which pulls into Soufriere Bay to retrieve them. Other popular excursions are a plantation visit, and a helicopter ride down the west coast for aerial views of the Pitons, plantations and craggy coastline.

BEACHES: North of Castries is the main resort area where excellent beaches include **Vigie Beach** (1-1/2 miles from Castries) and **Reduit Beach** on Rodney Bay where watersports equipment and bar facilities are available. South of Castries, a fine beach lies on **La Toc Bay,** where a Sandals resort is located.

DIVE & SNORKEL SITES: Diving off the island's west side is good except when river run-off decreases visibility following a heavy rainfall. A **Marine National Park** is located off Anse Chastanet near Soufriere Bay where a beach-entry dive or snorkeling excursion can be made to an underwater shelf that drops from 10 to 60 feet. Another good dive site is off **Anse Des Pitons** (below the Petit Piton) where a wall of coral drops to 200 feet. Dive operations are located at Vigie Marina, Marigot Bay and Anse Chastanet.

GOLF: There are two nine-hole courses on St. Lucia – one at Sandals St. Lucia on La Toc Bay, the other at Cap Estate Golf Club on the northwest end of the island.

SHOPPING: For duty-free shopping, visit the new harborfront shopping complex at Pointe Seraphine, where the selection of shops includes an outlet of Bagshaw's famous tropical clothing which is locally made of high-quality, hand-printed cotton. Bagshaw Studios is located at La Toc Bay, just north of the Sandals resort. Caribelle Batik,

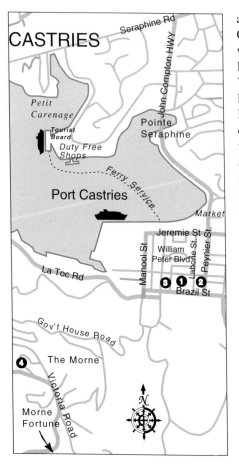

another famous name in Caribbean clothing, has a workshop and store at Howelton House, a Victorian Caribbean house located on Old Victoria Road, the Morne. Local crafts, such as baskets, wood carvings and pottery, are sold inside the public market at the head of the harbor. Official currency is the Eastern Caribbean dollar (EC$2.70 to US$1.00) but American dollars are widely accepted.

LOCAL SIGHTS: There is limited colonial architecture in Castries due to a 1948 fire that destroyed most of the town's wooden buildings. **(1) Derek Walcott Square** (formerly Columbus Square) is where a 400-year-old samaan tree stands in front of the **(2) Cathedral of the Immaculate Conception**, built in 1897. On the other side of the square, on Bourbon Street, is the colonial-style **(3) Central Library**. The wooden buildings lining Brazil Street on the square's south side were among the few to survive the last fire. They were built in the 19th century in the French fashion with gabled roofs and second-floor fretwork balconies overhanging the sidewalk. **(4) Government House** is situated west of the downtown, along Government House Road which snakes up a hillside called The Morne.

Island Attractions

Overlooking Castries is **Morne Fortune** (Hill of Good Luck), a key battleground during skirmishes between the English and the French. North of Castries, a short distance inland from Choc Bay, is the **Union** nature trail, interpretive center and small zoo with a pair of St. Lucian parrots. Near the island's northern tip is **Pigeon Island National Park**, the spectacular open-air setting for St. Lucia's annual Jazz Festival held in May. Visitors can wander among the ruins of Fort Rodney, or enjoy the beaches. Owned by the National Trust, the park's museum is housed in the former Officers Mess. Local history includes stories of the French pirate Francois Leclerc (call Jamb de Bois because of his wooden leg) who used a large cave on the north shore as a hideout. Britain's Admiral Rodney set sail from here in 1782 to defeat the French fleet off Guadeloupe in the famous Battle of Les Saintes.

South of Castries lies the lush, mountainous scenery so often associated with St. Lucia, including valleys filled with banana plantations and **Morne Gimie**, the island's highest peak at 3,117 feet. Beautiful **Marigot Bay** is where a British fleet once ambushed the French by camouflaging its ships with palm fronds. Today a fleet of pleasure yachts uses this sheltered bay as a base. Some scenes from the film *Dr. Doolittle*, starring Rex Harrison, were filmed at this idyllic location. South of here is the quiet fishing village of Anse-la-Ray.

Soufriere is St. Lucia's oldest town, established by the French in 1746. It lies at the base of the spectacular Pitons on the shores of Soufriere Bay. The town, with its old wooden buildings, colorful murals and a marketplace, is an authentic West Indian community. Nearby is **La Soufriere**, a dormant volcano which was about eight miles in diameter until it collapsed about 40,000 years ago. Entry is made on foot along the crater's west rim, and guides take visitors on a steamy tour of the active **Sulphur Springs** with its bubbling pools of ash. Also in this area are the **Diamond Falls** and **Mineral Baths**, originally developed by France's King Louis XVI when he had bathhouses built here for his troops. Today visitors can shower in the natural falls and soak in the mineral-rich baths.

Marigot Bay, where a British fleet once camouflaged its ships with palm fronds, is today an idyllic spot.

Photo Windstar Cruises / Gerald Brimacombe

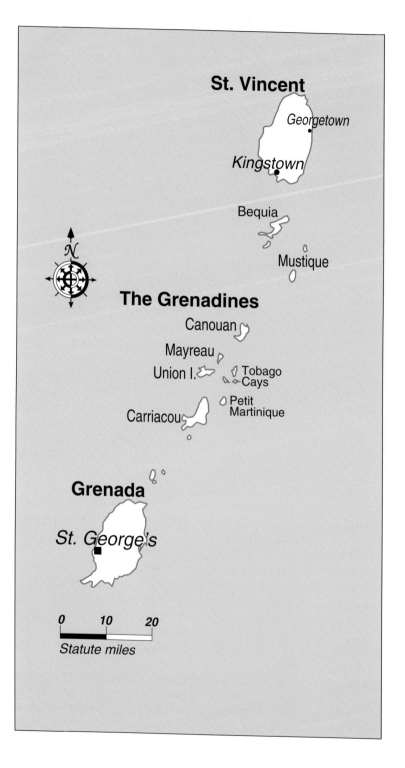

St. Vincent

Georgetown

Kingstown

Bequia

Mustique

N

The Grenadines

Canouan

Mayreau

Union I.

Tobago
Cays

Petit
Martinique

Carriacou

Grenada

St. George's

0   10   20

Statute miles

CHAPTER FIFTEEN

GRENADA

The Spice Island

Should you step on deck one evening while your ship plies the waters of the Southern Caribbean, you may detect the sweet scent of nutmeg being carried by the warm breezes. The aroma of spices – cloves, cinnamon, ginger – is often detected when passing Grenada, the Caribbean's Spice Island. A third of the world's supply of nutmeg is grown and processed here, the ripened pericarps picked from sweet-smelling evergreen trees that were introduced to the island more than 200 years ago by a French sea captain.

Many exotic plants were brought to the West Indies during the era of European colonization, including the breadfruit tree which Captain Bligh went to great lengths to collect in Tahiti and transport to St. Vincent. The plants and trees that thrive on Grenada (pronounced Gra-nay-da) and St. Vincent come in all varieties, from flowering to medicinal. Residents grow most of their own fruits and vegetables, and it has been said that even a nail would grow in the rich soil of St. Vincent. Rugged and fertile, St. Vincent and Grenada lie at either end of the Grenadines, a string of beach-ringed isles frequented by yachts and small sailing ships. Most of this island chain belongs to St. Vincent, while the southern islands of Carriacou (pronounced Carry-coo), and Petit Martinique come under Grenada's jurisdiction.

European settlement of Grenada began in 1650 with the French purchasing some land from the resident Caribs in return for knives and baubles. The Caribs soon had a change of heart however and their

Photo Fred Jensen

Ground nutmeg is made from the inner seed of the nutmeg fruit, and mace is made from the seed covering.

rebellion was swiftly put down. When defeat was all but certain, the remaining Caribs – men, women and children – threw themselves over a cliff now called Le Morne de Sauteur (Leaper's Hill). With that enemy exterminated, the French then had to fend off the British who seized control of the island in 1762. The French regained Grenada in 1779 but a few years later, under the terms of the Treaty of Versailles, the island was once again Britain's.

The next violent clash was caused by mounting tensions between British settlers and the French planters who remained on Grenada. A free colored Grenadian named Fedon, who owned a large coffee and cocoa estate called Belvedere in the mountains north of St. George's, plotted an uprising inspired by the French Revolution's principles of liberty and equality. His estate became Camp Belvedere as the insurrection swept across the island and rebelling slaves set fire to crops and buildings. The British governor was taken prisoner and executed. For a time, the entire island was under a siege of terror during which British settlers found safety in fortified St. George's, the island's only stronghold until reinforcements arrived and eventually quashed the rebellion. As British troops closed in on Camp Belvedere, mountain warfare ensued with specially-trained troops silently climbing under cover of darkness to the insurgents' armed camp which they attacked at dawn. Fedon and his men fled but all were eventually captured, except for Fedon who, it's believed, escaped by small boat only to drown at sea.

Following emancipation in the mid-1800s, the island became a British Crown Colony and in 1974 it gained independence as a full member of the Commonwealth of Nations. This was followed by a bloodless coup in 1979 and the establishment of the People's Revolutionary Government under radical leftist Prime Minister Maurice Bishop. His close ties to Cuba and the U.S.S.R. strained relations with the U.S. and other Caribbean nations, and Grenada was once again gripped by turmoil when, during an internal coup in 1983, the army seized control. Prime Minister Bishop, ten of his cabinet colleagues and an undetermined number of civilians were executed.

Within weeks the U.S., at the request of other Caribbean nations, invaded the island and quickly restored law and order. The U.S. military, which received the overwhelming support of the Grenadian population, also rescued some American medical students who had been stranded on the island during the coup. A general election in late 1984 re-established democratic government but the island's tourist trade suffered a serious blow from which it is still recovering.

The island capital is St. George's and its inner harbor, called The Carenage, is considered one of the prettiest in the Caribbean. Its historic harborfront warehouses are brightly painted, casting mirror images on the water where fishing boats and schooners moor alongside the seawall, their lines tied to bollards made from cannons. The town's cobblestone streets and walkways are lined with old churches and brick-and-stone warehouses, some roofed with red tiles brought as ballast by trading ships.

A hilltop view of St. George's with a ship moored in its harbor, called the Carenage, and another lying at anchor in St. George's Bay.

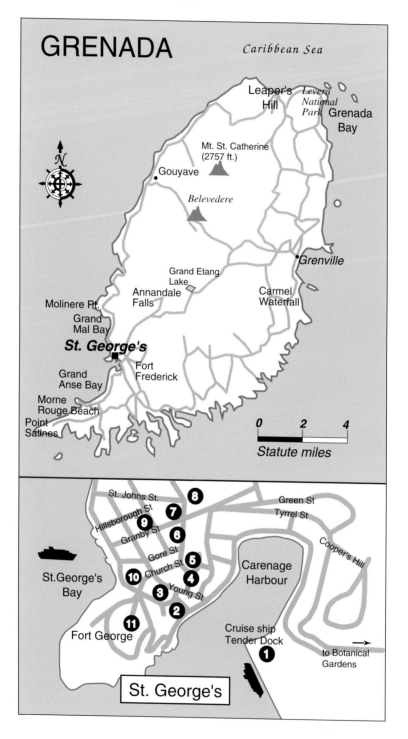

GRENADA

Caribbean Sea

Leaper's Hill

Levera National Park

Grenada Bay

Mt. St. Catherine (2757 ft.)

Gouyave

Belevedere

Grand Etang Lake

Annandale Falls

Molinere Pt.

Grand Mal Bay

St. George's

Fort Frederick

Grand Anse Bay

Morne Rouge Beach

Point Salines

Grenville

Carmel Waterfall

0   2   4

Statute miles

St. Johns St.

Hillsborough St

Granby St

Gore St

Church St

Young St

Green St

Tyrrel St

Cooper's Hill

Carenage Harbour

St.George's Bay

Fort George

Cruise ship Tender Dock

to Botanical Gardens

St. George's

Most cruise ships anchor in St. George's Bay and tender passengers ashore to the water taxi dock in the Carenage where a Tourist Information Center is conveniently located for disembarking passengers. A cruise ship pier is located just south of the water taxi dock.

Getting Around

English is the official language of Grenada, its population about 91,000, but a French-African patois is still used around the island, and many of the place names are in French.

The official currency is Eastern Caribbean (EC) dollar (approximately $2.70 EC to $1.00 US) but American currency and travellers cheques are widely accepted.

Card-operated phones are located at Grenada Telecommunications on the Carenage, and the card and coin phone booths located throughout the city are on the international direct dial system. A **(1) Board of Tourism** office is located at the pier on the Carenage, and a post office is located just to the east.

Rental car firms operating on Grenada include Avis (Spice Isle Rentals) on Lagoon Road. Driving is on the left and a local driving permit ($30 EC) can be obtained through most rental companies or at the Fire Station on the Carenage. Some of the roads on Grenada are in need of repair and are quite rough and bumpy in places.

Photo Fred Jensen

Market Square, where local buses depart, is situated amid the Georgian buildings, colonial churches and brick warehouses of old St. George's.

Local buses depart from Market Square and the Esplanade, the traditional ones painted bright colors with wooden seats. They cost between $1 EC and $5 EC (or 37¢ US up to $1.85 US), depending on the distance travelled.

Taxis holding one to four persons can be hired for $15 US per hour. Sample fares (in U.S. dollars) from the cruise pier to: downtown St. George's – $3; Botanical Gardens – $3; and Grand Anse Beach – $7. Water taxi fares are: Carenage to Grand Anse Beach – $2; across the harbor – $1.

Ship-organized excursions often include the 'Royal Drive' which traces the tour given to Queen Elizabeth on an official visit. This tour takes in Fort Frederick, the Morne Jaloux Ridge, the south coast and Grand Anse Beach. Another popular drive is the one to Grand Etang National Park and Annandale Falls. Boat excursions often include a catamaran cruise with a beach stop.

BEACHES: Just south of St. George's is **Grand Anse Bay** with two miles of beautiful white sand. World Wide Watersports in Grand Anse rents a wide variety of equipment and also has change facilities, as does the Flamboyant Hotel. The Ramada Renaissance Hotel and Coyaba Beach Resort are also located at Grand Anse.

At the north end of the island, at **Levera National Park**, is beautiful Bathway Beach, protected from the Atlantic surf by a reef barrier.

DIVE & SNORKEL SITES: Grenada has plenty of reefs and wrecks to satisfy snorkelers, novice divers and advanced divers, and a number of dive operations are located at Grand Anse Beach. **Morne Rouge Beach**, beside Grand Anse Beach, is popular with snorkelers.

An extensive reef lies south of Morne Rouge off **Point Salines**, its three main dive sites being The Hole, which starts in sand bars and descends 50 feet; the Valley of Whales, which contains hills of coral and canyon floors of sand; and Forests of Dean, where rays and octopus are often sighted. Snorkelers can explore the reef close to shore and gear can be rented at the Aquarium Beach Club, located on a quiet beach below Point Salines.

Molinere Reef, starting at 20 feet, is a good spot for snorkelers and novice divers. Other dive sites include wall dives at Grand Mal Point and Dragon Bay; Channel Reef at the entrance to St. George's Harbor; and numerous wrecks, including the *Bianca C* – a cruise ship that caught fire in 1961 and which, after all the passengers were evacuated, was sunk in 167 feet of water.

GOLF: The nine-hole course at that Grenada Golf & Country Club, near Grand Anse, is open to visitors and has scenic ocean views of both the Caribbean and Atlantic.

SHOPPING & DINING: The Spice Market is located near the pier on the Carenage and is a good place to buy gift baskets filled with spices. Other local items to look for on Grenada include batik, wood carvings, pottery and rum, as well as jams and jellies made from nutmeg and guava.

The Carenage is where a number of stores are located, selling Caribbean crafts and duty-free perfumes, china and crystal. A number of restaurants serving Caribbean cuisine are also located on the Carenage including the popular Nutmeg Restaurant & Bar.

Another good place for both duty-free goods and Caribbean handicrafts, including dolls, clothing and jewelry, is The Grand Anse Shopping Center.

LOCAL SIGHTS: A walking tour of St. George's

The Spice Market sells attractive gift items which are locally made.

will take you past many historical buildings, including the **(2) National Library** which has been at its present waterfront location, housed in a former warehouse, since 1892.

The **(3) National Museum**, housed in a brick warehouse built by the French in 1704, contains pre-Columbian exhibits including petroglyphs, and its gift shop carries books on the local history. Beside the museum is the Antilles Hotel, one of the oldest buildings in St. George's which was once a French barracks.

(4) Simmons Alley, a stepped pedestrian walkway, leads up to **(5) St. George's Anglican Church**, built by the British in 1825 using stone and pink stucco.

The residential **(6) Sedan Porches** were originally built open at each end so that people riding in sedan chairs could disembark without getting wet from the rain. The **(7) Houses of Parliament** and its neighboring Registry, built in 1780, are good examples of early Georgian architecture.

The town's **(8) Roman Catholic Cathedral** stands high on the hillside with an unobstructed view down St. Johns Street to the water. Local produce is sold at colorful **(9) Market Square** which is also the site of parades and political rallies.

(10) St. Andrew's Presbyterian Kirk, often called the Scot's Kirk, stands at the bottom of Church Street and was built in 1831 with help from the Freemasons.

(11) Fort George, at the entrance to St. George's Harbor, was built by the French in 1705, with later additions by the British. Its ramparts provide commanding views of the Carenage, and within its walls are tunnels, staircases and narrow passageways. Grenada's former leftist Prime Minister Maurice Bishop was executed inside this fort, which is currently used as headquarters of the Royal Grenada Police.

Island Attractions

The restored remains of **Fort Frederick** stand on the tallest point of a ridge overlooking St. George's, providing visitors with panoramic views of the coast and surrounding countryside. Built by the British around 1791 to protect the rear flank of St. George's from attack, it is the central fort in a chain of defence along Richmond Hill which included Fort Matthew to the north and two other fortifications to the south, said to be connected by tunnels.

The **Annandale Falls** cascade into a freshwater pool surrounded by tropical gardens and paths. Swimming and refreshments can be enjoyed here.

Grand Etang National Park is located in the central, mountainous part of the island, its centerpiece a crater lake surrounded by 2,000-foot mountain peaks. An Information Center provides audiovisual presentations on the flora and fauna of the park's tropical rain forest.

Carmel Waterfall, the island's highest at 75 feet, was recently developed. A walking trail with hand rails, botanical labels and benches leads to this once-hidden waterfall.

Grenada's spice plantations are concentrated at the north end of the island and a nutmeg processing station is located outside **Gouyave** on the northwest coast.

The 1994 opening of **Levera National Park**, on the rugged northeast coast, increased the island's protected area to 13% of its total land mass. Levera's pristine beaches and mangrove swamps provide habitat for sea turtles and a variety of birds. The islands of the Grenadines can be seen on the horizon, the two southernmost – Carriacou and Petit Martinique – forming a tri-island nation with Grenada.

ST. VINCENT & THE GRENADINES

Affectionately known as the Garden Island, St. Vincent is covered in tropical forests and has a thriving agricultural economy. Dominating the island's landscape is the 4,000-feet-high, still-smoldering *La Soufrière* volcano which last erupted in 1979. Over the centuries *La*

Soufriäre has blanketed the island with nutrient-rich ash which, combined with 80 inches of rainfall a year plus a hot tropical sun, creates fertile growing conditions. The main crop, bananas, is exported to Europe while other produce like sweet potatoes, yams and plantains are exported to neighboring islands.

The island's rugged topography and remote location has kept it off mainstream tourist routes. The small airstrip limits the annual flow of visitors and the lack of a site suitable for a larger one, coupled with a local desire to move into tourism slowly, ensure that St. Vincent will retain its antique charm for years to come. As a result of this low-key approach to tourism, the largest of the island's seven hotels has only 31 rooms.

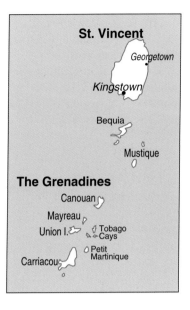

Legend has it that the original Carib inhabitants called St. Vincent *Hairoun* or 'Land of the Blessed' and most of the forested interior remains much like it was when Columbus sighted the island on January 22, 1493 – the feast day of the Spanish patron saint St. Vincent. For almost 200 years the island remained untouched by outsiders until 1675 when a Dutch slave ship foundered off the rugged east coast and the survivors, mostly slaves, were taken in by the Caribs. Over time, ex-slaves and indigenous people (Yellow Caribs) blended into a race known as the Black Caribs.

The British claimed the island in 1680, in a regional dispute with the French, but it was the French who established the first European settlement in 1719 at Barrouallie, on the leeward coast. The British, under Captain Braithwaite, attacked the settlement in 1723 but were defeated by a combined force of French and Carib fighters. Over the next 60 years, the island changed hands a dozen times until the Treaty of Versailles in 1782 officially ceded it to the British. St. Vincent remained under British rule until gaining independence in 1979.

In 1765, while under British rule, the noted botanist Dr. George Young established the first Botanical Gardens in the Western Hemisphere in the hills outside the island's capital, Kingstown. The Gardens were used to propagate herbs and medicinal plants, and as a quarantine area for plants exported to Kew Gardens in England. The highlight of Dr. Young's tenure occurred on January 23, 1793, when

Photo Michael DeFreitas

St. Vincent's Leeward Coast – where rugged slopes and fertile valleys run down to a tranquil Caribbean Sea.

Captain Bligh, returning to England from the South Pacific on the *H.M.S. Providence*, made landfall in Kingstown to unload 530 bread-fruit trees for the colonists. A sucker from one of those original bread-fruit trees still grows in the Gardens.

Other reminders of St. Vincent's colonial past are visible in and around Kingstown. Visitors to the island will find a number of well pre-served historical sites including the Court House, Government House, the Anglican and Roman Catholic Cathedrals (all circa 1820) as well as two forts: Fort Charlotte and Fort Duvernette (circa 1800). Remnants of a more distant past can be seen in the small archaeological museum in the Botanical Gardens which houses one of the best collections of pre-Columbian artifacts (Carib and pre-Carib) in the Caribbean.

The abolition of slavery in 1838 triggered an influx of immigrants from India, Portugal and the Middle East, further stirring the melting pot of cultures and races on the island. By the late 1800s the races had assimilated and today's cosmopolitan population of 100,000 is virtually free of racial strife. This racial mix has nurtured the second-largest Carnival celebration in the Caribbean, after Trinidad's renowned gala, and this takes place the first week of July.

Stretching south from St. Vincent, in a 60-mile arc, are the **Grenadines** – tiny islands ringed with white-sand beaches and coral reefs. Because of their small size and limited rainfall, the Grenadines remained uninhabited until the early 1800s when a band of French colonists established cotton plantations on two of them. **Bequia**, is the largest of the group (five miles long by two miles wide), with a population of 6,000. Its name is from the Carib word *becouya* – Island in the Clouds. The island became a busy whaling station in the mid-1800s when some seafaring Scots settled here. Port Elizabeth, in Admiralty Bay, is the center of island life and the nearby beaches can be reached by water taxi.

One of the oldest Catholic churches in the Windward Islands still stands on the tiny islet of **Mayreau**, situated about midway in the chain. Built around 1804 by the St. Heliers family from France, the church still functions as a Sunday gathering place for most of the island's 100 inhabitants.

The small, hilly island of **Mustique** was developed by international investors in the 1970s and is run as a private company, with each shareholder owning a piece of paradise. Princess Margaret and Mick Jagger are among the island's homeowners, who rent out their hillside villas when they're not there.

The four, deserted islets of **Tobago Cays**, surrounded by the huge Horseshoe Reef, have been declared a wildlife reserve. The brilliant white beaches and surrounding seas in shades of blue ranging from indigo to aquamarine, make this cluster of islands a tropical paradise for visitors arriving by sailing vessel.

Near the southern end of the chain is **Union Island**, with a population of 2,000. For decades it has been the port of entry for yachts plying the quiet waters of St. Vincent and the Grenadines, earning it the nickname 'Gateway to the Grenadines'.

Sandy Island off Carriacou, southern Grenadines.

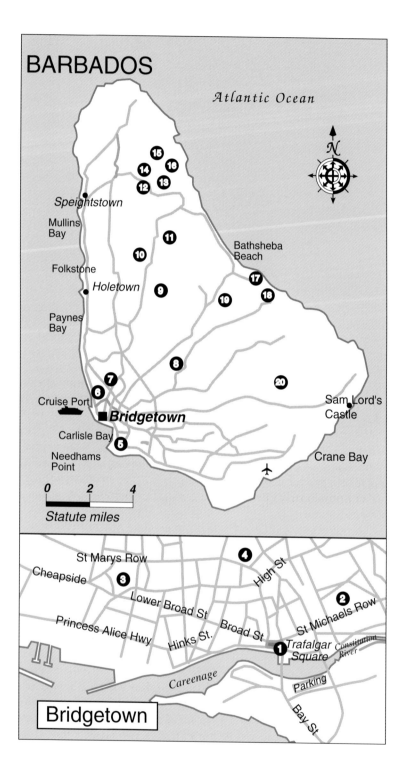

Chapter Sixteen

BARBADOS

Little England of the Caribbean

Barbados is perhaps the most British of the Caribbean islands. For more than three centuries the island was under continuous British rule, and its parliament, formed in 1639, is the third oldest in the English-speaking world (after Britain and Bermuda). An independent member of the British Commonwealth of Nations since 1966, Barbados is a stable democracy with a thriving economy and an impressive health care record. Cricket is the national sport, and the capital of Bridgetown has its own Trafalgar Square complete with Nelson's Column.

The similarities to Olde England continue outside of Bridgetown, where a drive along narrow winding roads, past village greens and cricket fields, is a step back in time to the days of the British Empire when wealthy plantation owners lived in Georgian-style great houses built of coral stone, their thick walls a barrier to the tropical heat and brutality of slave labor.

There were no permanent inhabitants on Barbados when the first English ship visited its western shores in 1625. Lying 100 miles east of the volcanic arc of Windward Islands, Barbados was at one time inhabited by Arawaks but the island escaped detection by migrating Caribs and, later, by Columbus. A coral island of ridges and hills, it began to form quite recently, geographically speaking. About 700,000 years ago, tectonic forces slowly pushed a section of seabed to the surface where this emerging coral cap was then fractured by two massive upheavals

The Morgan Lewis Mill, built in the 1700s to grind sugarcane, was one of hundreds that used to dot the countryside when Barbados was a prosperous plantation island.

which left a ridge running down the island's west side and a 600-foot-cliff on the east coast. The clay and soil deposits lying on this uplifted coral were the result of silt build-up from the Orinoco River in what is now Venezuela; the volcanic dust responsible for the soil's fertility was carried in the stratosphere over thousands of centuries from the islands of St. Vincent and St. Lucia.

The island remained in isolation, visited mostly by birds. The seeds left in their droppings and the coconuts that washed up on beaches were the source of vegetation which slowly took root, including the Bearded Fig Tree for which the island was named *Isla de los Barbados* (Island of the Bearded) by a passing Portuguese explorer in the early 16th century. When British settlers arrived in 1627 and established Jamestown near present-day Holetown, they initially planted tobacco, then switched to sugar cane. African slaves were brought in to work the fields when indentured servants began avoiding Barbados, partly because its planters had a reputation as cruel masters who paid meager freedom dues, but mainly because it was a white man's graveyard.

Europeans had no immunity to tropical diseases, several of which were brought over by the Africans, and the majority of white settlers perished within their first year on the island. Those who survived, how-ever, became extremely wealthy and Barbados dominated the sugar markets in England until the latter part of the 17th century. The island's easterly location (i.e. closer to England) and a coastline that was easily accessible from any point on the island, kept transport costs lower than on other islands. The island's location also helped preserve its British status, for the prevailing winds prevented enemy sailing ships from approaching the island's west side without tacking to and fro, making it difficult to stage a surprise attack.

The relative isolation of Barbados no doubt contributed to the independent streak of its early settlers. They resisted rule by outsiders, and this included Oliver Cromwell when he became Lord Protector of England. In defiance of Britain's Navigation Acts, Barbadians continued trading with Dutch shipping companies which gave them better prices and service, and Cromwell had to send a fleet to "subdue the barbarous Barbadians." The blockade lasted several months, the stubborn Barbadians refusing to allow any of the English naval officers to land. Eventually a meeting took place in 'Ye Mermaid Tavern' and the articles of surrender gave the islanders a protected market for their sugar in England, even after the monarchy was restored.

Barbados continued shipping sugar almost to the end of the 18th century, and the island's plantation era endures in the many historic mansions which have been preserved through the efforts of Barbados National Trust, founded in 1961 by an expatriate Briton and a group of interested Barbadians. The miniature counterpart to the colonial great house is the chattel house. These tiny structures, a miniature version of the Georgian-style manor house, appeared after emancipation when freed slaves built themselves moveable wooden homes.

Following the end of the slave trade in 1832, communities began to center around each parish's local church and school. Education became widespread and today 97% of the island's population is literate. Only 21 by 14 miles in size, Barbados is densely populated with about a third of its quarter-million population living in the Bridgetown area. Yet, once you're away from the busy streets of Bridgetown, the island's natural beauty, healthy climate and sense of gentility exert their appeal. Protected powdery beaches line the west side of the island, in contrast to the rugged east coast

The chattel house is a traditional Barbadian home, appearing in the 1800s when freed slaves built their own homes.

where Atlantic swells roll ashore. Inland, the rolling countryside of parks and gardens exudes a pastoral charm, as do the villages where parish churches swell with singing on Sunday mornings.

Barbadian rum is among the finest and oldest in the world, the locally produced Mount Gay brand first distilled here in 1663 by Abel Gay. The island's ideal climate has long attracted visitors, one of its most famous being George Washington when, in 1751, he accompanied his ill half-brother who came for a change of air, as was fashionable at the time. Much has changed since the days of British colonialism but the island's summer festival, called Crop Over, still celebrates the end of the sugar harvest – an annual event in Barbados for the past three and a half centuries.

Sugar remains an important export but tourism is well established, with more than 800,000 visitors arriving annually, half of these by cruise ship. The deep-water harbor, located about a mile north of Bridgetown's center, opened in 1961. It occupies Pelican Island, upon which pelicans once nested before it was joined to the mainland during the harbor's construction. The port's spacious complex contains a tourist information office and an assortment of shops carrying duty-free and locally made items.

The official currency is the Barbados dollar (worth approximately 50¢ US) but American and Canadian money is widely accepted.

Getting Around

Barbados is a very pleasant island to tour, whether by rental car, hired taxi or group excursion. The roads are in good condition, although they are generally narrow and winding, and visibility is sometimes restricted by bordering cane fields. Driving is on the left, roundabout lanes are common, and Bridgetown is best avoided during rush hour. A temporary licence (available through local car rental firms) costs $10 US.

Rental cars and taxis can be hired just outside the shopping complex where a number of companies have kiosks. Highly recommended is Johnson's Tours, founded in 1860, which maintains a fleet of rental vehicles and taxis, and also offers a variety of island tours.

Taxi rates (posted in the terminal building in Barbadian dollars) are fixed. Some sample fares, in US dollars, from the cruise port to: Bridgetown – $4; Hilton Hotel – $6; Crane Bay – $18; Sam Lord's Castle – $20; and Harrison's Cave – $20.

Ship-organized excursions usually include a countryside tour with popular stops being Gun Hill, St. John's Parish Church and one of the island's great houses. Also organized by most cruise lines is a visit to Harrison's Cave and a ride on the Atlantis Submarine.

SHOPPING: There is a selection of duty-free shops at the cruise terminal, and local arts and crafts are sold at **Pelican Village**, located on the main highway leading into town. In Bridgetown, the duty-free shops are concentrated on **Broad Street** and its side streets, where good buys can be found in crystal, fine bone china, jewelry, perfumes and clothing. Harrisons, established in 1854, is considered the island's premier store. Local handicrafts, batik, ceramics and original paintings and prints can be bought at various galleries, including Verandah Art Gallery, 'Creative Expressions' in The Shops of the Ginger Bread House, Colours of de Caribbean and Mango Jam Gallery.

Mahogany woodcarvings and sculptures can be found at Best of Barbados Shops (with a location at the Cruise Ship Terminal) and Potter's House Gallery in Shop Hill. Contemporary and traditional pottery is sold at various rural potteries, including Chalky Mount and Castle Pottery in St. Peter, Earthworks Pottery at Shop Hill in St. Thomas, and Fairfield Pottery in St. Michael.

BEACHES: The most sheltered beaches lie on the west coast, including **Mullins Beach** which offers glassy smooth water and good snorkeling, and **Paynes Bay** which is good for swimming and watersports. Restaurant facilities are available at both beaches.

South of Bridgetown, popular beaches include **Carlisle Bay Center** and the **Hilton Hotel** at Needhams Point.

A beach of sugary white sand and fairly big waves is located at **Crane Bay** on the southeast coast. Another beautiful beach washed by surf is **Bottom Bay**, which lies at the base of a cliff north of Sam Lord's

The Parliament Buildings and Trafalgar Square stand on the north side of the Bridgetown's historic harbor, known as the Careenage.

Atlantic swells roll ashore at Bathsheba Beach, in stark contrast to the island's calm Caribbean side.

Castle and is reached by some steps, as is the fine beach right below Sam Lord's – a Georgian mansion built by a 'gentleman pirate' and now part of a Mariott Resort. On the island's Atlantic coast, a dramatic sight is the pounding surf and eroded boulders at **Bathsheba Beach** where signs warn that swimming is dangerous.

DIVE & SNORKEL SITES: The **Barbados Folkestone Underwater Park and Marine Reserve** is just north of Holetown on the island's west coast. The park headquarters and interpretation center is in Folkestone, and the underwater park itself is divided into four zones – scientific, recreational, and a northern and southern watersports zone. The Recreational Zone contains a snorkel trail near shore and dive boats are available for trips to Dotting's Reef – part of a seven-mile stretch of intermittent banking reef that lies about 1/3 mile off-shore. South of the recreational zones, a 356-foot freighter has been sunk in 120 feet about a half mile from shore to form an artificial reef.

A number of wrecks lie on the bottom of **Carlisle Bay** where ships once anchored before the harbor was constructed; these include the *Berwyn* (scuttled in 1919) which is ideal for snorkelers.

Dive Boat Safari is located at the Hilton on **Needhams Point** and they offer beach and boat dives for all levels of experience. Drift diving is popular on the south coast along the barrier reef that starts at depths of 60 feet and lies from a half mile to two miles offshore. Hawksbill turtles are commonly sighted there. Non-divers can view the island's underwater world to depths of 150 feet aboard an Atlantis Submarine or enjoy a snorkeler's perspective of the near-shore reefs on board the Atlantis Seatrec observation vessel.

GOLF: The 18-hole course at **Sandy Lane Golf Club** is set in the upscale area of Sandy Lane Estate north of Bridgetown. A 6,533-yard, par-72 course, its signature hole is a 70-foot drop from tee to green. South of Bridgetown is the par-36, nine-hole course at **Club Rockley** which covers 2,736 yards.

LOCAL SIGHTS: Founded in 1628, Bridgetown stands on the banks of the Constitution River, its wide mouth forming a harbor called the Careenage where boats moor alongside. Spanning the Careenage is the Chamberlain Bridge, its south end graced with the Independence Arch. At the north end of the bridge is **(1) Trafalgar Square**, in the center of which stands a statue of Horatio Nelson which predates the one in London. The neo-Gothic Public Buildings on the north side of the square were erected in 1872 and they house the island's Parliament.

Other historic buildings in the downtown core include **(2) St. Michael's Cathedral** (rebuilt after it was destroyed by a hurricane in 1780), the 18th-century **(3) St. Mary's Church**, and the beautifully-restored **(4) Nidhe Israel Synagogue** which was originally built in 1654 and has won an American Express Preservation Award. Streets of interest include Hinks Street, with its old sugar warehouses, and Broad Street with its elegant shops and colonial buildings. A convenient parking lot is located between the two bridges on the south bank of the river.

Island Attractions

The Barbados National Trust preserves and operates a number of island attractions that have historic importance or natural beauty. These are indicated below with a star (*) and can be visited individually or by purchasing a mini-passport (US $12) that allows entry to a combination of attractions. Ship-organized tours also visit various National Trust properties (some of which are closed on Sundays and public holidays). In addition to those mentioned below, Trust properties include the Sir Frank Hutson Sugar Museum, Codrington College, Oughterson House & Barbados Zoo Park, and the elegant Francia Plantation House (near Gun Hill) which was built by a Frenchman for his bride at the turn of the century. In the historic Garrison area just south of Bridgetown are the **(5) Barbados Gallery of Art** and **The Barbados Museum*** which contains archaeological and historical exhibits as well as African and European decorative arts.

(6) The Mount Gay Rum Visitor's Center*, just north of Bridgetown, offers 45-minute tours which end with a sampling of the company's famous rum.

The authentic chattel houses at **(7) Tyrol Cot Heritage Village*** are centered around an 1854 mansion, the former home of Sir Grantley and

Lady Adams, and the village includes a popular market selling local arts and crafts.

In the 19th century, a series of signal stations were established by Britain's Royal Artillery along the island's high points to signal the approach of enemy ships or the safe arrival of cargo ships. The signal men communicated between stations using telescopes and flags. **(8) Gun Hill Signal Station***, situated on the highland of St. George with a magnificent view of the west coast, was built in 1818 and restored by the Barbados National Trust in 1982. On the hill below the station, visible from the road when exiting the premises, is a British Military Lion that was carved by British soldiers in the 19th century.

At **(9) Harrison's Cave*** trams take visitors on a spectacular subterranean ride past limestone stalactites and stalagmites that took millions of years to form. An underground stream of clear water runs through the cave, fed by rain that is filtered through 200 feet of coral before reaching a natural underground reservoir which is the island's supply of pure drinking water.

Administered by the Barbados National Trust, **(10) Welchman Hall Gully*** is an oasis of ornamental plants and trees nestled in a deep gully rimmed with cliffs. Located near Harrison's Cave, it was once part of a series of caves, the roofs of which collapsed to create the gully now filled with tropical plants and pathways. Its jungle setting is also a habitat for the Barbados Green Monkey which is frequently seen here in the early morning or late afternoon.

Members of Britain's Royal Family have visited Gun Hill Signal Station, which was built in 1818 to overlook the island's west coast.

Farley Hill National Park, officially opened by Queen Elizabeth in 1966, was once the most opulent plantation estate on the island.

The 50-acre **(11) Flower Forest** is a cross between a botanical garden and a nature trail. Located on a hillside of the Scotland District, its paths contain several seats, and walking sticks and umbrellas are provided. In addition to bar and restaurant facilities, the premises contain a Best of Barbados gift shop.

At **(12) Farley Hill National Park***, officially opened by Queen Elizabeth in 1966, visitors can wander the ruins of what was once the most opulent plantation estate on the island. Situated in the Scotland District at the north end of the island, the park's ridge-top location provides sweeping views of the surrounding countryside and the island's Atlantic coast. The mansion, built in stages in the 19th century, was gutted by fire in the late '50s shortly after the filming of *Island In The Sun* starring Harry Belafonte. Its stone walls remain, as do the trimmed lawns and narrow lanes shaded by a corridor of palm trees. The park is a cool and breezy place to enjoy a picnic lunch, just as Sir Graham's royal guests – Prince Albert and Prince George (later George V) – did in 1879.

Another restored signal station is located at **(13) Grenade Hall Forest & Signal Station*** in St. Peter. A panoramic view can be enjoyed from the signal station and the surrounding forest contains coral pathways for viewing the various species of trees, vines and herbs, their present and past uses illustrated with a series of signs.

Established in 1985 on four acres of mahogany forest, the non-profit **(14) Barbados Wildlife Reserve** includes a research center that focuses on conservation of the Barbados Green Monkey. The animals wander freely here and visitors are encouraged to take their time while walking quietly along the shady paths or pausing on a bench to wait and see which creatures appear.

One of the oldest great houses in the Caribbean, **(15) St. Nicholas Abbey*** is maintained by the National Trust. It was built by a British colonel around 1650 in the Jacobean style with Dutch gables and corner fireplaces – an unlikely feature for the tropics. Its second owner, Sir John Yeamans, colonized Carolina and became the third Governor of South Carolina. The current owner is Lieutenant Colonel Stephen Cave whose family has owned the estate since 1820. One of only three remaining great houses of its period in the Western Hemisphere, the ground floor is open for viewing and is furnished with English and Barbadian antiques. The wine cellar is now a gift shop.

(16) Morgan Lewis Mill*, a Barbados National Trust Property in the rugged Scotland District, is the only complete sugar windmill surviving in the Caribbean. Built in the 18th century to grind sugarcane, hundreds of such mills used to dot the countryside when sugar was 'white gold' and Barbados was Britain's most valuable possession in the Americas.

The six acres of individual tropical gardens at **(17) Andromeda Botanic Gardens*** contain rare and unique species of plants.

One of the oldest and most picturesque churches on the island, **(18) St. John's Parish Church** stands atop an inland bluff overlooking the east coast. Originally built of wood, its stone replacement was destroyed by several hurricanes. The present structure dates from 1836 and the churchyard contains the tomb of Ferdinand Paleologus, who was the great-grandson of Thomas, brother of the last Byzantine Emperor. Ferdinand served in the army of the King of England before sailing to Barbados where he was churchwarden from 1655 to 1656.

The original **(19) Villa Nova** was destroyed by a hurricane in 1831. Rebuilt in 1834, its previous owners include British Prime Minister Sir Anthony Eden and the Earl of Avon whose garden parties were attended by Lady Churchill and Queen Elizabeth.

(20) Sunbury Plantation House* is a beautifully-preserved great house built in the 1600s. Its original owners were the Chapmans, one of the first planter families on Barbados. The last owners, the Melvilles, lived here until 1985, although the residence was officially opened to visitors as a Heritage House in 1984. Carefully restored, the mansion is filled with mahogany antiques and all of its rooms are open for viewing. The grounds contain gardens, a gift shop, and a unique collection of horse-drawn carriages.

TRINIDAD & TOBAGO

Trinidad and Tobago, like Barbados, lie outside of the Windward arc of islands. These islands were in fact once part of the South American sub-continent, with Trinidad becoming an island as recently as 10,000 years ago when the last Ice Age ended and sea levels rose. The variety of flora and fauna is matched by the diversity of cultures found in this two-island nation. Unlike Barbados, which never changed hands once it became a British colony, the islands of Trinidad (named by Columbus for its three southeastern peaks) and Tobago (named for pipe tobacco by British settlers) were fought over and farmed by various nationalities which included the Spanish, Portuguese, Dutch, French and British.

Trinidad's capital, Port of Spain, is an amalgam of European, African and Indian heritage with cathedrals, mosques, markets and museums built in a diversity of styles – Moorish, neo-Gothic, Italian Renaissance, Victorian and West Indian gingerbread to name a few. There's even a German castle resembling the medieval castles of the Rhine which, along with the official residences of the prime minister and governor general, overlooks Queen's Park Savannah – the site of glittering revelry during Trinidad's famous Carnival when the Parade of Bands proceeds up Frederick Street on the final day of street parties and calypso competitions.

In contrast to the pulsating beat of Trinidad is the unspoiled holiday island of Tobago, 21 miles away but a world apart. Scarborough is the island's main port and nearby is Pigeon Point with its glorious beaches and famous Buccoo Reef where colorful coral gardens, popular with divers and snorkelers, can be viewed by glass-bottom boats.

The two islands, both of which prospered as producers of sugar cane during colonialism, were joined together under one government at the end of the 19th century and gained independence from Britain in 1962. Trinidad is the larger and more heavily populated of the two islands, with only 45,000 of a total 1.3 million inhabitants living on Tobago. Both islands boast lush rainforests, rare birds and brilliant butterflies, their colorful wings copied in the elaborate costumes of Trinidad's world-famous Carnival.

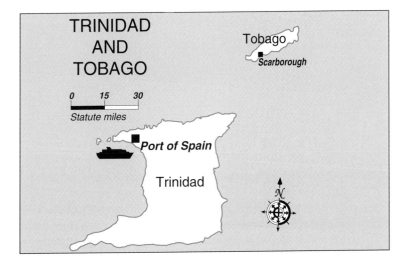

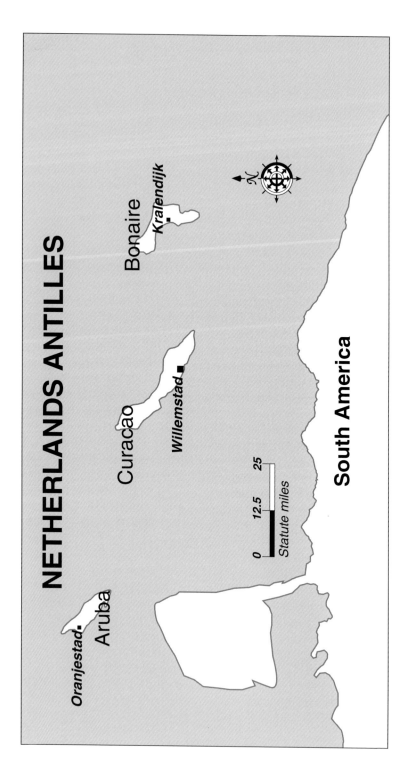

CHAPTER SEVENTEEN

THE DUTCH ABC'S

Aruba, Bonaire and Curacao

T
he Dutch islands of Aruba, Bonaire and Curacao (the ABC's) are true desert islands. They lie off the coast of Venezuela, outside of the hurricane belt, and – unlike the other Lesser Antilles – they receive little rain in summer, their vegetation consisting of drought-resistant cacti and divi-divi trees bent by the cooling trade winds. Their stark landscapes of wave-eroded rock formations and white-sand beaches are in contrast to the picturesque ports where Dutch gabled buildings, painted pastel colors, line the waterfront.

The islands' arid climate, interrupted by a brief rainy spell each winter, is one reason these islands were deemed 'useless' by the early Spanish explorers. They were inhabited at the time by Caiquetios, a tribe of peaceful Arawak Indians who lived in villages and caves, the walls of which contain pictographs they left behind. Their food came mostly from the rich bounty of the sea, the surrounding waters filled with colorful coral gardens and an abundance of fish. Other foodstuffs were obtained from mainland tribes in exchange for salt, one of the few natural resources found on these barren islands.

Located within 40 miles of the Venezuela coast, the ABC's are actually part of the Andes chain of mountains which snakes up the western side of South America and branches into smaller ranges at the north end of the continent. Underwater volcanic activity helped form the islands which consist of batholith rock as well as younger limestone which formed before uplifting slowly brought the islands to the sea's surface.

Natural resources on the arid ABC's include the aloe plant (below) and salt, piles of which are shown (left) on Bonaire.

The treasure-seeking Spaniards were the first Europeans to discover the ABC's when, in 1499, a Spanish sea captain en route to South America left some of his scurvy-afflicted sailors on one of the islands to die. When he returned less than a year later, he found them all alive and well. Hence the name Curacao – based on the Portuguese word for 'the cure'. Yet, despite its promising name, Curacao did not impress the Spanish for it was a dry, prickly place with no apparent gold deposits. Even the Valencia orange trees brought from Spain produced a bitter, almost inedible fruit when planted here.

It took the resourceful Dutch to see the potential of Curacao and make it an integral part of their trading empire. They seized the island in 1634, transferring the few Spanish settlers and Arawak Indians to the mainland, and took possession of Aruba and Bonaire a year or so later. Some Arawaks lived on Aruba where they maintained the cattle and horses that roamed freely on the island.

The Dutch West India Company was initially attracted to Curacao as a source of salt and hardwood, but the island soon became a base for raiding settlements on other Caribbean islands and the coastal mainland. Its sheltered harbor was fortified on either side at the entrance and, under the governorship of Peter Stuyvesant from 1642 to 1647, Willemstad became an important world port. With the soil unable to support sugar cane or other cash crops, Curacao's survival depended on trade, which came in the form of slaves. Throughout the latter half of the 1600s and well into the 1700s, Curacao was an enormous slave depot for the Caribbean and South America.

Meanwhile, Aruba was maintained as a vast cattle ranch, and corn was grown on Bonaire to feed the slaves passing through Curacao, which also became a commercial meeting place for pirates, American rebels, Dutch merchants and Spaniards from the mainland. As for those bitter-tasting oranges brought from Spain, it was discovered that their sun-dried peels contained an etheric oil which became the basis for Curacao's famous liqueur. The ABC's remained for the most part Dutch, briefly besieged by the British in 1804, and occupied by British troops from 1807 to 1814.

Slavery was finally ended on the Dutch Antilles in 1863 and the islands had to develop new resources. Trade with Venezuela became the mainstay of Curacao's economy and was helped greatly with the Dutch government's lifting of all import taxes on goods from the Netherlands, which local merchants could then exchange at a profit for Venezuelan products. On Aruba and Bonaire, the aloe plant became an important crop, its gel used in numerous pharmaceuticals, and the pods of the divi-divi tree were also exported for use in leather tanning.

Gold was another resource discovered on Aruba in 1824, when alluvial deposits were found in the quartz veins of its batholith rock. The island's mines, which operated for nearly a century, yielded more than three million pounds of gold. Black gold came to the ABC's following World War I when oil was discovered at Lake Maracaibo in Venezuela. The oil companies, seeking a stable place to locate their refineries and storage facilities, chose the nearby Dutch islands. When the demand for oil slumped, the islands developed yet another untapped resource which continues today – tourism.

Blessed with natural appeal – beautiful beaches, turquoise waters, colorful coral reefs, and a climate that's sunny and dry – the islands have added duty-free shopping, waterfront casinos and championship golf courses to their growing list of attractions. Their residents, who descend from a mix of races and cultures, are a people known for their racial and religious tolerance. They are also multilingual, learning Dutch – the official language – at school, and are often fluent in English and Spanish, as well as their native tongue of *Papiamento*, which is a lilting blend of Spanish, Portuguese, Dutch, English and African dialects.

All three islands are part of the Kingdom of the Netherlands but Aruba is no longer part of the Netherlands Antilles, of which Curacao is the capital and Bonaire is a member, along with the Leeward Islands of St. Maarten, Saba and St. Eustatius. Aruba, seeking more autonomy in connection with its oil revenues, became a separate entity in 1986.

CURACAO

Few Caribbean ports of call can surpass the arrival awaiting passengers at Curacao. Here the Queen Emma Pontoon Bridge swings open to allow ships to enter the canal-like entrance of St. Anna Bay and glide past the waterfront buildings of colonial Willemstad. A centuries-old capital, its channel-side streets are lined with gabled buildings which were painted bright colors in 1817 when the Governor complained that the sun's glare off the stark white buildings was giving him headaches. Initially founded as Santa Anna by the Spanish, the port's name was changed to Willemstad when Holland took possession of the island in 1634. Settlement grew on both sides of the channel with the eastern side called Punda and the western side called Otrabanda ('other side').

Ferry boats have long transported residents across the channel but in the late 1900s the American consul, Leonard Burlington Smith, suggested a pontoon foot bridge be built. Fixed at one end so it could open whenever a vessel had to pass, the bridge was completed in 1888. A toll charge was based on each person's ability to pay – those wearing shoes were charged 2¢ and those walking barefooted were free. It's said that the poor would borrow shoes to prove their ability to pay, while the rich would take off their shoes to save 2¢. Today there is no charge for either the bridge or the passenger ferries which run continuously throughout the day.

Both the Queen Emma Pontoon Bridge and a passenger ferry connect the two sides of Willemstad on Curacao.

Getting Around

Dutch charm and duty-free shopping await the visitor to Willemstad. The official currency is the Netherlands Antilles guilder (NAfl) but U.S. dollars are widely accepted. (1.78 NAfl = $1 US).

The cruise ships dock on the Otrabanda side of the channel and passengers can make their way to the Punda side on foot over the pontoon bridge, via the free passenger ferry which docks at Mathey Wharf, or by taxi (about $6 US) over the Queen Julianna Bridge which spans the harbor at a height of 185 feet. Taxis are unmetered and the fee should be agreed upon before departing. Sample fares, in US currency, from the cruise pier: Holiday Beach Hotel – $6; Curacao Caribbean Hotel and Las Palmas Hotel at Piscadera Bay – $7.

There are several tourist information booths along the Otrabanda waterfront, and the main office is located on the Punda side at the east end of Wilhelminaplein. A post office is directly east of the Central Market.

Organized ship excursions often include: a trolley train tour through the Punda section of Willemstad; an island tour with stops at the Curacao liqueur distillery and Curacao Seaquarium; a semi-submarine ride along coral reefs; and beach and snorkel excursions.

BEACHES: Curacao's southern coast is indented with beach-lined bays and coves. Private beaches charge a small entrance fee, as do some of the hotel beaches. A popular hotel beach close to the cruise port is **Holiday Beach**. Farther west is the private beach at Blauwbaai (**Blue Bay**) – considered one of Curacao's best with its white sand, shady areas and change facilities. More hotel beaches are located at **Piscadera Bay**, including the Sonesta Hotel, Las Palmas and Curacao Caribbean. Fine beaches east of Willemstad include **Princess Beach**, where a hotel is located, and **Seaquarium Beach** and **Santa Barbara Beach**, both private beaches with change facilities and snack bars.

DIVE & SNORKEL SITES: Excellent snorkeling and diving is available all around the island with visibility of 60 to 80 feet, and sometimes up to 150 feet.

The **Curacao Underwater Park**, ideal for both diving and snorkeling, protects 12-1/2 miles of unspoiled coral reef along which is an underwater nature trail and spectacular dive sites which include coral beds, sheer walls and shipwrecks. **Klein Curacao**, lying off East Point, is an uninhabited islet with beautiful beaches and good snorkeling and diving.

GOLF: A nine-hole course with sand greens is open mornings at the Curacao Golf & Squash Club just north of the Willemstad Harbor.

SHOPPING: Duty-free bargains in Willemstad include brand-name jewelry, watches, European fashions, perfumes, crystal, china, electron-

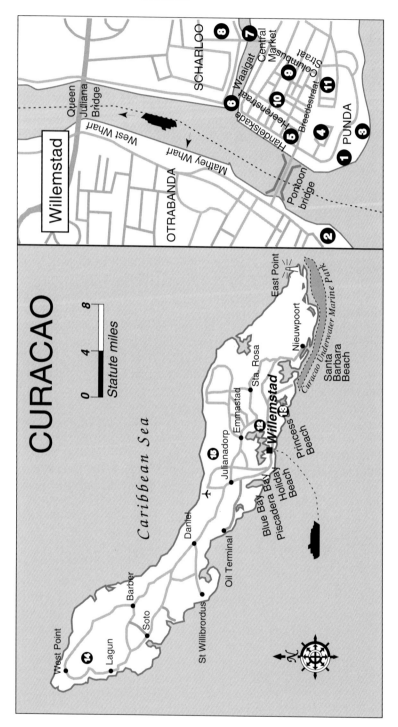

ics and cameras. Fine stores are located on Handelskade, Heerenstraat and Breedestraat, with more shops and boutiques located in the restored Waterfort Arches. Local crafts are sold at the Central Market (located in a large circular building east of the Floating Market) and at various shops in Punda such as Tropical Visions in the Penha Building. Along the Otrobanda waterfront, facing the cruise pier, are a number of shops selling duty-free liquor and local handicrafts, including pottery at the Arawak Craft Factory opposite West Wharf.

LOCAL SIGHTS: Located at the harbor entrance within the battlements of **(1) Waterfort** (built in 1634), and within hailing distance of ships entering the harbor, is the **Van der Valk Plaza Hotel** – one of only two hotels in the world that is covered by marine collision insurance. Still attached to the sea wall are iron rings once used to secure a chain that was stretched across the channel to prevent enemy ships from entering the harbor. During World War II, a steel net was stretched across the channel between Waterfort and **(2) Riffort** – built on the other side in 1838. Stretching east of Waterfort along the sea front are more old battlements, including the restored **(3) Waterfort Arches,** now housing shops and restaurants.

(4) Fort Amsterdam with its mustard-colored walls, was the center of the fortified town from 1648 to 1861. Today it's the seat of the Netherlands Antilles government. Its inner courtyard, entered through an arched walkway, is formed by the Governor's Palace (facing the water), the **Fort Church Museum** (opposite), and government offices on each side. In case of siege, the church was built with a cellar for provisions and an adjacent water cistern. A cannon ball fired in 1804 by English troops, led by Captain Bligh of *Bounty* fame, remains embedded in its front wall.

The much-photographed **(5) Penha Building**, golden yellow with white trim, stands at the corner near the east end of the pontoon bridge. One of Curacao's oldest examples of Dutch colonial architecture, the building was formerly a social club with a gallery overlooking the harbor. Other waterfront buildings along this block resemble the canal houses of Amsterdam, one of which houses **Gallery '86** – a showcase for the works of well-known artists of the Caribbean and Netherlands.

At the far end of the block is the **(6) Floating Market** where Venezuelan boats loaded with fruit, vegetables and fish sell their wares. At the east end of the market is the **(7) Queen Wilhelmina Bridge** which spans the Waaigat and leads to the former residential district of **(8) Scharloo** where wealthy merchants built opulent homes, their architectural styles ranging from 18th-century colonial to Victorian.

In 1651, a dozen Jewish families from Amsterdam arrived in Willemstad and by the early 1700s the local Jewish community numbered 2,000. The **(9) Mikve Emanuel Synagogue**, built in 1732 and similar in style to the old Portuguese one in Amsterdam, is today the oldest active synagogue in the Western Hemisphere. The Jewish Cultural Museum is entered off the synagogue's courtyard.

Other museums in Punda include the **(10) Postal Museum**, housed in a 1693 building at the corner of Keukenstraat and Kuiperstraat, and the **Numismatic Museum** on Breedestraat.

The town's central park, **(11) Wilhelminaplein**, contains a statue of Queen Wilhelmina, as well as shaded benches and a playground. Opposite the park's east side is the former Jewish Reformed Synagogue Temple Emmanuel (the **Temple Building**) and **City Gate**, which marks the boundary of Willemstad when it was a fortified settlement.

ISLAND ATTRACTIONS: Outside of Willemstad the attractions include beautiful beaches, secluded coves, village churches and restored land houses which are former country estates situated on hilltops so the owner could watch his slaves and signal his neighbors if trouble developed.

Popular attractions include the **(12) Curacao Liqueur Distillery**, located in the former colonial mansion of Chobolobo on the east side of Willemstad's harbor, and the **(13) Curacao Seaquarium** where visitors can view 400 species of sea life native to local waters, including various sharks and stingrays. Beside the aquarium is a full-facility beach of white sand.

At the north end of Curacao is **(14) Christoffel National Park**, a 4,500-acre nature reserve containing the island's highest point of Mount Christoffel (1,239 feet), Indian caves and trails.

The prehistoric caves at **(15) Hato** were recently opened to the public, their limestone terraces containing fossilized coral that formed before tectonic uplifting brought the submerged island to the sea's surface.

ARUBA

Once a cacti-studded cattle ranch, Aruba is today a holiday paradise with miles of blinding white beaches and crystal-clear turquoise waters. The island's first inhabitants, the Caquetio Indians, had established themselves at the mouth of Venezuela's Aroa River until repeated attacks by the Carib Indians prompted them to leave. Some of the tribe moved to the shores of Lake Maracaibo and still bear the name Arubaes. Others moved to the island now called Aruba.

The island's southwest coast has beach resorts, shopping malls and casinos; its rugged northeast coast is where wave action has carved coral cliffs into dramatic sea arches. In between lies a hilly desert of caves, cacti and scrub. Splashes of color are provided by flamboyant trees, in bloom from June through August, and gardens of homes which often contain a variety of tropical flowers. Wells tap into the island's water table but a huge saltwater distillation plant at Spanish Lagoon, once a hideout for pirates, is the island's main source of fresh water.

Getting Around

The cruise ships dock in the heart of Oranjestad, within easy walking distance of the shops, museums and other attractions.

Most major American car rental companies operate on Aruba, in addition to several local companies. Avis has an office at the cruise ship terminal. A valid driver's license is all that's required to rent a car. The island is 19-1/2 miles long by six miles wide, the main roads are paved, and driving is on the right. It's hard to get lost, and the divi-divi trees – bent by the trade winds – all point toward the island's leeward side where Oranjestad is located.

Official currency is Aruban florins but U.S. dollars are readily accepted island wide. The bank rate of exchange is fixed at 1.77 Afl. to $1 US. Banks charge to change traveller's cheques but stores and restaurants do not. Major credit cards are accepted at most establishments.

BEACHES: A short distance from Oranjestad, along the west coast's hotel strip, are two of Aruba's best beaches – **Eagle Beach** and **Palm Beach**, the latter touted as one of the best in the Caribbean and extremely popular for its good swimming and sailing. At the island's eastern tip are **Rodgers Beach** and **Baby Beach**, the latter being ideal for young children with its calm, shallow waters and shady areas.

Eagle Beach, not far from the cruise port, is one of many fine beaches to choose from on Aruba.

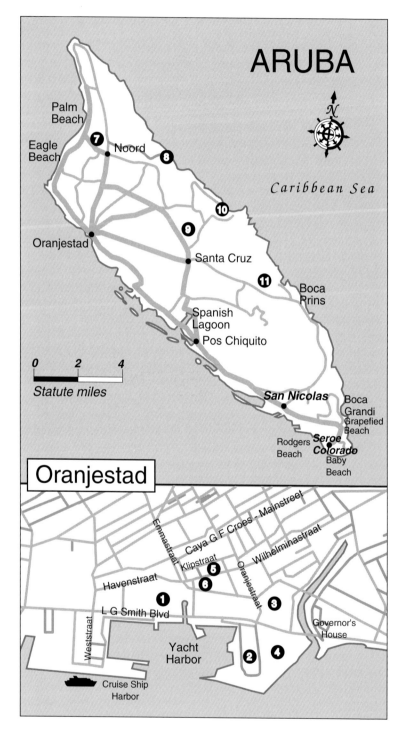

ARUBA

Palm
Beach

Eagle
Beach

Noord

Caribbean Sea

Oranjestad

Santa Cruz

Boca
Prins

Spanish
Lagoon

Pos Chiquito

0   2   4

Statute miles

San Nicolas

Boca
Grandi
Grapefied
Beach

Rodgers
Beach

Seroe
Colorado

Baby
Beach

Oranjestad

Emmastraat

Caya G F Croes - Mainstreet

Wilhelminastraat

Klipstraat

Oranjestraat

Havenstraat

L G Smith Blvd

Governor's
House

Yacht
Harbor

Cruise Ship
Harbor

Skilled windsurfers will want to head to the north coast beaches, such as **Grapefield Beach** and **Boca Grandi**. Picnickers will enjoy the romantic setting of **Boca Prins**, backed by sand dunes and pounded by the nearby surf.

DIVE AND SNORKEL SITES: Boat excursions can be taken from Oranjestad to **De Palm's Reef Island**, good for diving and snorkeling, and the *Antilla* World War II wreck is a popular dive site. Water excursions originating in port include the Atlantis Submarines; their catamaran transports passengers from Seaport Village Marina to the dive site where they board the submarine for a deepsea look at Aruba's coral reefs, shipwrecks and colorful marine life.

GOLF: A nine-hole course is located in San Nicolas and, at Tierra del Sol on the island's northern end, is a new 18-hole course designed by Robert Trents Jones Jr. A par-72 course with water on two sides, it has stunning sea views and is dotted with giant cacti and clusters of natural grasses.

SHOPPING: Shopping malls are located at the harborfront, in town and stretching north along the coast. **(1) Seaport Village Mall**, a five-minute walk from the cruise terminal, is Aruba's largest shopping and entertainment complex with dozens of stores, boutiques and a casino. The nearby **(2) Seaport Marketplace** is also popular with its shaded central walkway and sidewalk cafes.

Oranjestad's main shopping street is Caya G.F. Betico Croes, with its chic boutiques and cozy shops. International items to look for include cachet cosmetics and perfumes, designer fashions, china, crystal, fine jewelry, watches and cameras.

There are also good buys in embroidered tablecloths, Spanish porcelain, Danish silver and pewter, Dutch cheeses, Austrian figurines, Peruvian hand-knit sweaters, Brazilian semi-precious stones, Venezuelan shoes and handbags, Columbian emeralds and leather, and locally made aloe vera products. Clay pottery and other local artwork is sold at Artesania Arubiano on L.G. Smith Boulevard.

LOCAL SIGHTS: (3) Fort Zoutman is the oldest building in Oranjestad, erected in 1796 and named for a Dutch Rear Admiral. Added to the fort in 1868 was **King Willem III Tower** which served as a lighthouse and now houses a heritage museum. A weekly festival of folkloric dancing is held here on Tuesday evenings.

The gardens of waterfront **(4) Queen Wilhelmina Park**, adjacent to the Seaport Marketplace, contain a marble statue of the former Dutch queen gazing toward the Governor's home.

Wilhelminastraat contains interesting colonial architecture including the **(5) Protestant Church**, built in 1846. Across the street is the **(6) Archaeological Museum** containing artifacts and pottery of the island's first Indian inhabitants.

Photo Michael DeFreitas

The Seaport Marketplace is located near the cruise pier in
Oranjestad, Aruba.

ISLAND ATTRACTIONS: (7) Santa Anna Church in Noord was built in the 1770s and its hand-carved oak altar, neo-gothic in design, won the exhibition award in Rome in 1870.

The **(8) Chapel of Alto Vista**, built by a Spanish missionary, is a place of pilgrimage situated on the north coast overlooking the sea.

The interesting rock formations at **(9) Casibari** can be climbed via some steps to the top for a view of the island and the Haystack.

Aruba's famous landmark is the **(10) Natural Bridge**, made of coral and carved by the sea on the island's windward coast. The arch is over 100 feet long and stands 23 feet above sea level.

(11) Arikok National Park contains natural and man-made paths, a restored *cunucu* (countryside house), a traditional stone well and the Natural Pool, near Boca Keto, which is surrounded by rocks and filled with sea water. Horseback excursions lasting 2-1/2 hours across Aruba's countryside can be taken with Rancho Del Campo.

BONAIRE

Boomerang-shaped Bonaire is one of the best islands in the Caribbean for diving and snorkeling. The entire island is a protected marine park and its coral reefs are home to more than a thousand different species of aquatic creatures, including sea horses and turtles. There are over 86 charted dive sites on the island, many of these located on the sheltered western side of the island, clustered north of Kralendijk and around the offshore islet of Klein Bonaire. Reefs and wrecks, beach dives and drop-offs – the variety of dive sites and the clarity of the water is spectacular. Conditions are also ideal for snorkelers with little current and plenty of shallow-water snorkeling sites.

The island capital of **Kralendijk**, meaning 'coral dike', is a quiet place where about 2,000 of the island's 12,000 residents live. Shops carrying duty-free and local items are found at the Harborside Shopping Mall and along the main street which runs parallel with the waterfront. Historic sights include Fort Oranje, two churches and a museum. Wild donkeys and goats roam free on this unspoiled island where the centuries-old industry of salt mining has been joined by oil bunkering and tourism.

Bonaire's land-based attractions are as fascinating as its underwater world, for the island is home to one of the largest flamingo colonies in the Western Hemisphere. More than 15,000 flamingos nest in the island's salt pans and, in addition to two flamingo sanctuaries, a 13,500-acre game preserve (Washington-Slagbaai National Park) has been established at Bonaire's north end. Here iguanas and green-tailed lizards can be viewed in addition to flamingos and other birds such as yellow-winged parrots, often seen perched on the giant cacti which grow as high as 30 feet.

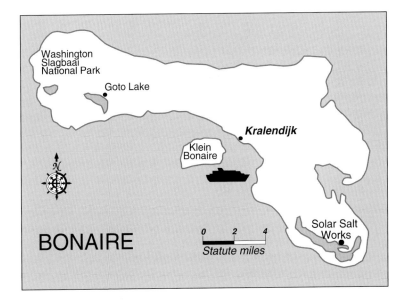

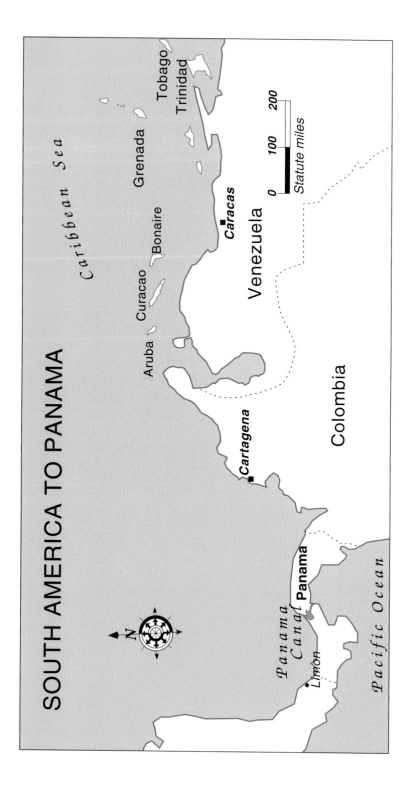

CHAPTER EIGHTEEN

CARACAS/CARTAGENA

Cities of Conquest

T he sight of native villages set on stilts above the water prompted an early Spanish explorer, when exploring the northern coast
of South America in 1499, to name the area Venezuela – 'little
Venice'. Venezuela is, however, anything but little, with its 350,000
square miles of scenic wonders, including Angel Falls – the highest
uninterrupted waterfall in the world at 3,200 feet. Venezuela's
Caribbean coastline is nearly 1,800 miles long and its offshore islands
include Margarita, famous for pearl fishing.

Venezuela is also a country of great wealth. The lowlands around
Lake Maracaibo are rich in oil deposits which, since 1918, have been
developed by Dutch, British and American interests, with large
amounts processed in the nearby Netherlands Antilles. Still, the majority of the country's 20 million inhabitants live in poverty, their shacks
covering the hillsides of suburban Caracas where monumental architecture and modern skyscrapers attest to the city's historical greatness and
continued growth.

Caracas, with about six million residents, is the capital of Venezuela.
The city is situated on a mountain plateau of a coastal range which is a
spur of the Andes. An earthquake destroyed much of the city in 1812,
shortly after the country declared its independence from Spain under
patriot leader Francisco de Miranda. This setback helped the royalist
forces but South America's great liberator, Simon Bolivar, continued
the revolutionary cause from his base at Cartagena on the Colombia

An equestrian statue of Simon Bolivar, South America's great liberator, stands at one end of Bolivar Square in Caracas.

coast. His victory over Spanish forces in 1821 won independence for Venezuela and its neighboring territories, and they formed the federal republic of Greater Colombia.

In 1830, Venezuela became a separate state, and subsequent power struggles among the landholding class resulted in corrupt regimes ruling the country until 1947 when, for the first time, a president was elected by direct popular vote. This was followed by a military coup, but democracy was restored in 1958. Inflation and unemployment are ongoing problems, and social unrest erupted into riots in 1989 when falling oil revenues prompted the government to make cuts in social services.

La Guaira is the port of access to Caracas, connected by a modern and scenic highway that hugs the mountainsides and provides spectacular valley views along the 45-minute drive. A colonial port, La Guaira's historic buildings include the 17th-century Customs House and the Casa Boulton, which houses a museum tracing the town's history since its founding in 1589. However, the majority of passengers visiting La Guaira promptly head to Caracas or other outlying areas, such as **Rancho Grande National Park,** with its dense tropical forests, and **Colonia Tovar**, an isolated village settled by German farmers in 1843.

City tours of Caracas include a visit to **Bolivar Plaza**, named for Venezuela's national hero who was born in Caracas to a wealthy Creole family. Amid the fountains and mosaic walkways stands a magnificent statue of Bolivar on horseback. At the opposite end of the shady square is the Hallway of Heroes – towering statues of black stone which stand in two facing rows. Numerous government buildings surround the plaza, including the golden-domed Capitol with its famous Elliptical Hall and ceiling paintings that depict the final battle of the war of independence. The nearby Cathedral is a 19th-century reconstruction of the original built in 1595.

Getting Around

The cruise lines offer a number of ship-organized excursions from La Guaira, including half-day and full-day city tours, but for passengers wanting to tackle Caracas on their own, the round-trip taxi fare is about $50 U.S.

The official currency is the *bolivar*, with the U.S. dollar buying approximately 170 bolivars, although this exchange fluctuates. There are 100 *centimos* to the *bolivar*. Spanish is the official language but English is widely spoken.

SHOPPING: For shoppers, good buys can be made in handcrafted leather goods, including coats and jackets, as well as handbags, wallets, shoes and belts. Venezuelan souvenirs to look for include hand-embroidered t-shirts, woolen throw rugs, gold jewelry and pearls from Margarita Island. Visitors whose city tour includes a stop at the Cristalart Glass Factory can choose from a wide variety of intricate ornaments and elegant vases which are crafted on site.

A child plays in Bolivar Square, amid the statues, sculptures and fountains.

CARTAGENA, COLOMBIA

Cartagena (pronounced kar-ta-hay-na) is an historic walled city of shady plazas, Iberian-style palaces and narrow cobblestone streets. Founded by the Spanish in 1533, Cartagena de Indies was named for an important Mediterranean port in Spain which was established in ancient times by the Carthaginians.

For two centuries, from the mid-1500s to the mid-1700s, Cartagena was one of Spain's most prized New World ports. Two fleets would sail from Spain each August, one heading to Veracruz in the Gulf of Mexico, the other calling at Cartagena to load gold and silver arriving from Portobelo. When Spanish ships pulled into port loaded with goods from the home country – wines, cheeses, books, clothing and porcelain – Cartagena took on a circus-like atmosphere. The townspeople would crowd the docks where bankers, merchants, agents, pedlars and prostitutes all sought a piece of the action. Bidding wars for Spanish products often ensued, with local merchants paying fantastic prices. A few months later the fleet would sail for Havana, its ships now loaded with gold, silver and precious gems, where it would rendezvous with the other fleet for the journey back to Spain.

A series of forts and massive stone walls, which now divide the Old City from the newer part, were built over time to defend the port against marauding pirates and enemy fleets. Its history is a bloody one of sieges and sackings, starting with its fall to the English privateer Sir Francis Drake, who took Cartagena in 1586, after doing the same to its Mediterranean namesake the year before.

Drake's successful attack and pilfering of Spanish treasures in the Caribbean prompted an enraged King Philip II to hire an Italian engineer named Antoneli whose task for the next 20 years was to make sure it didn't happen again. A series of forts were built to defend Cartagena from sea approaches and the city remained impregnable for more than a century, until the famous French buccaneer Jean Du Casse arrived in 1697 with 700 men and direct orders from the France's King Louis XIV to go ahead and attack. After a fierce battle, the Spanish surrendered to the joint force of French pirates and soldiers, the latter collecting the loot of gold and silver, then refusing to share it with the pirates who turned back to the city and sacked it again.

In 1741, an unsuccessful British siege was led by Edward Vernon who was able to storm the harbor but whose troops, including a North American regiment led by George Washington's half brother, succumbed to dysentery, malaria and yellow fever before a final assault could be staged.

Independence was declared here in 1811, the first city in Colombia and Venezuela to officially defy Spain's rule. It became known as the

Founded in 1533, the walled city of Cartagena, with its Spanish churches and colonial buildings, was named an 'Historical and Cultural Heritage of Humanity' site by UNESCO in 1985.

Republic of Cartagena, a base from which Simon Bolivar launched his military campaign to liberate Venezuela. The walled city built by Spanish colonists was, ironically, besieged and captured by Spanish forces in 1815, but the rebel forces regained Cartagena in 1821 and the former treasure city of the Spanish Main was incorporated into Colombia. Its importance waned until the 20th century when oil refining brought new-found wealth to the city.

Getting Around

Cruise ships enter Cartagena Bay south of Isla de Tierra Bomba and most of them dock at the cruise ship pier in residential Manga. From the pier there are three options for seeing the city – a ship-organized tour, hiring a bilingual guide or taking a taxi.

Ship-organized city tours are conducted on buses that load at the dock. Passengers wishing to hire a bilingual guide can identify the 'tour guides' by their blue caps with a licence number on the front. They line up on the dock and some drive their own cars while others have a taxi driver with whom they work. If you simply want to take a taxi, the drivers who work alone are generally dressed in brown and speak limited English. They too are lined up in the dock area. Agree on a price with your guide or cab driver before setting off, and be sure to avoid anyone offering you a trip for 'one dollar'.

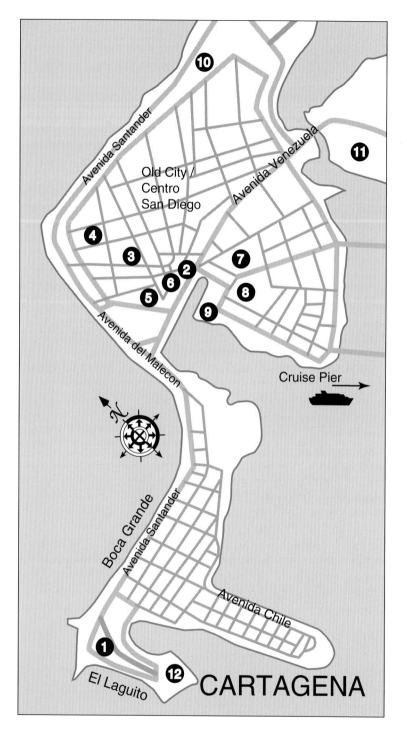

The dock area is patrolled by port police (dressed in green uniforms) who control smuggling, theft and drug pushing. Passengers should not be intimidated by their presence, but are advised to take reasonable precautions before heading ashore which includes refraining from wearing any expensive jewelry, especially showy necklaces.

SHOPPING: Cartagena is not a duty-free port but local products worth shopping for include leather goods, ceramics, silver jewelry, semi-precious stones and, of course, emeralds. Colombia is the world's leading producer of emeralds and those sold at Cartagena are unique in that centuries-old goldsmithing techniques are used to create handcrafted items of jewelry.

The **(1) Pierino Gallo Shopping Center** at **El Laguito** is the place to shop for quality merchandise. A number of reputable jewelers are located here, including Greenfire, Colombian Emeralds International and H. Stern. The center's other stores carry fine leather goods, pre-Columbian art including beadwork and ceramic pieces, gourmet coffee products, pottery, hand-painted plates and appliqued t-shirts.

In downtown Cartagena, an interesting shopping experience can be had bartering with street vendors or at boutiques housed in medieval dungeons. The **Portal of Sweets**, located in the arches facing the **(2) Clock Tower**, is a noisy passageway filled with white candy stands as well as newsstands, shoeshine boys and watch repairers.

LOCAL SIGHTS: The Old City was laid out in the traditional Roman grid scheme with one property often stretching an entire block, its owner's name given to the street out front.

(3) Plaza Bolivar is the center of the Walled City. Here you will find the main Cathedral, the Palace of the Inquisition with its museums, and the Gold Museum with an excellent collection of pre-Columbian gold work. Nearby is the **(4) Church of Santo Domingo** – the oldest in the city – and the **(5) Church of San Pedro Claver**, named for a Jesuit monk who was canonized 200 years after his death in the mid-1600s for his life's work of defending the African slaves.

East of Santo Domingo Church is **(6) Plaza de la Aduana** and the **(2) Clock Tower**. Following the waterfront, you will see **(7) Parque del Centenario** to your left, the **(8) Cartagena Theatre** straight ahead and to your right, on the waterfront, is the **(9) Convention Center**. Other highlights of a city tour include the fortifications at **(10) Las Bovedas** and a visit to **(11) San Felipe de Barajas**, a fort dating back to 1657, which provides an excellent view of the city, as does the 17th-century monastery at La Popa Hill.

Cartagena's beach and hotel strip, the **Boca Grande**, is directly south of the city's historic core. The upscale **(1) Pierino Gallo Shopping Center** is at the far end of the strip, in between the Hotel Las Velas and the **(12) Hotel Cartagena Hilton**.

The Panama Canal

One of the world's great engineering feats, the Panama Canal took more than 20 years to build at a cost of thousands of lives. Completed in 1914, its opening marked the end of a centuries-old era in which ships had to round treacherous Cape Horn at the southern tip of South America when travelling between the Pacific and Atlantic Oceans. Today it takes ships eight hours to transit the Canal's six massive locks, during which they are raised and lowered 85 feet. Another attraction of transiting the Panama Canal is the crossing of island-dotted Gatun Lake where passengers have the opportunity to view tropical plants and exotic wildlife. In addition to a pilot boarding each ship before it enters the canal, a lecturer also embarks to explain the remarkable history of this man-made 'ditch'.

As long ago as 1524, King Charles V of Spain ordered a survey of the Isthmus of Panama to determine the feasibility of a faster, safer route for sailing ships. But it wasn't until 1881 that the first major effort at building a canal took place when the French public underwrote a project led by Ferdinand de Lesseps, builder of the Suez Canal. His plan to dredge a sea-level trench proved to be a financial disaster and national tragedy for France with an estimated 20,000 lives lost – almost all from disease – and thousands of middle-class investors losing their life savings. Lesseps, once the hero of his country, died a broken man in 1894. His son Charles was sent to prison and his family henceforth never again spoke of the Panama Canal.

It's a tight fit for large cruise ships entering the immense locks of the Panama Canal, where man-made channels, lakes and dams comprise one of the world's great engineering feats.

The Canal's Gaillard Cut is a narrow, eight-mile channel with massive locks and a lush shoreline of tropical rain forest.

A successful attempt to build a shortcut was finally launched in 1904 when U.S. President Theodore Roosevelt led the drive to take over the task. American construction of a lock canal commenced on land leased from the newly-created Republic of Panama, formerly a state of Colombia. This strip of land, called the Panama Canal Zone, extends for five miles on either side of the canal. The surrounding terrain of low, lush hills is a pleasing sight for cruise passengers but was a breeding ground for malaria and yellow fever before the U.S. military cleared miles of brush and drained swamps in the area to eliminate swarms of disease-carrying mosquitoes. Because of slides, especially near the Culebra Cut, the canal must be constantly dredged. The canal was managed by the U.S. until 1979 when it was turned over to Panama under the terms of a treaty. In the year 2000, control of the canal will transfer to Panama for the canal's neutral operation.

Popular ports of call near the Panama Canal include Costa Rica's Puerto Limon, where passengers disembark to travel inland to the capital city of San Jose, which is set on a plateau 3,800 feet above sea level. The country's volcanic mountains, lush valleys and virgin tropical rain-forests support such an abundance of flora and fauna – including 10% of the world's butterflies – that nearly one quarter of its total land area is preserved within national parks or reserves. One of Latin America's most politically stable nations, Costa Rica has a democratic government, no army, good roads and safe drinking water. Its Spanish heritage dates back to 1563 when Spain's conquest of this region began.

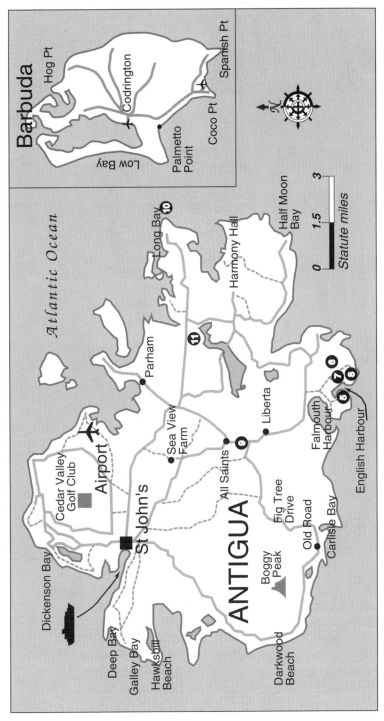

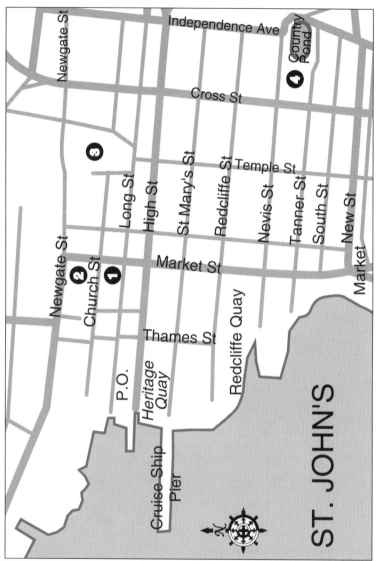

Port Attractions:

(1) Museum of Antigua and Barbuda
(2) Police Station
(3) Anglican Cathedral of St. John the Divine
(4) Country Pond

Island Attractions:

(5) Nelson's Dockyard
(6) Dow's Hill Center
(7) Clarence House
(8) Shirley Heights
(9) Tyrells Catholic Church
(10) Devil's Bridge
(11) Betty's Hope

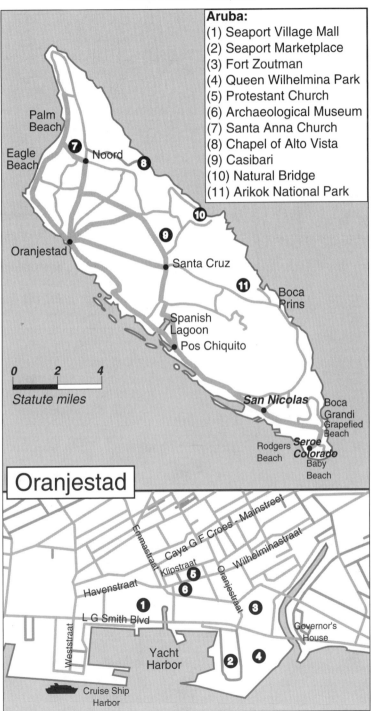

Aruba:
(1) Seaport Village Mall
(2) Seaport Marketplace
(3) Fort Zoutman
(4) Queen Wilhelmina Park
(5) Protestant Church
(6) Archaeological Museum
(7) Santa Anna Church
(8) Chapel of Alto Vista
(9) Casibari
(10) Natural Bridge
(11) Arikok National Park

Palm Beach
Eagle Beach
Noord
Oranjestad
Santa Cruz
Spanish Lagoon
Pos Chiquito
Boca Prins
Boca Grandi
Grapefied Beach
San Nicolas
Rodgers Beach
Seroe Colorado
Baby Beach

0 2 4
Statute miles

Oranjestad

Ennastraat
Caya G F Croes - Mainstreet
Klipstraat
Wilhelminastraat
Havenstraat
Oranjestraat
L G Smith Blvd
Weststraat
Yacht Harbor
Governor's House
Cruise Ship Harbor

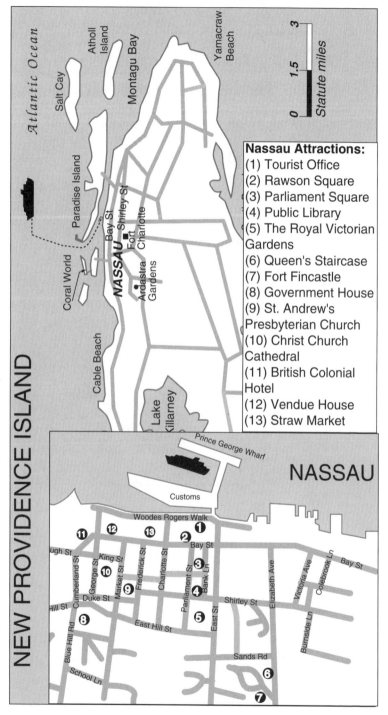

Atlantic Ocean

Salt Cay

Atholl Island

Montagu Bay

Yamacraw Beach

3

1.5

0

Statute miles

Paradise Island

Coral World

Cable Beach

Shirley St

Bay St

NASSAU

Fort Charlotte

Ardastra Gardens

Lake Killarney

Nassau Attractions:
(1) Tourist Office
(2) Rawson Square
(3) Parliament Square
(4) Public Library
(5) The Royal Victorian Gardens
(6) Queen's Staircase
(7) Fort Fincastle
(8) Government House
(9) St. Andrew's Presbyterian Church
(10) Christ Church Cathedral
(11) British Colonial Hotel
(12) Vendue House
(13) Straw Market

NEW PROVIDENCE ISLAND

Prince George Wharf

Customs

NASSAU

Woodes Rogers Walk

Bay St

ugh St

King St

George St

Cumberland St

Duke St

Hill St

Blue Hill Rd

School Ln

Market St

Frederick St

Charlotte St

Parliament St

Bank Ln

East St

East Hill St

Shirley St

Elizabeth Ave

Victoria Ave

Burnside Ln

Colebrook Ln

Bay St

Sands Rd

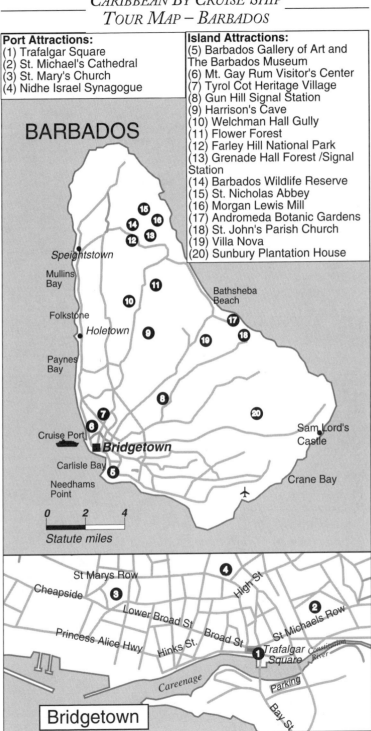

Port Attractions:
(1) Trafalgar Square
(2) St. Michael's Cathedral
(3) St. Mary's Church
(4) Nidhe Israel Synagogue

Island Attractions:
(5) Barbados Gallery of Art and The Barbados Museum
(6) Mt. Gay Rum Visitor's Center
(7) Tyrol Cot Heritage Village
(8) Gun Hill Signal Station
(9) Harrison's Cave
(10) Welchman Hall Gully
(11) Flower Forest
(12) Farley Hill National Park
(13) Grenade Hall Forest /Signal Station
(14) Barbados Wildlife Reserve
(15) St. Nicholas Abbey
(16) Morgan Lewis Mill
(17) Andromeda Botanic Gardens
(18) St. John's Parish Church
(19) Villa Nova
(20) Sunbury Plantation House

BARBADOS

Speightstown
Mullins Bay
Folkstone
Holetown
Paynes Bay
Bathsheba Beach
Cruise Port
Bridgetown
Carlisle Bay
Needhams Point
Sam Lord's Castle
Crane Bay

0   2   4
Statute miles

Bridgetown

St Marys Row
Cheapside
Lower Broad St
Princess Alice Hwy
Hinks St.
Broad St
High St.
St Michaels Row
Trafalgar Square
Constitution River
Parking
Careenage
Bay St.

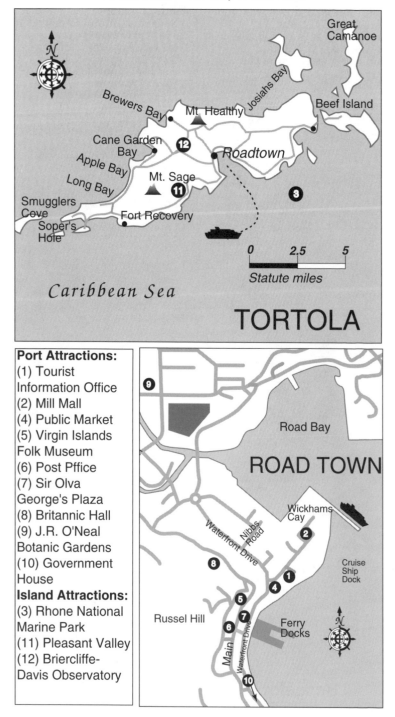

CARIBBEAN BY CRUISE SHIP
TOUR MAP – BVI's, TORTOLA

Great Camanoe

Josiahs Bay

Brewers Bay

Mt. Healthy

Beef Island

Cane Garden Bay

⑫

Roadtown

Apple Bay

Long Bay

Mt. Sage

⑪

③

Smugglers Cove

Soper's Hole

Fort Recovery

0   2.5   5

Statute miles

Caribbean Sea

TORTOLA

Port Attractions:
(1) Tourist Information Office
(2) Mill Mall
(4) Public Market
(5) Virgin Islands Folk Museum
(6) Post Pffice
(7) Sir Olva George's Plaza
(8) Britannic Hall
(9) J.R. O'Neal Botanic Gardens
(10) Government House
Island Attractions:
(3) Rhone National Marine Park
(11) Pleasant Valley
(12) Briercliffe-Davis Observatory

⑨

Road Bay

ROAD TOWN

Wickhams Cay

Waterfront Drive

Nibbs Road

②

Cruise Ship Dock

⑧

①

④

⑤

Russel Hill

⑦

⑥

Ferry Docks

Main

Waterfront Drive

⑩

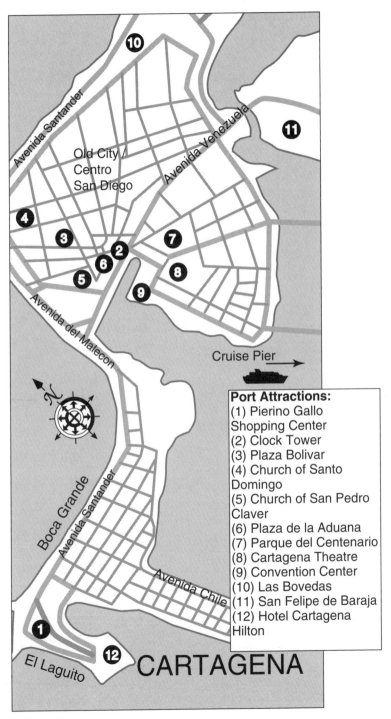

CARIBBEAN BY CRUISE SHIP
TOUR MAP – CARTAGENA

Old City /
Centro
San Diego

Avenida Santander

Avenida Venezuela

Avenida del Malecon

Avenida Santander

Boca Grande

Avenida Chile

Cruise Pier

El Laguito

CARTAGENA

Port Attractions:
(1) Pierino Gallo Shopping Center
(2) Clock Tower
(3) Plaza Bolivar
(4) Church of Santo Domingo
(5) Church of San Pedro Claver
(6) Plaza de la Aduana
(7) Parque del Centenario
(8) Cartagena Theatre
(9) Convention Center
(10) Las Bovedas
(11) San Felipe de Baraja
(12) Hotel Cartagena Hilton

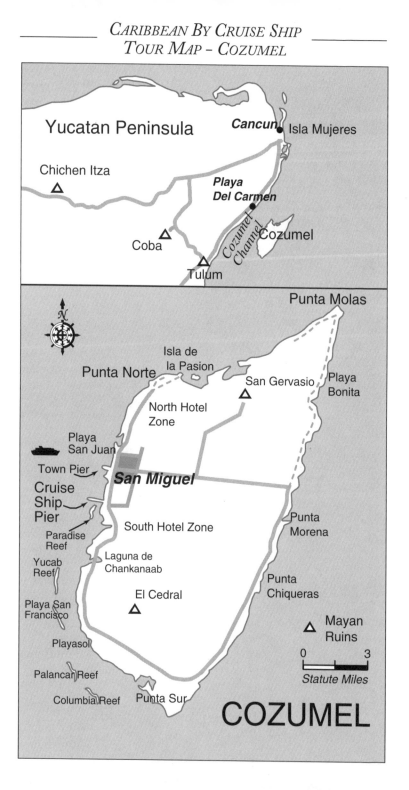

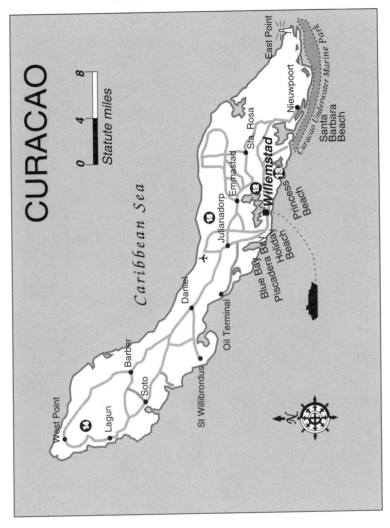

ISLAND ATTRACTIONS
(12) Curacao Liqueur Distillery
(13) Curacao Seaquarium
(14) Christoffel National Park
(15) Hato

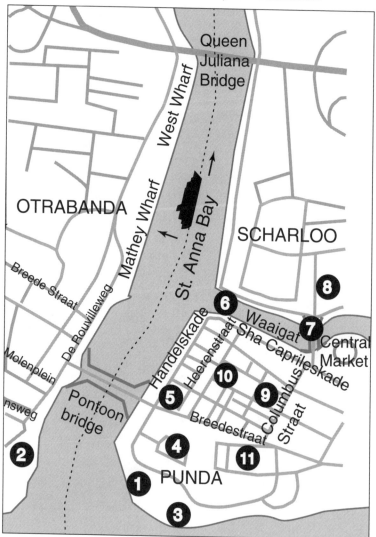

Willemstad Attractions:
(1) Waterfort
(2) Riffort
(3) Waterfort Arches
(4) Fort Amsterdam
(5) Penha Building
(6) Floating Market
(7) Queen Wilhelmina Bridge
(8) Scharloo
(9) Mikve Emanuel Synagogue
(10) Postal Museum
(11) Wilhelminaplein

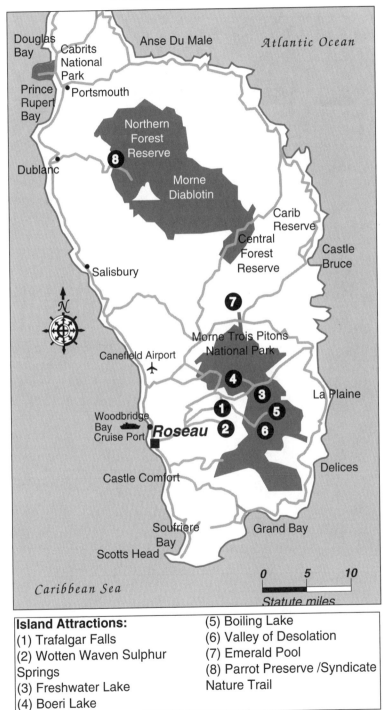

CARIBBEAN BY CRUISE SHIP
TOUR MAP – DOMINICA

Douglas Bay
Cabrits National Park
Anse Du Male
Atlantic Ocean
Prince Rupert Bay
Portsmouth
Dublanc
Northern Forest Reserve
Morne Diablotin
Carib Reserve
Central Forest Reserve
Castle Bruce
Salisbury
N
Morne Trois Pitons National Park
Canefield Airport
La Plaine
Woodbridge Bay Cruise Port
Roseau
Castle Comfort
Delices
Soufriere Bay
Scotts Head
Grand Bay
Caribbean Sea

0   5   10
Statute miles

Island Attractions:
(1) Trafalgar Falls
(2) Wotten Waven Sulphur Springs
(3) Freshwater Lake
(4) Boeri Lake
(5) Boiling Lake
(6) Valley of Desolation
(7) Emerald Pool
(8) Parrot Preserve /Syndicate Nature Trail

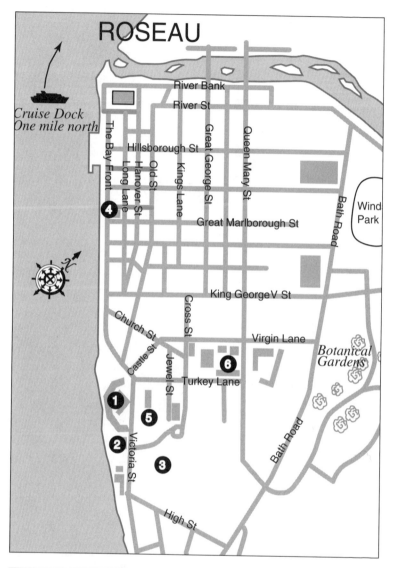

Roseau Attractions:
(1) Fort Young
(2) Public Library
(3) Government House
(4) Court House
(5) St. George's Church
(6) Cathedral of Our Lady of Fair Haven

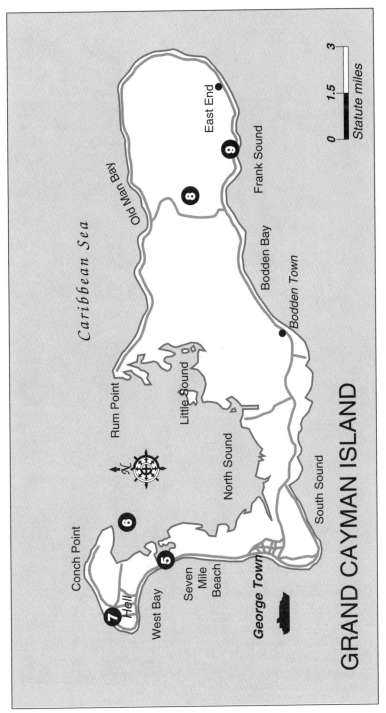

GRAND CAYMAN ISLAND

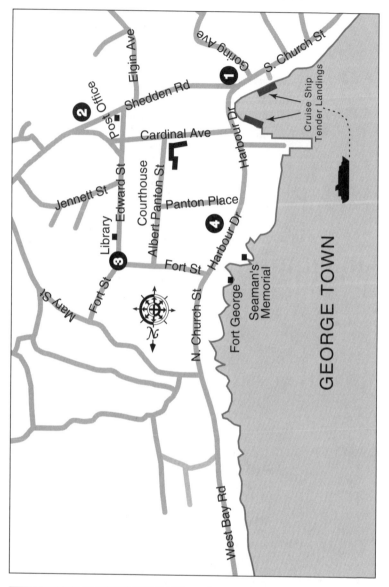

Georgetown Attractions:
(1) Cayman Islands National Museum
(2) Elizabethan Square
(3) Clock Tower
(4) Elmslie Memorial Church

Island Attractions:
(5) Government House
(6) Stingray City
(7) Cayman Turtle Farm
(8) Botanic Gardens
(9) The Blow Holes

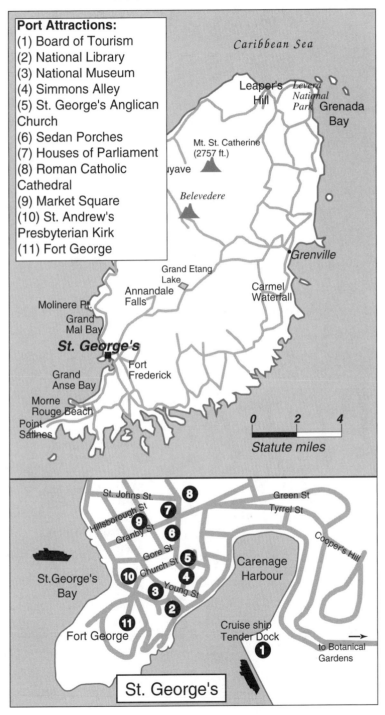

Port Attractions:
(1) Board of Tourism
(2) National Library
(3) National Museum
(4) Simmons Alley
(5) St. George's Anglican
Church
(6) Sedan Porches
(7) Houses of Parliament
(8) Roman Catholic
Cathedral
(9) Market Square
(10) St. Andrew's
Presbyterian Kirk
(11) Fort George

Caribbean Sea

Leaper's Hill
Levera National Park
Grenada Bay

Mt. St. Catherine
(2757 ft.)

uyave

Belevedere

Grenville

Grand Etang Lake
Annandale Falls
Carmel Waterfall

Molinere Pt.
Grand Mal Bay

St. George's
Fort Frederick

Grand Anse Bay

Morne Rouge Beach
Point Salines

0   2   4
Statute miles

St. Johns St
Green St
Tyrrel St
Hillsborough St
Granby St
Gore St
Church St
Young St
Cooper's Hill

Carenage Harbour

St.George's Bay

Fort George

Cruise ship Tender Dock

to Botanical Gardens

St. George's

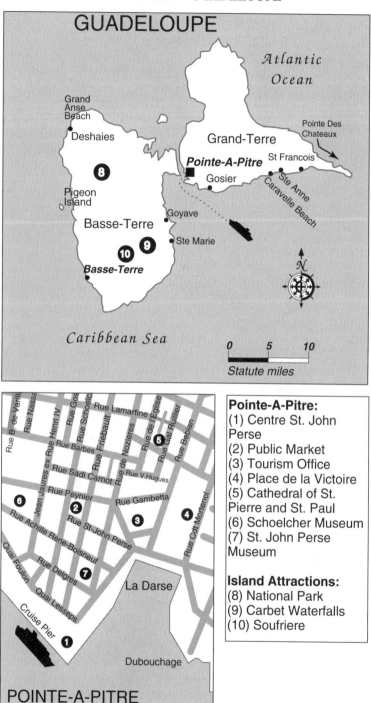

GUADELOUPE

Atlantic Ocean

Grand Anse Beach

Deshaies

Pointe Des Chateaux

Grand-Terre

Pointe-A-Pitre

St Francois

Gosier

Ste Anne

Caravelle Beach

Pigeon Island

Goyave

Basse-Terre

Ste Marie

Basse-Terre

Caribbean Sea

N

0   5   10
Statute miles

Pointe-A-Pitre:
(1) Centre St. John Perse
(2) Public Market
(3) Tourism Office
(4) Place de la Victoire
(5) Cathedral of St. Pierre and St. Paul
(6) Schoelcher Museum
(7) St. John Perse Museum

Island Attractions:
(8) National Park
(9) Carbet Waterfalls
(10) Soufriere

Rue B. de Varill
Rue Nassa
Rue Gos
Rue Schoelch
Rue Lamartine
Rue de l'Eglise
Rue Gal Ruillier
Rue Bebian
Rue Henri IV
Rue Barbes
Rue Friebault
Rue de Nozieres
Jean Jaures ex Rue
Rue Sadi Carnot
Rue V.Hugues
Rue Peynier
Rue Gambetta
Rue Cdt Mortenol
Rue Achille Rene-Boisneuf
Rue St-John Perse
Quai Foulon
Rue Delgres
Quai Lessaps
Cruise Pier
La Darse
Dubouchage

POINTE-A-PITRE

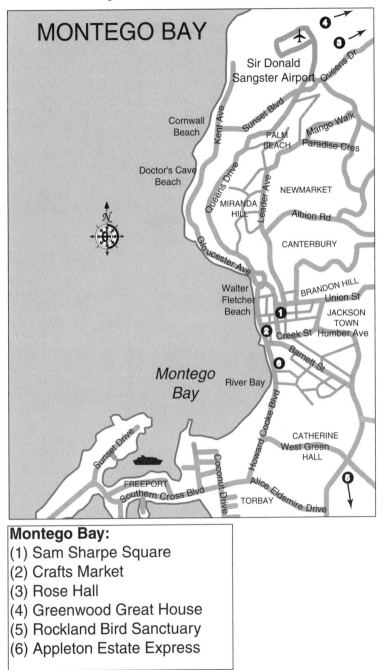

Montego Bay:
(1) Sam Sharpe Square
(2) Crafts Market
(3) Rose Hall
(4) Greenwood Great House
(5) Rockland Bird Sanctuary
(6) Appleton Estate Express

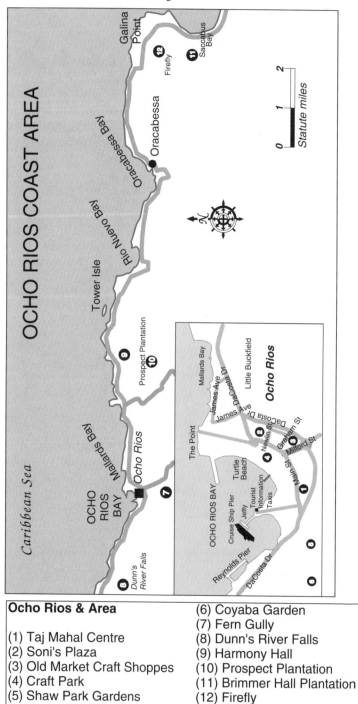

Ocho Rios & Area

(1) Taj Mahal Centre
(2) Soni's Plaza
(3) Old Market Craft Shoppes
(4) Craft Park
(5) Shaw Park Gardens

(6) Coyaba Garden
(7) Fern Gully
(8) Dunn's River Falls
(9) Harmony Hall
(10) Prospect Plantation
(11) Brimmer Hall Plantation
(12) Firefly

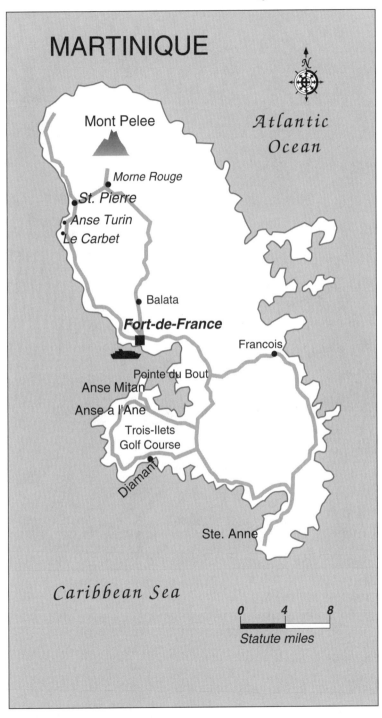

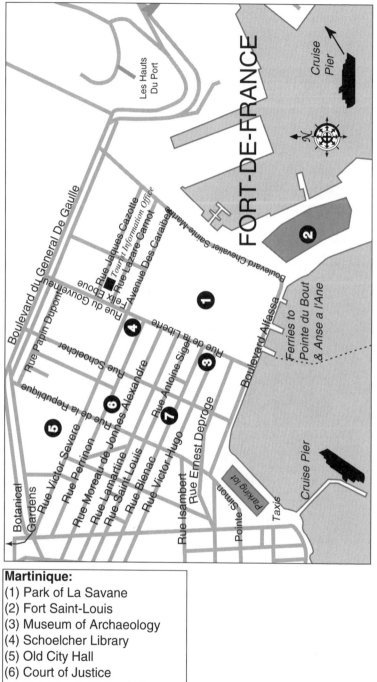

Martinique:
(1) Park of La Savane
(2) Fort Saint-Louis
(3) Museum of Archaeology
(4) Schoelcher Library
(5) Old City Hall
(6) Court of Justice
(7) Saint-Louis Cathedral

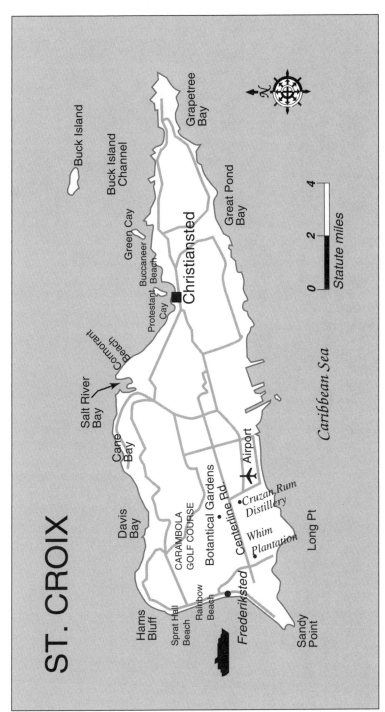

ST. CROIX

Buck Island

Buck Island Channel

Green Cay

Buccaneer Beach

Protestant Cay

Cormorant Beach

Salt River Bay

Cane Bay

Davis Bay

Hams Bluff

Sprat Hall Beach

Rainbow Beach

CARAMBOLA GOLF COURSE

Botanical Gardens

Centerline Rd.

Frederiksted

Sandy Point

Long Pt

Whim Plantation

Cruzan Rum Distillery

Airport

Christiansted

Great Pond Bay

Grapetree Bay

Caribbean Sea

Statute miles

0   2   4

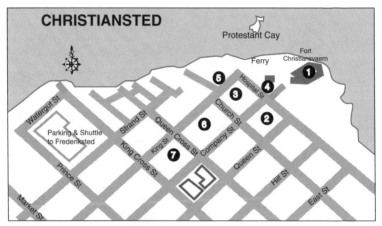

CHRISTIANSTED

Christiansted Attractions:
(1) Fort Christiansvaern
(2) Steeple Building
(3) Danish West India & Guinea Company Warehouse
(4) Customs House
(5) Scale House / Visitors Bureau
(6) Government House
(7) Lutheran Church

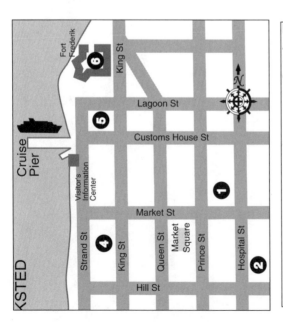

Frederiksted Attractions:
(1) St. Patrick's Catholic Church
(2) Holy Trinity Lutheran Church
(3) St. Pauls Anglican Church
(4) Victoria House
(5) Customs House
(6) Fort Frederick

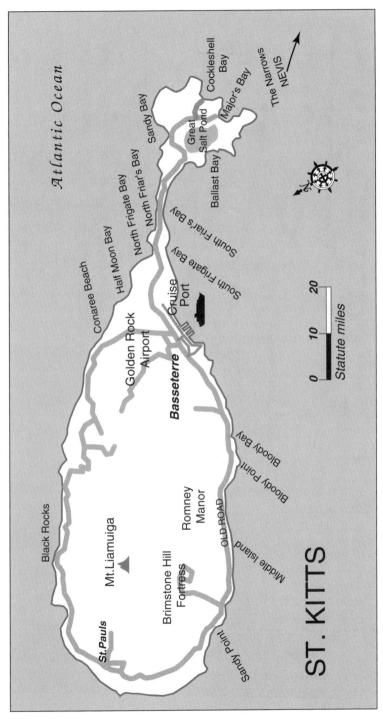

ST. KITTS

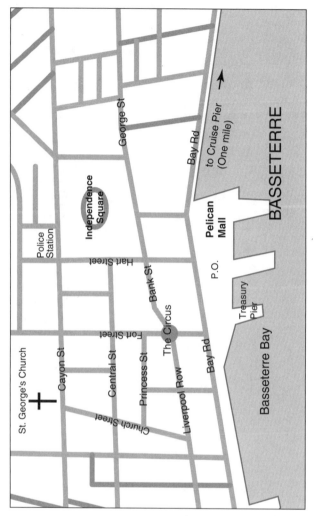

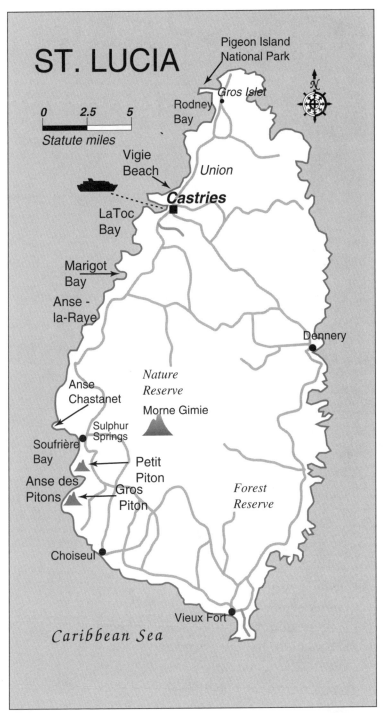

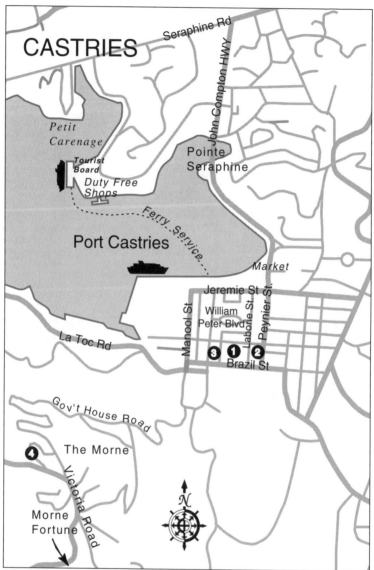

Castries Attractions:
(1) Derek Walcott Square
(2) Cathedral of the Immaculate Conception
(3) Central Library
(4) Government House

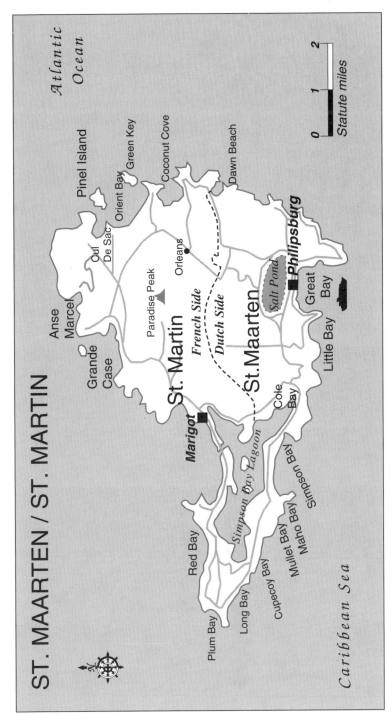

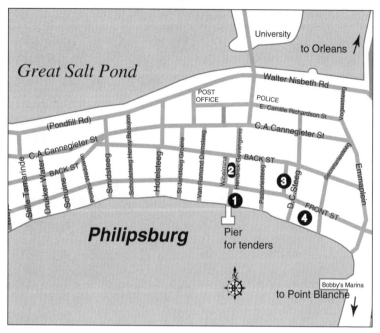

Philipsburg Attractions:

(1) Cyrus Wathney Square
(2) Courthouse
(3) Old Street Mall
(4) Pasanggrahan Royal Guest House

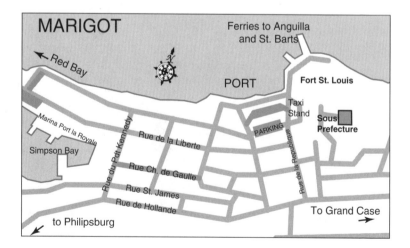

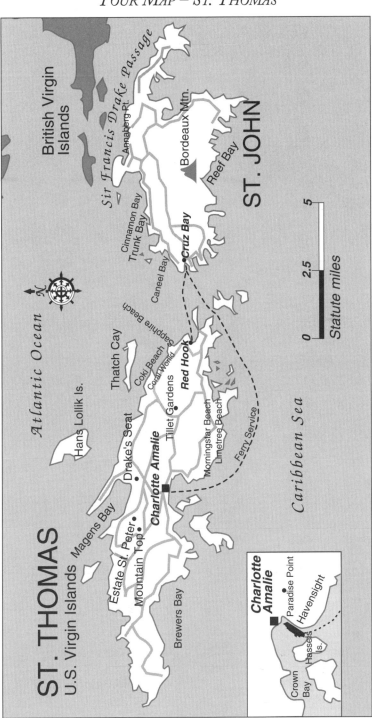

ST. THOMAS
U.S. Virgin Islands

Atlantic Ocean

British Virgin Islands

Sir Francis Drake Passage

N

Hans Lollik Is.

Thatch Cay

Magens Bay

Estate St. Peter
Mountain Top
Drake's Seat

Brewers Bay

Charlotte Amalie

Tillet Gardens

Coki Beach
Coral World
Sapphire Beach

Red Hook

Morningstar Beach
Limetree Beach

Ferry Service

Caneel Bay

Cruz Bay

Trunk Bay
Cinnamon Bay

Annaberg Pt.

Bordeaux Mtn.

Reef Bay

ST. JOHN

Caribbean Sea

0   2.5   5
Statute miles

Charlotte Amalie

Paradise Point

Havensight

Hassels Is.

Crown Bay

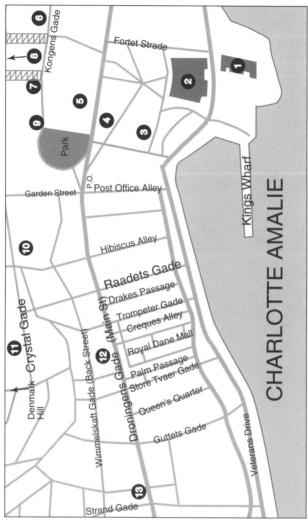

Charlotte Amalie Attractions:

(1) Legislature Building
(2) Fort Christian
(3) Emancipation Garden
(4) Grand Hotel
(5) Frederick Lutheran Church
(6) Government House
(7) The 99 Steps
(8) Skytsborg (Blackbeard's Castle)
(9) Hotel 1829
(10) St. Thomas Reformed Church
(11) Beracha Veshalom U'gemilut Hasidim
(12) Camille Pissaro Building
(13) Market Square

CARIBBEAN BY CRUISE SHIP
TOUR MAP – SAN JUAN

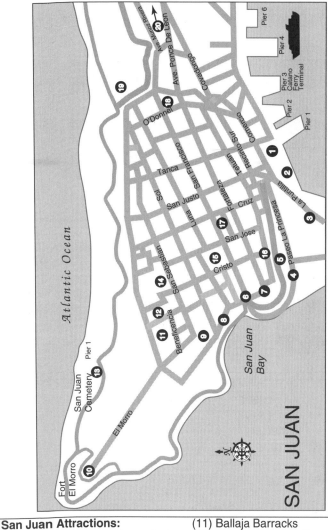

San Juan Attractions:
(1) La Casita (Visitor Information)
(2) Aduana
(3) El Arsenal
(4) Paseo La Princesa
(5) La Princesa
(6) La Puerta de San Juan (San Juan Gate)
(7) La Fortaleza (The Fortress)
(8) Plazuela de la Rogativa (Plaza of the Religious Procession)
(9) Casa Blanca (White House)
(10) El Morro

(11) Ballaja Barracks
(12) Plaza del Quinto Centenario
(13) San Juan Cemetery
(14) Plaza de San Jose - San Jose Church
(15) San Juan Cathedral
(16) Capilla de Cristo (Christ Chapel)
(17) Plaza de Armas (Army Plaza)
(18) Plaza de Colon (Columbus Plaza)
(19) San Cristobal Fort
(20) Capitol Building

OTHER CRUISE BOOKS FOR YOUR TRAVEL ENJOYMENT FROM OCEAN CRUISE GUIDES

Alaska By Cruise Ship – The international bestseller used by cruise passengers and travel agents around the world. Includes details on wildlife, native culture, glaciers, ports, cruise routes and much more. Over 200 photographs, 35 maps, 368 pages.
2nd edition ISBN 09697991-2-8
$18.95 US. $24.95 CDN

The Complete Cruise Handbook – Discover the world of cruising with this introduction to destinations, cruise lines and ships. Maps, color photography and charts round out this volume which makes cruise options easier to understand.
ISBN 0-9697991-1-X
$11.95 US. $14.95 CDN

AVAILABLE AT LEADING BOOKSTORES

TO ORDER DIRECT USE THIS FORM:

Add $2 per book for S&H and 7.25% tax if CA resident or 7% GST if CDN resident. Bulk quantity rates available on request.

Name _____

Address _____

City, State or Prov., _____

Code_____ Total Cost (Book total + S&H + tax)_____

Check Enclosed ☐ American Express ☐ Visa ☐ MC ☐

Card # _____Exp Date _____

Signature _____

IN USA:	IN CANADA:
OCEAN CRUISE GUIDES	OCEAN CRUISE GUIDES
Box 3098	614 – 888 Beach Avenue
San Clemente, CA 92674-3098	Vancouver, BC V6Z 2P9
Phone: (714) 361-0224	Phone: (604) 685-0593
Fax: (714) 361-9627	FAX: (604) 685-2479